MODERN MILL

(COPYRIGHT)

THE NEW ART PUBLISHERS
77 QUEEN STREET, BRISBANE, Q'LD.

WITHDRAWN

Teaching from the Beginning

THE MEASURING, MAKING, BLOCKING, CLEANING, DYEING, DESIGNING, RE-MODELLING. All the Correct Millinery Stitches, Equipment, Materials, etc., Fully Detailed. The Correct Methods of Finishing and Trimming all types of Hats—Adults and Children's—Making head linings, Ribbon trimmings, Lining under Brims, Wiring Edges, Blocking and trimming Straw Hoods. Blocking, Cleaning, Trimming Felt Hoods. Making Braid and Straw Hats. Making Brims and Crowns separately and in one piece. The Cutting to Measure of Stitched Hats, Outer Coverings, Interlinings and Brims Pressing. Making Berets, Girls' Hats. Infants' and Toddlers' Bonnets. Cutting and Making Boys' Hats and School Caps, Child's Bonnets. Boys' Stitched Hats—Cleaning and re-modelling all types of hats. MAKING HAT STIFFENING. The correct Straws—all varieties Detailed. Cleaning and Renovating Flowers and trimmings. Cleansing all types Straw and Felt Hats. Renovating Velvet. Making and Renovating Wedding Veils. Making Millinery with and without Hat Blocks. Making shapes for Velvet and Grosgrain Hats. Veiling and Various Trimmings. Making Flowers, etc., etc.

AN ENCYCLOPEDIA OF ALL MILLINERY AND FLOWER MAKING

Foreword

THIS book has been written and illustrated for several reasons, **firstly** in response to the insistent demand of ex-students and students of "Modern Designers Academy" of Dressmaking and Millinery. For a permanent record in concise form of the thorough advanced modern methods instructed at the Academy or by thorough postal tuition, and to provide a standard work of reference in "Millinery" which in itself forms a thorough course of study for those desiring to thoroughly learn "Millinery," and **secondly by request** from those who have taken **"Dressmaking," "Dresscutting," "Ladies' Tailoring," "French Flower Making," "Shirt and Pyjama Cutting"** (Boys, Youths, Men's), and various other Trade Courses (by the same author) and gained knowledge and earning power from the thorough instructions contained therein.

It is not pretended that a work of this description can ever entirely replace a sound individual training as offered those who can attend **"Modern Designers Academy"** personally, but within its scope as outlined above, it is hoped that it will fill a breach which has long existed in trade literature. There is an ever increasing demand for "Milliners" and "Dressmakers," and both trades offer great opportunities and remunerative careers, for those thoroughly trained in any branch of the Millinery or Clothing Trades.

Thirdly, for women and girls who desire to make their own Millinery or Children's Millinery, or to make for others and earn a livelihood.

Every care has been taken in details to produce a book which will remain useful throughout the years. Nothing is included that is not eminently practical and in accordance with the best professional practice. In order to obtain the best results, and the greatest advantage from its possession, each subject must be thoroughly studied, and practical experiments made at each stage. If this is done, knowledge, and consequently earning power, should be vastly increased. Throughout this work a logical reason is given for anything that is done, and if the instructions are carefully followed satisfactory and successful results will be obtained. This Course reveals all the short cuts and secrets of making Millinery, and for those who cannot attend the Academy for private tuition it will assist to give knowledge of Adults and Children's Millinery.

You may think that Millinery is beyond your power of accomplishment, that Hat Making requires a great amount of creative ability and specialized training. This is not so. Anyone who is really interested can learn Millinery. Creative talent and the correct training are necessary for anyone to become a Milliner. Any girl or woman with average good taste and judgment can very quickly learn to copy various styles from Fashion Plates, or designs seen in shop windows, styles to suit her own requirements. The knowledge is not difficult to attain. Anyone of average intelligence can master it.

THIS IS A COURSE OF INSTRUCTION IN MILLINERY MADE EASY. It is based on time-saving ideas, to help both the beginner and the already trained milliner; whatever your skill, ambition or interest in Millinery, you will find all the answers to your problems in this thorough Course of Instruction of **"MODERN MILLINERY MADE EASY."**

As Millinery, like Garments, dates quickly and styles change with every passing phase of fashion, I have dealt only with simple styles, enabling the student to understand thoroughly the making and finishing, blocking, cleaning and trimming of a variety of hats.

INDEX

Index—Continued

STUDY LESSON (Lesson 1).

Equipment used in the Making of Millinery

The necessary equipment for the making of Millinery is as follows:—

Wooden Hat Blocks of various shapes and sizes. The most important shapes are Sailors (Plain) ; Gutted Sailor Crown; Round Sailor Crown; Domes, Ring Tams, Split Tams (Beret) ; Small Tams. These are the general types in use. The Brim Boards are as follows: Small 9in. to 10in. Coolie; Small 9in. Saucer Brim; Plain 10in. to 11in. Brims; Sailor Small Brim; Sailor Large Brim; Coolie Brims 14in.; Large Brims 18in.; Medium Deep Coolie Brim, 11in. to 12in.; Large Coolie Brim, 14in.; Casablanca Block; Casablanca Centre Block; Sports Brim, 14in.; Fancy Brims, 12in. to 14in.; Collars; Stands; Pins used for holding the Crown Block to the Brim Block, and many other types of Blocks too numerous to detail here. The ones listed are the most used type of Hat Blocks and Brim Boards.

A SUBSTITUTE. Many substitutes can be provided for Hat Blocks:—

(1) **For a Sailor Crown.** The upturned Saucepan of the Around Head Measure required.

(2) **For a Dome Crown** on a Basin of the same shape.

(3) **A Flower Pot** turned upside down.

(4) **A Basin can be filled with Plaster of Paris,** and when the plaster sets it is removed from the Basin and covered with Felt or Blanket.

(5) **The Crown of an old Felt Hat** stuffed with sawdust and the lower edge of the Crown tacked to a piece of Board.

(6) **The Crown filled with Cotton Wool** and attached to a piece of board as above. These Blocks, if made to a 19in. Around Head Measurement, can be padded to larger head fittings by adding additional layers of blanket or felt. Note also: Wooden Hat Blocks can be enlarged to several sizes by placing a felt crown over the block or several felt crowns till correct measurement is obtained. This avoids having to purchase several Blocks of the same shape but of different sizes. The Block can in this manner be built up from a 19in. around head measurement to larger sizes desired.

Children's Bonnet Crown Blocks can be built up in this way to use for adults' sizes. (The price lists of Wooden Hat Blocks is given in the Re-modelling Section.)

A Pair of Pliers used for cutting the millinery wire.

A Sharp Knife, Old Razor or Razor Blade used for cutting the felt. Note: The use of scissors will flatten and flute the edges of the felt. **The felt must have a clean, smooth cut edge.**

Millinery Needles. For sewing Straws and Braids, millinery needles No. 4 and No. 5 and No. 6 are used.

For Fine Work, such as edges and finishings, slip stitching, etc., No. 7 and No. 8 millinery needles are the best.

For Trimmings, No. 4 needle is the best to use.

Pins for Millinery. The best British steel pins (fine steel pins 2in. in length are best for millinery).

Note.—Important. Do not keep pins in a tin as the tin container will discolour the pins, causing them to leave dark lead-like marks on the work. Keep pins in a glass jar or cardboard box. Do not use pins that have rusted. They will spoil the work.

Drawing Pins, the brass type are best as they will not bend or break when being used. They are inexpensive and sold in small boxes at stationers or department stores.

An Ordinary Iron, electric or any type available used for pressing and blocking straws and felts, steaming, etc.

A Kettle for steaming.

Stiffening referred to as Millinery Stiffening (glossy finish). This can be purchased in small bottles and tins, also in ¼ gallon and 1 gallon tins, from all Millinery Supply Departments. It must be kept airtight as it evaporates quickly and is used for straw hats, etc. Note: You can make your own stiffening (not varnish), using Gum Arabic crystals (obtainable from chemists). To make the stiffening (which is suitable for felt hats and stiffening materials that do not require a shiny finish), place the crystals in a jar, cover the crystals with cold water. Place lid on jar and leave for a day. Then strain through a piece of voile or thin calico and place the stiffening in a bottle ready for use. This type of stiffening is not used for straws requiring a glossy finish, but is excellent for felts.

✓ **Millinery Varnish** is used for varnishing straws and stiffening straws, laces, etc. This is also referred to as stiffening solution, and has been previously referred to.

Millinery Solution referred to as rubber solution, used for sticking ribbon to hats, seams of straws, etc., has a sticky rubber appearance, similar to bicycle solution for mending rubber tubes. Obtainable from Millinery Supply Departments or stores.

Raw Starch for stiffening fabric hats, laces, etc.

◆   ◆   ◆

STUDY LESSON (Lesson 2)

Hoods and Capelines

Referred to as Body Hats. Body Hats are Hats that have the Brim and Crown woven all in one piece. There are a large variety available in both Straws and Felts.

1. The Process of Manufacture. This varies with the type of hat. Most of the better straws, such as "Panamas," "Leghorns" and "Tuscan Straws," etc., are hand-woven by native workers. Felt Hoods are made entirely by machinery, as are sewed body hats.

2. The Tests of Quality. Straw Body Hats vary in quality with the fineness of the straw used and with the expertness of the weaver. Among the Felt Hoods the better quality of Felt Hoods are fine and close and need little stiffening. The cheaper grades of Felt Hoods are loose and coarse; a great deal of stiffening must be used to give them body.

3. The Varieties of Felt Hoods. Felts are made of a wool or wool and cotton composition which is subjected to heating, beating and pressure processes. The fur of the rabbit makes an excellent Felt Hood, and this is extensively used, especially in the making of high grade men's Felt Hats. The fur is stripped from the skin and machine treated. The felt composition, when made, is rolled out into sheets. The Hoods or Body Hats are blocked from sheets of felt with specially made steel machines. The imported Felt Hoods are made in Switzerland and France. Beaver and Velour Felts are made with beaver and rabbit fur in the composition. The finest quality Velours and Felts are made in Switzerland.

STRAW BRAIDS. STUDY LESSON.

4. Special Varieties. The various Braids used in millinery are many kinds. **Chenille Braid** is a soft woven braid obtainable in a large variety of colours; a velvety thread is interwoven with the straw or cotton forming a plait. There is a variety of widths. This braid is sold in bundles and the amount of yardage in each bundle varies with the width of the braid. A narrow "Chenille Straw Braid" will have more yards in a bundle than the wider braid used in a variety of Shapes and Berets. There is usually a gathering thread on the edge.

Yarn Braids. These are used mainly for Sports Hats; obtainable in various colours.

Leghorn Straw. These are hand woven.

Tuscan Straw.

The **Leghorn Straw,** named after Leghorn, Italy, where it is woven; a very fine bearded wheat straw is used. The finer the straw and the smoother the weaving the better quality is the hat. These are sold only in the hood, which are large and expensive, but outwears a dozen cheaper types of straw. They will stand continuous cleaning and re-blocking. To satisfactorily re-block these straws they must be soaked for several hours in water. (**The straw of the Leghorn Hat** is first woven into fine strips of braid, and these are woven into Hats.)

The **Tuscan Straw** is a very finely woven golden, natural coloured straw braid, usually made in lace-like patterns. These, too, are always sold in the Hood and are the expensive variety.

Panama. This is also sold only in the Hood. They are hand woven by native workers of Panama, Cuba, China and many other islands. A fine special grass is used; the weaving is done under water. The genuine is very fine. (There are imitations.) These are cheaper than the genuine Panama. They vary in size and are made for children, women and men. The widths of the brim also vary.

Panamas are hard to block. The straw of the Panama does not stretch easily. It is hard straw. They last for years and can be cleaned easily and re-blocked and re-trimmed They require to be soaked in water many hours before re-blocking and will not hurt to be left in water several days, which will help to make the straw softer. The straw will stiffen when it dries. Therefore no stiffening is necessary for Panamas. Panamas are used mainly for Sports Hats.

Pedal Straw has a dull finish. It is a fine plaited straw; being a soft straw it can usually be made up without damping. There is usually a draw thread along the edge. It is necessary with this straw to use a foundation or shape to support the straw, especially the crown. The wiring of the outer edge of the brim is sufficient support for the brim. The amount of straw in the bundle is 10 to 12 yards. A variety of colours and widths are obtainable.

Ramie Straw. A cheap coarse straw obtainable in a variety of colours. This straw is made up and sewn and blocked by steaming and pressed into shape; obtainable in bundles of 10 yards. Breaks very easily and requires careful handling.

LESSON 3.

Straw Braids

Straw Braid. This is obtainable in a variety of colours and widths. These vary from 1 inch to 4 inches. This straw is sold only by the yard. The straw is very pliable and has more give than some other varieties. It is obtainable in fancy or plain weaves, also in a rough or smooth finish. It is ideal for making small hats and berets. The straw must be steamed while blocking.

Viska Straw is silky finished, similar in appearance to Pedal Straw, sold in the Hood; obtainable in different colours or natural.

Bankok Straw appears similar in weave to Panama, having a finer, more even appearance and a silky finish. Sold in the Hood. **There is genuine Bankok and imitation. When blocking genuine Bankok the Hood requires pulling gently,** and it is not easy to pull down on the block. Treat the **Bankok** in the same manner as **Panama.**

Cellophane Straw. This straw is a highly glazed variety, and is sold in bundles of 9 yards to 10 yards, or by the yard; obtainable in a variety of colours. It is obtainable in fancy or plain weaves and is often combined with other types of straw. This straw must be moistened only by the steam from a kettle. The straw is brittle and breaks away easily. Care must be taken when sewing and preparing this straw. This straw is easy to make up in the hand or on a foundation. To join (see Straw Section).

Parisisol Straw. Greatly resembling glazed Bankok Straw; sold in fairly large-sized Hoods.

Mottled Straw. A natural straw, very easy to work; sold in the bundle. Must be damped for working.

Pedaline Straw. A glossy finished Pedal Straw.

Horse Hair and Crinolines have the appearance of coarse, loosely woven lace or net, obtainable in bundles consisting of from 10 to 12 yards.

The very narrow Crinoline Straw is obtainable in bundles of 36 yards. There are many widths, and it can be obtained with 2 or 3 widths ready sewn together. Ideal for Cocktail or Picture Hats, and can be obtained in a large variety of colours. This straw is rather difficult to handle as it becomes sticky when it is damp. Great care must be taken when blocking Crinolines—the hood has a tendency to spring up when it is placed on the block. It must be securely pinned down on the block with drawing pins before attempting to block or steam it. If the Crinoline is made into a hat, with a brim, and the Crinoline is not combined with other straw, the Crinoline must be mounted over Millinery Net or Tulle.

Raffia. Ideal for Garden Hats, very soft to work. It is treated with glycerine; obtainable in natural and bright colours. The bundles contain 18 to 20 yards of Raffia. It is plaited in 5 to 8 strands. It is made up in the hand, beginning from the tip and working outwards. The brim and crown are worked in one piece; damp on the wrong side as work is proceeded with. Much moisture will be absorbed while working. Keep damping. Also makes lovely table mats, baskets and handbags.

Rush Straws. Is finished with a rough basket work appearance; ideal for Children's Hats and Garden Hats. Obtainable in hoods and bundles. Must be well wet to handle. If dry will break easily. Soak the straw for 24 hours. It can then be either blocked or made in the hand; this will depend on whether you have bought a hood or the straw braid. Various colours are available.

Hemp Straw has the appearance of rough canvas; a variety of colours are obtainable. Sold only in hoods, small or large sizes. It is easy to handle, but must be thoroughly wet by soaking for several hours. It can then be moulded over the hat block.

Paper Pulp Imitation Straw. A rough surface straw used in cheap hats. It can be bought in the hood and by the yard. It tears easily even when inserting the needle in it. It is difficult to handle. It must be moistened by steam, as wetting it causes it to break apart. Obtainable in a variety of colours.

Chip Straw. A very cheap straw, attractive for Garden or Beach Hats. This straw has a rough surface. Sold in bundles and by the yard. It takes usually 7 to 8 yards to make a large size hat. Easy to make up and can be made up in the hand as Raffia Straw. Use glycerine on hands while working and it is easier to handle the straw. A variety of colours are obtainable.

Straw Cloth: Sold by the yard, 12 ins. to 18 ins. in width. It is an imitation of straw and is used over a shape similar to material. A variety of colours are obtainable.

Yarn Braid is obtainable in a variety of colours, plain and mixed. Excellent for Sports Hats. The entire hat can be made of Yarn Braid.

Felt Braid is used mainly to trim Felt Hats. The edge of the braid is usually cut in a pattern of points and scallops.

Satin Straw is woven of a composition with a smooth and shiny surface, resembling Shiny Straw.

Lisere Braid has a harder finish and more shiny than Milan Braid. For feathered, trimmed or tailored hats and for cellophane and lacquered plumed trimmed hats it is very attractive. Lisere Stripping is used for combination sewing with hair or Crinoline Braid. Variety of colours may be obtained.

Hair Braids with beautiful designs and colours are obtainable in beautiful patterns. White hair, with designs in natural Tuscan Braid, has a dainty effect and is very pretty in combination with Chiffon, Georgette or Lace flower-trimmed hats. Designs of Satin Straw or Hair Braid can be worn in models to wear with street dresses.

Paribuntle sold in the hood, and **Baribuntle,** similar to Paribuntle, sold in hood.

Racello Swiss hoods. **Racello Italian** hoods.

Racello Banding, sold by the yard in bundles of 10, 12 and 24 yards, also by the yard. The width is 1 in. to 4 ins.; a variety of colours.

Rapal Braid, narrow, sold in bundles of 48 yards to 72 yards; also by the yard.

Rapal Braid Banding, sold in bundles of 10, 12 and 24 yards; also sold by the yard. Width 1 in. to 3 ins.; obtainable in a variety of colours.

Rapal Straws. This straw can be interwoven at the cut edges to neaten.

Baku, excellent combined with Crinoline.

Sizol, also suitable combined with Crinoline.

"Knotty Sizol," very smart. Ideal with Crinoline and Velvet trims, or Lace straw.

"Tagel Straw," lovely combined with Crinoline and Velvet trims.

"Chenille" or **"Wool Braid,"** sold by the yard. Ideal for small berets and hats.

"Grosgrain" is 18 ins. wide. Is excellent for berets, hats, bonnets.

Lame is 36 ins. wide. Suitable cocktail and evening wear hats and toques. Obtainable in gold, silver and brocaded gold and black, also silver and black, and a a large variety of colours. Pastel and other shades. Ideal for swathed and draped effects.

LESSON 4.

The Various Types of Millinery Wires

(All Are Fully Detailed)

1. **Steel Wire,** which is a heavy spring wire, covered or uncovered, suitable only for the wiring of sailor or mushroom brims; not easy to handle.

2. **Cable Wire** is a fine steel wire covered with a padding and a silk wrapping; used mainly in trimmings and machine work.

3. **Brace Wire** is used more than any other one wire. It is a silk-bound medium-fine wire which is very firm. It is used for wiring frames and for facing edges.

4. **French Wire** is much like Brace Wire, but is finer and not so stiff. It is largely used for wire-edged finishes and for many soft hats.

5. **Lace Wire** is very fine silk-wrapped wire, used for wiring lace, ribbon and bows and for very soft Infants' Bonnets and Children's Hats.

THE CORRECT USE OF MILLINERY WIRE.

This is bought in coils (black and white) as wire is always covered. White wire is used for white and light Straws, black for black, navy and dark coloured Straws and Felts. When working with the wire, there must be no kinks. The wire must be absolutely smooth. It is necessary to hold the wire over the arm, and holding the wire (see illustration in another lesson—Wiring Hat Brim) firmly between the thumb and finger of one hand, run the wire between the thumb and finger of the other hand, smoothing it out into a circle large enough to fit around where required on the hat.

Note.—When re-modelling hats, do not replace the old wire; discard it, and replace it with a new piece. You will find it more satisfactory than trying to straighten the old piece. Hat wire is not expensive, 6d. to 9d. per roll at any department store.

To Cut Wire.—Place the wire between the blades of the cutters or pliers and give the pliers a sharp, firm grip and the wire will be cut without tearing the covering of the wire. The correct method of joining the wire together is dealt with in another lesson.

STUDY EACH LESSON CAREFULLY. PRACTICE IS NECESSARY.
CONTINUAL PRACTICE WILL SHOW THE BEST RESULTS.

LESSON 5.

Various Millinery Materials, Widths, Textures, Etc.

"**Espartra.**" Sold by the yard, 36 ins. in width, strengthened on the wrong side with a starched muslin; used for Hats and Bonnets shapes. "**Leno**" is 27 ins. in width and also sold by the yard. It is made of closely woven cotton or gauze; used mainly for the underbrims of hats or bonnets that are lined with silk or velvet. "**Buckram**" is 27 ins. to 36 ins. wide and is sold by the yard; obtainable in black or white. It is a coarse open fabric, straw-like in appearance, woven over cotton, very stiff. Used for shapes for Bonnets and Hats. Buckram is heavier and cheaper than Espartra. "**Book Muslin,**" usually 36 ins. to 40 ins. in width, very stiff, transparent, and fine; used mainly as a foundation for Children's Millinery and Hat Crowns. "**Stiff Millinery Net**" is usually about 27 ins. in width and sold by the yard; a large mesh stiffened net used mainly for Children's Caps, Bonnets and Hats. "**Mull**" is 27 ins. wide, used by English manufacturers of millinery. A soft muslin mainly used to bind edges of Espartra or Buckram shapes to avoid the wire showing through the covering of hat.

◆ ◆ ◆

LESSON 6.

Classified Construction of Fabrics and Velvets

1. **Velvet has the most gorgeous colour effects,** and is favored more than any other fabric, both as a hat or the trimmings of a hat. Its rich deep pile gives depth of light and shadow. The shadows cause one colour to have many different lovely tints.

2. **Plushes.** These are referred to as Hatters' Plush. It is similar in appearance and finish to "Soleil," but has a much longer nap. It is used for strictly Tailored Hats, "Boaters" and plain types, and is usually sold in colours suitable for street wear.

3. **Satin Soleil in black** is one of the smartest materials for tailored types of hats. It has a high lustre.

4. **Satin is also favoured for the covered hat,** and also for millinery trimmings and children's millinery.

5. **Baronet Satin is a Fibre Satin,** with a high almost metallic finish, which combines beautifully with Plush and with Shiny Straw.

6. **Brocaded Satin,** often also referred to as Embossed Satin, the Brocaded Satin having a tinsel thread woven through it, forming a design. The Embossed Satin is similar, only no tinsel threads are interwoven. It makes lovely evening or cocktail trimmings and smart Turbans and Toques for wearing with suits and coats.

7. **Duchess Satin** is used combined with velvet, mainly as a trimming.

8. **Fancy Materials.** There are many different types. The main varieties are Gold and Silver Brocades, Embossed Velvet, Georgette and Satin mixtures; all are ideal for trimming. These are expensive and rich in appearance.

9. **Astrachan.** Used mainly to trim small hats or caps for winter wear.

10. **Ribbons.** Both wide and narrow. Moire Ribbon, Silk Petersham and Velvet, Taffeta, Satin. All are excellent trimmings for millinery.

LESSON 7.

The Essential Stitches used in Millinery

These are all important, and must be thoroughly practiced on spare material and clearly understood before attempting to commence making millinery.

Diagram 1 clearly illustrates Tacking. To tack or baste, often referred to as basting, meaning a stitch to hold two parts together temporarily before the actual sewing. It is necessary, when tacking, to take up half as much as the needle has passed over. Tacking is an uneven running stitch, small or large, whichever is required.

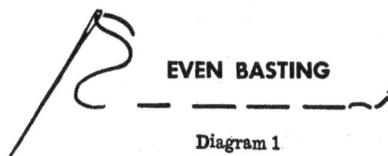

EVEN BASTING

Diagram 1

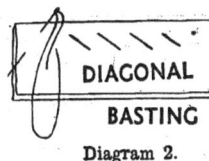

DIAGONAL BASTING

Diagram 2.

Diagram 2 clearly illustrates Side Way Basting Stitch. The stitches are made sideways, as illustrated, and are used for holding two parts together.

RUNNING STITCH

Diagram 3

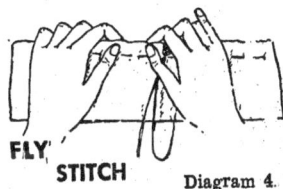

FLY STITCH

Diagram 4.

Diagram 3 clearly illustrates the running stitch. This stitch is an even stitch, about $\frac{1}{8}$ in. to $\frac{1}{4}$ in. in length. This stitch is used for joining two parts together where there is little if any strain on material. Take up on needle the same quantity of material as needle passes over to keep stitches even.

Diagram 4 clearly illustrates a stitch referred to as Fly. Running stitch gathering—small even tacking stitches. Hold the material between the thumbs and the first fingers of both hands. The material is held taut by the left hand, the thimble propelling the needle, which must not be drawn through until a long length of stitches is on the needle. This stitch requires practice and is used for all branches of millinery requiring gathering.

Diagram 5 clearly illustrates Shirring, which is used on the under brims of Children's Hats and Bonnets. Three rows of machine gathering are placed about $\frac{1}{8}$ in. apart and drawn up, pulling the three under threads, not the top threads. Groups can be used of three rows at intervals of $\frac{1}{2}$ in., $\frac{3}{4}$ in., or 1 in. apart.

Diagram 6 clearly illustrates Back Stitching. The needle is inserted into the material and about 4 threads picked up. It is then taken back to the length of the stitch and brought on to the length of the stitch beyond where the previous stitch came out. This stitch is a strong stitch, and is ideal for joining velvets or material requiring strength.

SHIRRING

Diagram 5-

Diagram 6.   BACKSTITCHING

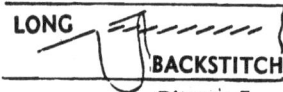

LONG BACKSTITCH

Diagram 7.

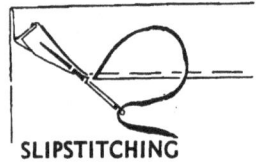

SLIPSTITCHING

Diagram 8.

Diagram 7 clearly illustrates the long Back Stitch. When making this stitch it should be from $\frac{1}{4}$ in. to $\frac{1}{3}$ in. in length. The cotton must be left loose. This stitch is used for joining soft materials.

Diagram 8 clearly illustrates Slip Stitching. It is important to take up one stitch on the surface of one side of the material, then, immediately opposite, taking either stitch through the single fold. It is used for an invisible join, such as required in edges of velvet hats or the join in head linings.

Diagram 9 clearly illustrates Whipping Stitch. This stitch is used for edges. The needle is taken over the edge of the material. It is necessary to take several stitches on the needle before drawing the needle through. This stitch is used to prevent the edges ravelling, and also for drawing up georgette, lace and soft materials.

WHIPPING STITCH

Diagram 9.

Diagram 10 clearly illustrates the Catch Stitch. This stitch is worked from right to left. Take on the needle a small portion of the material on the wrong side of the material, then a similar portion on the fold on the right side of the material. This stitch is used for fixing down the edges of a fold of velvet or heavy material.

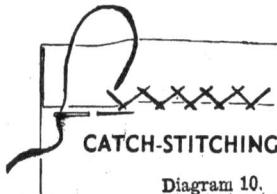

CATCH-STITCHING

Diagram 10.

Diagram 11 clearly illustrates the Button Hole Stitch, referred to as the wire stitch. This stitch is used for fixing wire on the edge of buckram or for wiring ribbon or lace, etc. Take the stitch through, then pass the needle through the back of the loop before drawing the thread tight. The stitches are placed about ⅛ inch apart.

BUTTONHOLE STITCH

Diagram 11.

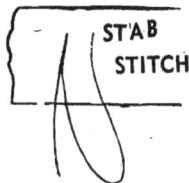

STAB STITCH

Diagram 12.

Diagram 12 clearly illustrates the Stab Stitch, so called because the needle is stabbed through from one side to the other, a strong stitch, and is used for securing trimmings.

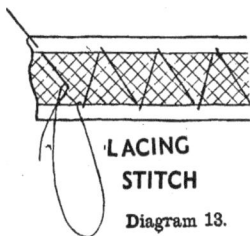

LACING STITCH

Diagram 13.

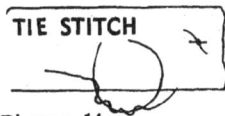

TIE STITCH

Diagram 14.

Diagram 13 clearly illustrates the Lacing Stitch, used for fixing material over Espartra, Buckram, stiff net or fine Braid. The material is first fixed over the Espartra, net or Buckram. The edges are then caught by the needle, being taken from one side to the other of the raw edges.

Diagram 14 clearly illustrates the Tie Stitch. Pass the needle through the material from the right side, leaving a length of cotton, then bring the needle through from the wrong side close to the first stitch, and secure by taking together in a knot. This is used mainly for fixing the tips of feathers, lace, flowers, or any light trimmings.

B

LESSON 8.

Important Hints Essential to Remember

Study carefully the various stitches used in millinery. Each stitch has its special use. When sewing, use strong silk or cotton. Remember, a good hat completed without a head lining will soil quickly and spoil. The joins in all linings must be kept at back of hat. All joins must be neatly finished.

When cutting velvet on the "bias" or "cross" grain, place the velvet on the table with the selvedge top and bottom. Fold over the cut edge of the velvet, forming a triangle, so that it runs level with the top selvedge edge. Note carefully that the shade of the velvet runs the same way when joining the velvet. Velvet must always be cut on the "bias" or "cross" grain for all millinery purposes. Fine net, chiffon, tulle, etc., will have to be handled carefully, and the less handling the better. When trimming a hat with ribbon, take care to see that the join in the ribbon is placed on the hat where trimming, a bow, or flowers will cover it. The Tie Stitch is used for all light trimmings. The Back Stitch is used for joining velvets and heavy similar materials. The long Back Stitch is used for joining soft materials. When binding edges of hats made of stiff material shapes, the Mulling (binding) must be cut on the the "bias" or "cross" grain. Do not combine wrong colours when trimming hats. Make sure the colours blend nicely.

A short, stout figure will look shorter in a large hat. High trimming does not suit a long face. High trimming suits an oval face. To overtrim a hat is not smart. If you are really going to learn Millinery, it is necessary to study various models in the shops. Learn also to create ideas. Buy only good trimmings, the best quality straws, braids and felts.

When tacking velvet, use only a fine silk thread; this avoids marking the velvet.

Avoid joins in material that has to be shirred.

To succeed, practice and more practice is necessary. Millinery, like Dressmaking, is an art. Your success depends entirely on yourself.

This thorough Course teaches you all Millinery; but practice alone can only make you a good milliner.

LESSON 9.

The Correct Method of Taking Head Measurements (Women's)

Diagram 1

SIDE to SIDE

Back to Front

Diagram 2.

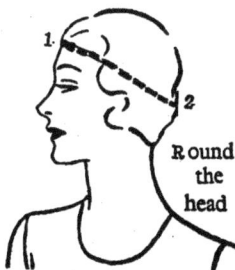

Round the head

Diagram 3

Use a Dean tape measure and be assured of the correct measurements. (Note: If the measurements are not taken correctly, the hat will not fit correctly. The correct fit depends on correct measurements.)

To take the side to side head measurement. Diagram 1 clearly illustrates by heavy dotted line from 1 to 2 the correct position that this measurement must be taken in over the top of the head from ear to ear of wearer.

Diagram 2 clearly illustrates the correct method of taking the back to front head measurement from 1 to 2 shown by heavy dotted line.

Diagram 3 clearly illustrates the around the head measure 1 to 2 shown by heavy dotted line. The tape measure must be placed around the head of wearer. This measurement must be taken on the position where the headline of hat is worn. (Note: This measurement can also be taken from the inside of the hat that fits the wearer by standing the tape measure on its side inside the hat.)

(Note Diagram 2: This measurement is taken from the forehead across the top of the head to the back of the head. To simplify taking this measurement, I advise students to tie a piece of ribbon around head at position that headline of hat will come to and measure from the front of ribbon on head to the back of ribbon on head. This will greatly assist to locate the correct position. Note with the rapid change of fashions these measurements will vary a little.)

The head measure from side to side and the back to front must always be measured before commencing the making of a hat. Take careful notice of the fashions and various styles and types of hats and the positions they are worn on the head. You will soon learn the correct position to take the measurements in. If you have a Dome Hat Block you can practice taking measurements on this block. It will greatly assist you to master the art of taking the correct measurements.

Note carefully in diagrams the correct position that measurements are taken in. Always check the measurements and remember to allow a little for the head lining or petersham innerband at headline of hats. Write measurements down and check; if not correct, alter the ones you have written down. Accuracy is essential for successful results.

A scale of measurements is given for adult measurements. (Note: The children's measurements are given in the section dealing with children's hats and bonnets.) You can compare the measurements taken with these. Also these are given for practice purposes and for the making of ready-to-wear hats.

(Copyright)

LESSON 10.

A SCALE OF MEASUREMENTS

THE SCALE OF HEAD MEASUREMENTS (SIZES)—WOMEN'S AND MISSES.

	Head Measurements	Front to Back Measure	Side to Side Measurements
For Small Adults	21 ins.	15 to 15½ ins.	14½ to 15 ins.
Or Misses	21½ ins.	15 to 16 ins.	15 ins.
For Adults	22 to 22½ ins.	15 to 16 ins.	14½ to 15 ins.
For Larger Head Sizes (with Long Hair) ..	22½ to 23 ins.	15 to 16 ins.	14½ to 15 ins.
	23½ to 24 ins.	15½ to 16½ ins.	15 to 15½ ins.

* * *

POINTS TO REMEMBER FOR BECOMINGNESS.

It is essential to always try on and readjust the hat to suit the individual. Harmony of line. Important. Becomingness depends greatly upon the degree to which lines of the hat harmonise with the wearer's physical lines.

(1) **Harmony of Line with Face Contour.** The hat must be made and trimmed so as to preserve a balanced proportion. A small face must not wear a top heavy type of hat. A long face oval requires soft width without length. A wide face oval takes proportionately wide brims and trimmings.

(2) **Harmony with Costumes.** A hat must harmonise in style and material with the costume it is designed for. A hat may be worn for street or dress according to the material used. Evening material for evening wear. Street material for street wear is correct.

LESSON 11.

The Principles of Line in Millinery

1. General Principles. In all millinery line gives to the hat that intangible thing referred to as "style"; a hat may be pretty and becoming to its wearer, yet have no line or style. In choosing a hat or its trimmings, it is always best to know exactly what you want.

2. Harmonising of line with the Frock or Costume. It must be remembered that a hat is but one unit of a costume. It must be just right to make a complete and perfect ensemble, the line of the hat must be in harmony with the general lines of the rest of the costume or frock.

3. The Harmonising of Hat Lines with the General Style. The correct mode of hairdressing, this is always a determining factor in the matter of becoming line. Various styles of hairdressing make the lines of the head entirely different. Naturally the lines of the hat must then be adjusted and adapted to each manner of dressing the hair. Different qualities are required in a hat to make it comfortable. This changes the line of the crown, and the brim line must be changed to correspond. Fashion silhouette. Styles in line will change with the seasons. What is smart and fashionable this year may be out of fashion next year.

THE PRINCIPLES OF LINE AS APPLIED TO THE INDIVIDUAL.
Objects to be Attained.

1. The real purpose of any hat is to add to and enhance the good points of its wearer.

2. Beauty of Line in the Hat. Beauty of line in a hat is the goal for which all designers strive. The choosing of that hat with good lines which brings out and compliments the good and minimises the bad points of the wearer is the task of the milliner.

3. Conformity with Fashion Dictates. In selecting a hat it is necessary to choose one in keeping with the lines of the rest of the wardrobe. Sport lines for golf, tennis, and sports clothes; dressier, softer lines for dress suits and frocks, always in line as in other matters of dress. The paramount thing is to have such harmony that the clothing is but a fitting frame for the pictured individual, and the observer conscious only of the personality of the wearer not the garments. The really successful hat is one which has style, line, good workmanship and becomingness.

NOTE: A wide face oval needs wide soft crowns trimmed with soft draped trimmings, not severe. A wide high forehead requires wide brims, straight or bent, and draped soft crowns; large "sailors" are becoming. A narrow face oval. The hat becoming to the narrow face oval is one that will soften the lines of the face. (Note: The features of a narrow face oval have a tendency to be sharp and shorten the length of the face. Many of the small brim types are becoming).

The Round Face. The hat for a round face should be so designed as to add to or lengthen the face oval. The crown must always be wider than the face at its widest point. A narrow crown makes the face appear larger.

Study carefully each figure type. Try to design hats to suit the personality of the wearer.

LESSON 12.

COLOUR HARMONY

COLOUR COMBINATIONS SUITABLE FOR VARIOUS TYPES.

The effect of colour is such as to make us see others as interesting persons of outstanding individuality. Colour as we know attracts, and colour is one of the greatest helps in bringing out all possibilities of beauty. The first principle to remember in choosing colours for an individual, is that you are working for just one thing—the beautifying of that person.

The beauty of a given colour combination, or garment, is non-essential if it does not greatly improve the looks of the wearer. Each colour must be considered in relation to the other for the effect desired. The colour combinations must be harmonious, both in themselves and as applied to the wearer. The desirable colours for a hat are those that give the wearer a rosy glow of health. The answer to this is rose, red, or pink. The less obvious is certain blues for certain types; certain greens, browns, tan and black, and navy for others. Why not select hats in colours that will enhance the expression of one's temperament?

◆ ◆ ◆

A List of Colour Combinations Suitable for Various Types.

A Brunette Type can wear rose, flame, fuchsia, or amethyst shades, jade green, olive, navy blue, golden yellow, honey shades, chartreuse, mole, dark or medium grey, mid blue.

Blonde Types can wear rose, flame, red, purple, pink, black, navy blue, mid blue, sky blue, jacaranda blue, beige, sand, natural, golden brown, tobacco brown, cocoa brown, olive and huntsman green, jade green, gold, tan, cinnamon brown.

Red Haired Types can wear golden yellow, burnt gold, cinnamon, tan, beige, sand, natural, cream, tobacco brown, leather brown, black, grey, orange, jade green, peacock olive, dull greens, buttercup yellow, honey.

Greys trimmed with green all can be combined into harmonious colour effects.

The correct colours for the various types is important. Study carefully this important feature in millinery.

LESSON 13.

Fashion Forecast for Spring, Summer, Autumn and Winter Wear

LOVELY STRAWS

FLOWER, FEATHER, RIBBONED TRIMMED

•

LARGE AND SMALL BRIMS

•

ALL ARE POPULAR

COLOURS THAT BLEND ARE THE IMPORTANT FEATURE OF ALL MODEL HATS.

A few suggestions are given here. **A wide brimmed Cream Baku Straw,** the edge of brim bound with nut brown velvet; a wide velvet bow of same nut brown velvet across front of brim, and a touch of brown veiling around crown, making a lovely model.

(Copyright)

LESSON 14.

Fashion Forecast for Spring, Summer, Autumn and Winter Wear

A Black Tagel Straw, medium brim, trimmed with several velvet roses on side of crown and down to brim edge; velvet ribbon in a deeper shade than the roses encircles the crown of this smart model.

A large brimmed fine Rapal Straw, trimmed with veiling and clusters of flowers under the brim, finished with a tie under chin with velvet ribbons; and matching velvet ribbon loops on crown and upper brim.

A beautiful model Flower Hat. A small coronet entirely covered with flowers in lovely pastel shades. Veiling to tone draped over flowers and tied under the chin. Smart for all occasions.

A smart model of Straw and Grosgrain combined, a Sailor shape in white or natural Straw. The Grosgrain in navy or colour desired is draped around crown; a large bow with wired edges finishes the model.

A lovely large brim model made in natural Baku Straw, trimmed with satin or Grosgrain. The crown is high; the satin ribbon or Grosgrain is around the crown and pulled through and tied in a bow on the underbrim; various colours are used as desired.

A smart Bonnet of shiny Black Straw, with the edges of brim bound with pink Petersham ribbon, and clusters of feathers around the crown.

A large Picture Hat of Leghorn Straw, trimmed with velvet ribbon and roses.

A large brimmed Fine Tagel Straw, trimmed with striped wide Taffeta ribbon bow.

A rust shade Velour Felt, large brim turned up in front, caught with a gold clasp; trimmed with green feathers across back of crown and brim.

A navy Velour Felt, high crowned; rolled brim on both sides, with white ostrich feathers around crown falling over brim at side.

◆ ◆ ◆

LESSON 15.

"Bandeaux" and Their Many Uses

VARIOUS TYPES OF "BANDEAUX"

1. A "**Bandeau**" is a separate narrow band made of matching material to be placed under the hat at the headline at various angles to tilt the hat, or as a trimming. The hat, with the aid of a "bandeau," can be tilted off the face or over the face, off the side of the head or over the side of the head. It also aids in making the hat fit firmer to the head of wearer. It can be used to make the crown of the hat larger or smaller, and saves time in the work of taking a hat to pieces to alter the head fitting. It is also used to attach trimmings to when trimmings are desired across back of hat at the under brim, at the headline of hat or at the side of hat in same position at under brim. These little "bandeaux" are easily made; the best materials to use are Espartra, Buckram, and if you have none on hand, a firm piece of Skirt Webbing will serve the purpose for the small side type of "bandeau." The shape of the "bandeau" is then covered with matching material.

  (1) **Straw Braid.**   (4) **Felt.**

  (2) **Velvet.**   (5) **Grosgrain.**

  (3) **Silk.**   (6) **Petersham Ribbon.**

There are various types of "bandeau" (made into a band), which is made to the measurement of the head of the wearer, covered with silk or soft material on the inside and matching material of the hat on the outside. This is attached inside the headline of the hat. The Buckram or Espartra interlining requires to be 1 in. or 1½ in. when finished width, and covered with a matching material (allowing for the usual joining allowance). This straight "bandeau," when fixed into position, will have three parts of the width showing below the headline of the crown of hat. If a wider "bandeau" is required to give more height to the crown, this can be added accordingly. A Sailor Hat with a "bandeau" across the back trimmed with flowers, feathers, or soft rich velvet sewn on the "bandeau," makes an entirely new and different hat. The small Pill Box model, too, can be changed into an entirely different model with an added "band..."

2. The Straight "Bandeau" is cut to the measurement from ear to ear around the back of head, or it can be measured from side to side by standing the tape measure on edge inside the headline of crown of hat and measuring from side to side around the headline. The usual length for a straight "bandeau" is half of the around head measurement, less 1 in. The width, finished, from 1 in. to 2 ins.

◆ ◆ ◆

LESSON 16.

"Bandeaux" and Their Many Uses

Interlined Buckram or Espartra covered with matching material.

3. The Back "Bandeau." This is straight on the edge that fits into the crown at headline of hat, and approximately 2 ins. to 2½ ins. wide in the centre, sloping off to nothing at ends. The length 5 ins. to 7 ins. Cut on cross of Espartra or Buckram and covering with matching material. These "bandeaux" can be wired for extra firmness. (Refer to Shape Making if wiring the shape of "bandeau.") This "bandeau" is used to tilt the hat forward or attach trimmings to.

4. The Side "Bandeau" is used for lifting the brim at side of hat, also to attach trimmings to. Often if you tilt your hat and see the effect in the mirror it appeals to you instantly. Why not wear it that way? You can with the aid of a "bandeau." Then, for a change, you may prefer to wear it tilting over your eyes and turned up at the back, trimmed across the "bandeau" at back with flowers, feathers or bows. Viewing the different angles in a mirror you will find the one that suits you best. You can then make your model as you desire it. To make the side "bandeau," cut a strip of Buckram or Espartra on the bias 6 ins. long and 2½ ins. wide, cut both ends to points; the centre will be 2½ ins. wide, graduating off to nothing at the pointed ends. Cover with matching material. Pin in position. Test the head fitting, then securely sew the "bandeau" inside the crown at headline of hat. (Note: If wearing a "bandeau" that is not having trimming attached completely covering it, a fancy scalloped shape may be preferred, especially if the brim edge of hat is scalloped.) This gives a smarter effect to your hat, completely in harmony with the rest of your hat. A tilt in the hat may be becoming to some and not to others. All this must carefully be studied when making millinery; so much depends on the correct line. All scraps of Buckram and Espartra must be saved. There are many uses for them, and some day they will be just right to make all the "bandeaux" you require. The sizes and shapes of "bandeaux" will probably alter a little according to the styles of the hats. The ones dealt with are the main types in general use when "bandeaux" are required.

Last year's model made new. The hat with a forward tilt may be the present fashion, or a sideway tilt may suit you best. These can easily be adjusted by the aid of a "bandeau."

◇ ◇ ◇

CAN YOU ANSWER THESE QUESTIONS?

1. What is a "bandeau"?
2. What is a "bandeau" used for, and why?
3. How is a "bandeau" made, and what material is it made from?
4. What kind of wire must be used for small millinery flowers?
5. What materials are most suitable for making small flowers?
6. Why must all spare pieces of material be saved, and what use can they be put to?
7. What type of elastic is the correct type to use for millinery?
8. What type of needles are the correct type for millinery?
9. What type of pins are the correct type for millinery, and why are they used?
10. What material is used in the making of bridal veils?
11. How much material is generally required to make a bridal veil?

LESSON 17.

Making of Straw Hats

This Section of the Course deals with the Making of Straw Hats.

(Diagrams appear on following pages.)

All important details are explained to assist you as you progress with the work. A list of so-called Straws is given and the correct treatment for same. Many so-called Straw Hats are not really made of straw at all. Some types of straw are made by hand. Many are imported from overseas, and there are many substitutes which are classed as straw, but many are imitations and even treated paper. It is important to cut off a small piece of straw before beginning the hat: (1) **Will it stand rain and heat;** (2) **will it stand cleaning and reblocking;** (3) **can it be successfully dyed and cleaned.** There are so many and varied materials for making millinery that it would not be possible to deal with them all. I have dealt with those in general use, and a variety here in this course which will enable the student to clearly understand millinery and its underlying principles. The making up of Straws is dealt with in this section and are listed here.

1. Straw Plait, or often referred to as Braid, can be purchased by the yard and also in bundles of 12 yards or more.

2. The Correct Method of Blocking Straw Hoods. (A hood is the hat already made up, ready to block and make into any desired shape.)

3. The making up of Straw into a shape, with the crown and the brim in the one piece. The crown is commenced from the centre and is referred to as the tip.

4. The Crown and the Brim made separately, the edge of the brim is neatened or finished by stretching the Petersham ribbon; the edge is wired and bound with the Petersham ribbon, or a bias binding can be used.

5. The Crown and the Brim made separately. The crown is commenced from the centre tip and the brim is commenced from the outer edge of brim.

6. The Varnishing of Straws. Note: When making up hats of Straw Plait (Braid), the coarser Straws are much more easy to handle than fine Straws.

7. The quantity of Straw required to make various types of hats will depend on the width of the Straw and the size of the hat required.

8. For a large hat with a 21 in. to 23 in. head measurement and a 3 in. to 3½ in. brim, at least 12 yards of 1 in. to 1¼ in. wide Straw would be required. If the Straw is wider less will be required.

9. Commence to make the Crown. Prepare the same as directions given for Felt Hats. When the Straw has been selected, and strong cotton to match it, the hat is commenced by making the crown. Commence in the centre (tip) by first dipping the end of the Straw in warm water and binding the end securely with strong cotton, as **clearly illustrated in Diagram 1.** The amount of wetting the Straw varies with the different varieties of Straw being used. Commence by working from right to left; begin to form a circle holding the Straw in place on the block with brass drawing pins, damping the Straw on the wrong side as often as required during the making up of the crown. The Straw must be overlapped over the first row of Straw at least one-third of its width. Ease the Straw to make it lie flat. **Do not ease too much.** This will cause the Straw to become fluted at its outer edge, and if the Straw is held too closely the circle will not lie flat. Pin firmly with drawing pins.

Making of Straw Hats

(Diagrams appear on following pages.)

Diagram 2. To avoid having the Straw fluted at edges and the circle not lying flat on block, test the Straw by pinning a complete circle of Straw and laying it flat on your table before stitching it.

The Straw is woven diagonally and naturally is elastic to a degree, and will stretch, and ease, in the same manner as material cut on the bias or crossways grain.

If requiring an oval shaped crown, make a circle which will measure about 3 ins. across; the centre front and the centre back must be marked with coloured cotton or white.

Then the Straw must be overlapped slightly more than one-third of its width at the sides of the crown. **See Diagram 3.**

The Stab Stitch is used to sew the Straw together. This stitch must be sunk into the plait. The cotton must not be showing.

Care also must be taken to avoid splitting the Straw.

This stitch is stabbed into the Straw from the right to the wrong side of the Straw.

Continue working until the tip is the size required.

Leave the plait hanging as in **Diagram 3.**

Press the Straw on the wrong side.

Placing Straw on a blanket or towel, the Straw must be placed under a clean cloth. Use a warm iron.

The Diagram 8 clearly illustrates the crown made on a wooden block.

The shape is the **Dome Block** and can be obtained in various sizes and head fittings. (See price lists of all blocks.)

All blocks are made in first quality timbers and are guaranteed first quality at lowest prices in Australia.

For the Dome Shape Crown, work on the block by wetting the Straw and pinning it down firmly with the drawing pins. When the crown is shaped, sew the Straw carefully to hold its shape. Press with a damp cloth and not too hot an iron. When dry, stiffen, and remove from block. Brims may be sewn over wooden brim boards by attaching the first row of braid with drawing pins, then sewing each row of the braid to the previous row. If you have no wooden brim board on hand, a bread board or a Buckram brim will serve the purpose.

(Note: Brim boards are made in a variety of shapes and sizes.)

♦ ♦ ♦

A special course of instruction is available, **"French Flowers Made Easy,"** teaching the Art of Flower Making. Lifelike flowers can be made for millinery or home decorations. The complete course is available for £3/3/-. Write to the Secretary for full particulars. You can save the cost of the course on the first flowers you make. These can all be made cheaply, and there is always a demand for beautiful flowers. It really pays to learn to make beautiful flowers. The lessons are thorough and fully explained, making the "French flower" easy to learn and a pleasant pastime hobby as well as a profitable one. When you have completed this thorough course of "Modern Millinery Made Easy," you will want to learn the art of artificial flower making at home in your spare time. You will be both pleased and proud to be able to make all the flowers you need, and many as gifts or to sell. Also to make beautiful Cushions and Home Decorations which this course can teach you.

DRYING THE STRAW

SAILOR TYPE FLAT.

It is essential that the braid be thoroughly dry before removing the shape from the hat block. The shape will be lost and the stiffening or varnish will not have the same new look.

The Shellac Finish. This can be made by purchasing shellac and covering it with methylated spirits in a jar till dissolved. Do not place near naked light. The transparent shellac may be used on all coloured Straw hats. The shellac will restore the shine that is lost when the Straw is soaked. There is no need to buy hat stiffening. It is less expensive to make your own. The directions have been given. All Hats, Straws, Braids, Trimmings, Flowers, Veiling, etc., can be purchased at all leading department stores. Felt hoods in a variety of colours. Velours and Felts also are obtainable. These are reasonably priced and can be made into the latest styles for the cost of only a few shillings.

The Sideband. First re-mark the centre back and the centre front. It is necessary to commence the sideband about 2 ins. before reaching the centre back. It is necessary to slope very gradually, and cease easing the straw, as the first row will take all the strain of the curve; it must be sewn both evenly and firmly. Continue to work down the side of the crown, underlapping the straw one-third its width. Test the head fitting as the work is proceeded with. It is necessary to watch carefully that the crown is not pulled into a smaller size, as this frequently happens if this is not carefully watched. It is easy to make the crown even if the centre back is plainly marked. Measure off a piece of straw the length of the head size measurement, marking with a pin and leaving the plait hanging. Arrange this length in position, pinned all round before commencing to sew. Continue until you have the crown the right depth required. Then commence the brim. This can be made all in one or separate from the crown. The crown can be joined to the brim later.

The Hat Brim. For a simple hat that does not vary much in the width of the brim, the brim and crown can be made as one piece, instead of crown and brim separately.

The Brim all in one with the Crown. Commence to shape the brim about 2 ins. before the centre back. **See diagram dealing with each step.** Study carefully. The straw must be eased on to the lower edge of the crown, and sew it very securely, as great strain is set up on the hat when removing it each time from the head, and unless firmly sewn the crown will part from the brim. This easing is done with the thumb and finger of the left hand and must be perfectly even, and sufficient to make the brim stand out at right angles to the crown. The straw, of course, must be kept underlapped one-third of its width and the stitches close together and secure. Each stitch must be hidden on both the upper and under side of the straw, and the long stitch lying between the two thicknesses of the straw plait.

Straw must be eased sufficiently to allow the brim to lie perfectly flat on the table. It must not be fluted, or rippled, but perfectly flat. If a mushroom brim or turn up brim is required, the straw is eased less. This will cause the straw brim to turn up or down as desired. **The width of the brim.** This must next be considered. For a brim that is the same width all around, continue to work until the brim is the width required. The stitches must be kept hidden on both the upper and undersides of the brim. Once the correct width has been obtained the remaining straw at the back can be cut off, leaving an end of at least 2 ins., which must be worked in under the edge of the brim neatly. **For a brim that is required narrower at the back of brim and also the front.** The straw must be overlapped in these places the same as when making the oval tip. If a wire is required at the outer edge of brim, it must be put on at this stage of the work. **See Fixing Wire in Diagram 9.**

LESSON 20.

WIRING EDGE OF BRIM

To wire the edge of the brim. Take a measurement $\frac{1}{4}$ in. inside the brim edge; a length of millinery wire (white for light coloured hats, black for dark hats) must be cut off, the measurement of around brim of hat, adding $1\frac{1}{2}$ ins. for overlap and joining. Join the wire in a circle, overlapping $\frac{3}{4}$ in. each end over the other. Bind with self shade cotton (see **Diagram 1,** Joining the Wire), neatly attach the wire $\frac{1}{4}$ in. from edge of the brim. **The stitch is illustrated and explained in beginning of the course.**

THE CORRECT METHOD OF
JOINING HAT WIRE
DIAGRAM I

Do you know the name of the stitch used when wiring brims? Try to remember them; each has a purpose and must be used in their correct places.

The wire, when fixed securely to the brim (under), must then be covered by either Petersham ribbon or straw. To cover wire with straw, make a circle of straw plait to fit the edge of the brim. Note this circle of straw must be carefully and correctly joined, not just sewn together. First damp the ends of the straw, then unpick about $1\frac{1}{2}$ ins. of straw at each end of piece. Then the two ends are replaited together. A bodkin can be used. Thread straw strands through eye of bodkin and weave the straw joining it flat and neatly. (**See Diagram 10.**) When finished, press the join on wrong side of straw (as pressing previously described) and fix the circle to the edge of the brim covering the wire. The brim must then be pressed.

Holding the brim the wrong side up flat on the table over a soft pad, press as previously detailed. The hat is next placed on the block and the crown pressed all over with a damp cloth and medium hot iron. (See Wiring Brims and Head Lines in Shape Making section.)

The headline can be strengthened and softened in several ways; a piece of Petersham ribbon, same colour as the hat, about 1 in. to $1\frac{1}{2}$ ins. in width and cut $1\frac{1}{2}$ ins. longer than around head measure and allow for head measure to allow for joining. Join this into a circle and then the edges are mulled (Mulling directions are dealt with in another lesson.) Next sew the ribbon into the hat $\frac{1}{8}$ in. above the headline so as ribbon will not show when hat is on wearer. Also note the stitches must not show on the outside of the hat.

LESSON 21.

WORKING WITH STRAW

Diagram 1.

Diagram 1 clearly illustrates the end of the straw braid securely bound with cotton to avoid fraying.

Diagram 2 clearly illustrates the commencement of the straw tip.

Diagram 3 clearly illustrates the correct method of forming the tip of crown or an oval for a tip of a straw hat crown.

Diagram 4 clearly illustrates the correct method of sinking the stitch into the straw braid. This is the "stab stitch."

Diagram 5 clearly illustrates the 1st row of sideband, pinned in correct position.

Diagram 6 clearly illustrates the centre front and centre back of the tip of crown. The arrow shows where to commence the side band about 2 ins. from the centre back. This avoids a sudden sloping of the straw. The straw is graduated off.

Diagram 7 clearly illustrates the centre back of crown placed over the brim of hat.

Diagram 2.

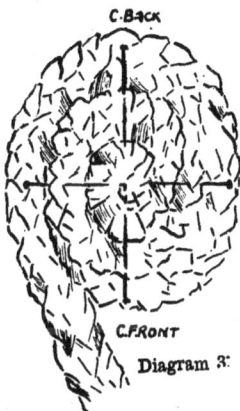

C.BACK

C.FRONT

Diagram 3.

Diagram 4.

Diagram 5.

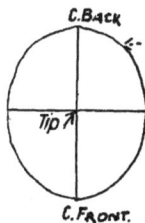

C.BACK

Tip

C.FRONT.

Diagram 6

C BACK.

Diagram 7

WORKING WITH STRAW

(Continued)

Diagram 8 clearly illustrates the crown left with the piece hanging which must be worked in gradually under the edge of the inner edge of the brim.

Diagram 9 clearly illustrates the correct method of covering the edge of brim with the straw, neatening the outer edge of the brim.

Diagram 10 clearly illustrates the correct method of making a neat join by plaiting the straw ends (1st method).

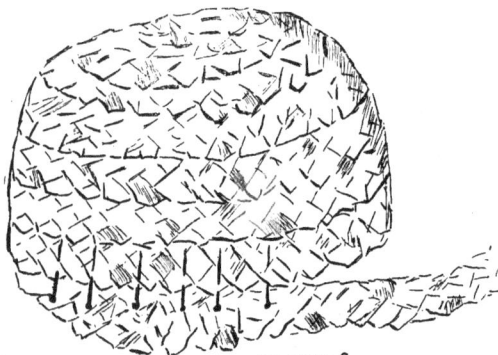

Diagram 8.

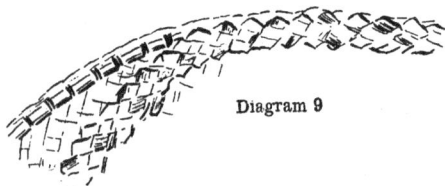

Diagram 9

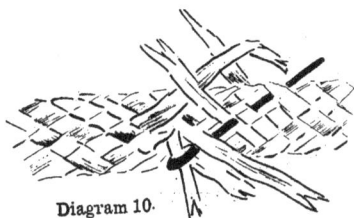

Diagram 10.

WORKING WITH STRAW

(Continued)

Diagram 11 clearly illustrates (2nd method) the joining of fine straws showing the wrong side of the straw.

Diagram 12 clearly illustrates (3rd method) the join stuck in position (wrong side).

Diagram 13 clearly illustrates correct method of joining fine straw (1 in. overlap) with rubber solution, sometimes referred to as Millinery Solution (used for sticking ribbon).

Diagram 14 clearly illustrates the correct method of filling in the spaces with straw at the sides of a large brim.

Diagram 15 clearly illustrates the separate brim with centre front and back marked.

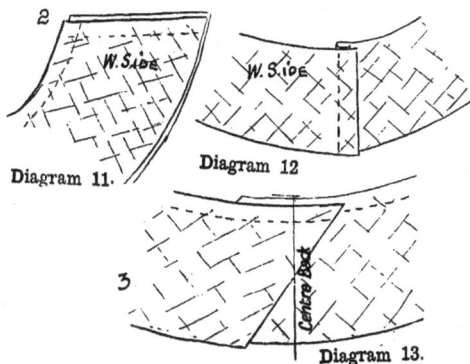

Diagram 11.

Diagram 12

Diagram 13.

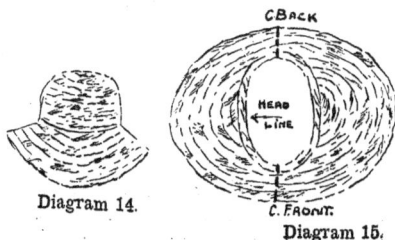

Diagram 14.

Diagram 15.

CAUTION.—*When using Millinery Solution for sticking purposes (Ribbons are often attached to a Felt Hat by means of Millinery Solution), do not use any glue or a substitute, as it will stain the hat. Only the correct Millinery Solution must be used.*

C

LESSON 22.

Mulling the Brim Edges

Another method is to cut crossways, a strip of Espartra the measurement of the head measure required, allowing 1¼ ins. for overlapping. Join into a circle and mull the edges. (Mulling is explained in a previous lesson.) This piece of Espartra is sewn into the inside of the hat about ⅛ in. above the headline of the hat. The stitch must not show on the right side of the hat. A piece of leno or net can be blocked as explained; a piece about 12 ins. square is suitable. Trim off all the rough, uneven edges when it is blocked and place the net or leno down onto the tip or top of crown of hat. This hat crown, just blocked and placed inside hat crown, should not come down as far as the headline; about half way down is sufficient. It can be stitched in place, using as few stitches as possible along its lower edge. Stitches can be avoided if the hat is well blocked with the leno or net crown inside it. The hat is ready to trim and to fix in the head lining. **Note** that with finer types of straw, such as Tagel or similar type, it is difficult to work the straw in the manner dealt with in previous lessons.

For Coarse Straw, the crown and brim must be made separately and the crown joined to the brim when finished. This method is excellent where a large brim is selected in the design of the model being made.

Moulding the Crown Shape on the Block. Commence the tip the same way as making the tip in coarse straw. (See Diagram.) It may be fixed by running on the right side (Tagel) machining, or hemming cheap Tagel on the wrong side. When you have made it 3 ins. across, place it wrong side upwards on the block. Secure to block with a drawing pin in the centre of the crown, then continue working the straw in position, pinning it to the previous row with the hat still on the block. In this case the last row will always overlap the previous row for one-third its width. Continue working down the crown until it is the required depth. When at about 2 ins. from the centre back of crown, cut off remaining straw, leaving only 2 ins. of straw. This end is gradually slanted off over the crown. It is very important to mark the centre back, and the centre front of the crown. Next turn the crown right side out. Prepare a pattern for the brim, or work on a brim board, whichever is easier. If using a pattern, as explained in another lesson, cut the pattern out on firm brown paper. Join the pattern up in the centre back. Commence working 2 ins. from the centre back, arranging the straw around the outer edge of your pattern. The right side of the straw must be upwards, facing the worker. Fix firmly by a running stitch, worked from the right side of the straw. If hemming is used, tack first; remove the straw from the paper pattern and hem the straw on the wrong side. Continue working until the pattern is completely covered. **Note carefully:** If a brim is large and of uneven and fancy shape, spaces will be left where the brim is the widest. These must be carefully filled in with the short lengths of straw. (See Diagram.) It is most important in all cases that the last row of straw on the brim must be a complete unbroken circle holding the short pieces of straw in position. Another 1 in. must be added to form a headband to slip inside the crown of hat. First mark the centre back and centre front, then the pattern can be removed.

Next wire the outer edge of the brim as for wiring coarse straws, but instead of using support wire, use Lappet wire No. 2. The support wire is too heavy for this type of brim. The covering of the wire is treated in the same way as for coarse straws, but the straw covering the wire must have a back join instead of plaiting the two ends of the straw together. **A crossways or bias binding** may be preferred, which is detailed in another lesson, also a binding of ribbon or Petersham can be used. Where this is used, it is necessary to press the brim edge on the wrong side over a soft pad; avoid pressing the headband piece, which must be left standing, and it must keep its shape. Next place the crown of hat on the block right side outwards, and press gently under a thick cloth. **Remove the crown from the block only when it is thoroughly dry.** As the head line must be strengthened, use one of the methods detailed in a previous lesson. See diagram clearly showing this important detail in shape making section.

To Join the Crown and Brim together. The crown edge is slipped over the brim and attached to the rim of straw left for that purpose. When stitching together, use ¼ in. back stitch long stitches on the inside, and no stitches must show on the outside of the hat. **Remember, neatness is essential for all good first class work.**

◆ ◆ ◆

LESSON 23.

The Correct Method of Underlining the Under-brim

A soft finish to the under-brim is often desired, especially in Bridesmaids' and Children's hats; a fine tulle or net, pleated or ruched around the under-brim, gives the soft effect desired. If preferred, Georgette or Chiffon may also be used, and Val. lace is very soft for Bridesmaids' hats. The under-brim may be fixed in two ways— **The under-brim described with or without a piping wire, or it may be caught to the outer edge of the brim; the last row of straw covering the raw edges.** Owing to the "give" in material generally used for the under-brims, a back join in material is not necessary. Even a hat with a shaped brim may have the tulle or net stitched to the shape of the brim; that is, if the tulle or net is placed on in a fold and not gathered on the under-brim.

The Correct Method of Blocking Straw Hoods. A straw hat ready made up for blocking is referred to as a **"Straw Hood"** and a large variety of sizes and colours are procurable both in imitation and genuine straws. When blocking straw hats the hood or straw hat may be treated in two ways. **(1) It may be held over the steam of a kettle; (2) It may be soaked in warm water.** It is wise to test a small piece of the straw to see which is the most suitable method. When blocking, care must be taken when placing the hood on the block, as fine straws are harder to handle and will split easily. In this case it is wise to place the hood on the block before damping it and to steam it. Many straws are woven diagonally from the centre of the crown to the edge of the brim, and it is then necessary to work the hood firmly on the block, using the palms of both hands to work the crown down on the block and pulling the brim fairly hard and diagonally working with the thread as it is woven. This is hard work, but you will be pleased with the result when the hood is blocked. If much fullness or a ripple is formed in the brim this can be made into a pleat as a part of the design of the hat. If only a slight fullness, this can be pressed out with a warm iron over a clean cloth. After you have blocked the crown and you are perfectly satisfied with the result, and the string is tied tightly around it at the correct headline position, you can then decide if it is possible to keep the brim of the hat in one piece, or cut it off and make a separate crown and brim. If possible, do not cut it off, but leave it all in one piece as straw frays easily and it is much better to avoid a join at the headline or at a back seam. When the side band is too deep for fashion it must then be cut and joined, or a deep folded tuck effect can be placed around the top of the crown close to the tip of the crown.

(Copyright)

LESSON 24.

For the Crown and Separate Brim

Cut off the brim of the hat, leaving 1 in. turning below the string around the headline of the crown, and only when the crown is dry must it be removed from the block. If the edge is to be covered with ribbon, flowers, or any trimming, it may be left raw and cut off at the headline. Great care must be taken not to stretch the crown before it is sewn to the headband. If the lower edge will not be covered with trimming, it can be neatened with a binding of Petersham ribbon. First it is necessary to join the ribbon in a circle; press the seam; and see that the halves and quarters are pinned into position so that the crown will not be stretched. First pin into position at the centre front, then the centre back, and then the both sides, with the pins at right angles to the edge. Next turn in one raw edge at the centre back and then overlap the other edge. On a straw hat it is necessary for the edge of the brim to be turned in and pressed while the hat is still damp. Then the prepared Petersham may be fixed in position. A small amount of millinery solution must be applied to the undersides of the brim and to the Petersham ribbon. This must be left to get nearly dry, and then a second coat of solution must be applied to both the hat and the ribbon. Press together till the solution is set. Some types of straw being coarse, invisible ties may have to be added every 1 in. around the outer edge, or to invisibly stitch all around the brim.

To Stretch Petersham Ribbon. First dip the ribbon in cold water; remove from water; place it in a curve in a clean cloth, the wrong side upwards; then press with a hot iron. At the same time, stretch the outer edge of the Petersham ribbon with the iron at the same time as the inner edge of ribbon is being shrunk. **Note:** Silk Petersham ribbon up to 1½ ins. wide can be treated in this manner. For wider widths a gathering thread is necessary; this must be run along one edge before the Petersham is dipped in the water. If a small circle is required, it is impossible to shrink or stretch any other ribbon than Silk Petersham. When buying ribbon, care must be taken to buy the correct ribbon. **Petersham ribbon is a firm ribbon with fine ribs,** mainly used for all millinery purposes. (See section of course teaching Various Ribbon Trimmings.)

The Brim of Hat separate from the Crown. First make a paper pattern. (See section of course Pattern Cutting for Various Hats). Note carefully: That if the design of the hat you have selected to make has a brim which lies nearly flat, it may be made without a join or seam in the back. If desiring the brim to droop, pleats may be ironed in the brim to shape it into a droop brim. A brim with much shaping must have a seam at back. Lay the pattern selected on the straw brim; outline the headline and outer edge with chalk or tacking cotton; mark the centre front and back; allow ¾ in. for turning at headline and ¾ in. on the outer edge. If a join at back, allow 1 in. at position of join for seam and neatening. The allowance of ¾ in. at outer edge of brim allows for any fraying, and even a little less can be allowed on some straws that do not fray much. Naturally the back join would depend upon the class or type of straw being used. **The Diagrams 10, 11, 12 and 13 clearly show the various methods of joining different types of straws. Diagram 10 clearly illustrates the plaiting of a straw join. Diagram 11 illustrates a join for fine straw. Diagram 12 also illustrates the correct method with the turning glued in position with solution. Diagram 13 illustrates the joining of fine straw with rubber solution.** Complete these joins as illustrated in the diagrams. They can be pressed under a cloth when finished.

Wire the headline of hat, if desired, with support wire (see diagram How to Wire in another lesson) or a strengthening wire can be joined up and attached to the head. (This also has been explained in another lesson.) It is important to test the head size as the work is proceeded with.

LESSON 25.

The Correct Method of Finishing the Outer Edge of Brim

The Correct Method of Finishing the Outer Edge of Brim: (1) It is important to turn in the raw edge while straw is damp. Tack firmly and press. "Stab stitch" firmly to band, or machine around with a cotton that is a perfect match. This is important. All cottons used must match.

(2) When hat is finished, the edge of brim can be bound with a Petersham ribbon stretched and stuck on with solution. This method is soft and excellent for small or large hats. For a wide brim the edge must be wired before finishing with ribbon.

The Correct Method of Binding the edge of Brim with Petersham Ribbon. This is generally used to bind the edges of brims of hats that have been wired. A narrow width of Petersham ribbon is best, but not less than ⅛ in. in width. Cut off a length of the ribbon sufficient to go around the outer edge of hat brim, not forgetting to allow 1½ in. extra for the turnings. Place the right side of the Petersham ribbon to the upper edge of the brim, first turning in the raw end before commencing to sew. The **"Back Stitch"** is the stitch used to fix it in position. The long stitches must come on the Petersham ¼ in. from the edge of the brim, and the short stitches must show on the the under side of the brim. While working, hold the Petersham slightly tight when reaching the centre back of the brim. Any extra ribbon must be cut off. Turn in the raw end to meet exactly at the back, then carefully slipstitch this join. Next turn the Petersham ribbon over on to the other side of the brim, then press firmly with a damp cloth and a hot iron, taking care not to mark the Petersham with the iron. Next pin the edge of the Petersham ribbon to come exactly on the row of running stitches, with pins stabbed in to avoid marking the hat. Next fix in position with slip-stitching (the stitch must be neat); then the pins are removed. Finally, press under a damp cloth from the underside of the hat. Note: Petersham ribbon will mark very easily if it is pressed on the right side.

The Edge of Brim Wired and Bound. First measure the outer edge of the paper patterns you have used for the brim; next cut off a length of Lappet (No. 2 is best for fine straws), then measurement of the outer edge of brim, allowing 1½ ins. for overlapping of wire. Join the wire in a circle and finish neatly as detailed and illustrated in previous lesson. Next place the circle of wire under the brim. Fold the damp edge of the straw over the brim, so that the wire comes to the tacked outline; next **"wire stitch"** to stitch through the double straw. Use strong cotton and follow directions (in a previous lesson giving detailed correct methods of wiring). Next trim off the raw edge closely. The wire must be neatened by Petersham ribbon binding; a **Crossway** or **Bias Binding; a Velvet Binding.** To cut material on the cross or bias, refer to the lesson dealing with this important subject. Note: It is important when pinning the cut pieces to see that the shade of the velvet runs all the one way. Note: **Velvet having** a pile, has a dull way look and a shiny way look. If cutting material with a rib or stripe, the join must be made down the rib or the stripe of the material. When cutting the bias binding for the brim, and if it is required, ⅛ in. wide on top and under, turnings must also be allowed for, and also loss in stretching. Therefore it must be cut 2 ins. in width to allow for turnings. When correctly joined up, it must be joined into a circle to fit tightly around the outer edge of the brim. The join must be neatly and carefully made.

"Back stitch" the join carefully together and press upon the join. This binding must be carefully joined, and must not be too loose or too tight. It must fit around the brim perfectly, without strain or bulges. After the binding is sewn in a circle, fold the binding in half lengthways. Cover with a cloth and press. Next pin the binding on the edge of the brim; the right side to the upper-side of the brim. The

The Correct Method of Finishing the Outer Edge of Brim

(Continued.)

raw edge of the binding and the brim must be equal. Fix the binding in position with pins stabbed into the binding and the straw brim, and avoid marking the binding and the straw. The stitches used for fixing are **"back stitches"**; stitches must be $\frac{1}{2}$ in. long. The long stitch must be on the upper side of the brim. Press gently under a damp cloth, taking care not to mark the binding. Next turn the binding over on the outside of the brim and slip hem into position. **See Diagrams 17 and 18,** clearly illustrating the important detail. Fine silk must be used to match the braid. You will find it easy to pull the binding over the raw edges, and to regulate the binding so as to avoid lumps and unevenness—as it is cut on the cross—it will give or stretch to a degree. When completed, press under a thick cloth and over a soft pad.

 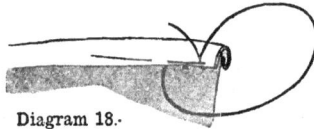

Diagram 17.   Diagram 18.·

Diagram 17 clearly illustrates the binding stitched in place at the outer edge of the brim (showing right side upward of brim).

· **Diagram 18** clearly illustrates the underside of the brim with the binding correctly slip-stitched in position.

To Join the Hat Brim to the Crown. First pin the centre front and centre back of brim. The crown must be placed over the brim. Stab the pins in to hold firmly, then tack securely, and try hat on. You can then see if it is necessary to make any alterations. Then fix securely together with **"Back Stitch"** or **"Stab Stitch."** The stitch must be firm and secure and invisible from the right side, and should be worked at about $\frac{1}{2}$ in. from the edge. Sometimes two rows are advisable when a binding is used, then the stitch should come just at the place where the binding is fixed on to the crown of the hat. An end of silk or cotton is left hanging inside the hat when starting to sew as this enables the finished end to be tied off securely. Next place the hat on the block and press around the headline. This is only possible with fairly manageable straws, or for a hat with a turned down brim. It must be possible to work the type of straw when it is damp (as if it were being shrunk). Place the hat on the block; tie a string around the headline, and tack a centre front and centre back mark. Block the crown while the hood is still damp and continue working. The brim must be pulled out sharply from the headline. When the shape for the outer edge of brim has been decided on, mark with pins. Fix a piece of wire to edge of brim with wire stitch. You can shape the brim as you work; also fix the wire to brim, which can be eased or stretched on to the wire. Study the lessons dealing with wiring. The raw edges must be trimmed off after wiring.

Next press the crown on to the block with a warm iron, covering the straw with a thick damp cloth. **The hat must remain on the block until thoroughly dry,** then varnished. The finishing of headlining and strengthening the headline have been dealt with in another lesson.

The Correct Method of Finishing the Outer Edge of Brim

(Continued.)

The hat can be trimmed before a closed type of headlining is inserted in the crown of the hat. Consider carefully when lining a hat; select trimmings to blend with the colour of the hat.

THIS IS IMPORTANT!—DO NOT OVER-TRIM.

Dainty trimmings look smarter, and there is always a large variety of trimmings and ornaments to select from. Flowers, feathers, ribbons, especially velvet, are always fashion favourites.

For a tailored frock or suit, select a model that is the plainer type. For afternoons or special occasions, a smart hat must be chosen. For late afternoon and night wear the smaller types are popular.

Large types do not suit everyone. Learn to choose the right style and type of hat for each personality. Study fashion magazines and window displays, and note carefully what is being worn. You can obtain many new ideas from a shop window, and even improve on many of the models.

If a swathed trimming is required this must, of course, be cut on the "bias" or "cross" of the material. This is usually pinned at one end and the length pulled around the crown into folds or pleats. The finished ends may be covered with various ornaments.

♦   ♦   ♦

DO YOU KNOW THE ANSWERS TO THESE 10 QUESTIONS?

1. What type of straw is Pedaline Straw?
2. What type of straw is Bangkok Straw, and how is it sold, and what are the two types of Bangkok?
3. What type of straw is mottled English Straw, and how is it sold?
4. What is Straw Braid, and in what widths is it obtainable?
5. What type of straw is Paribuntle and how is it sold?
6. What is the best type of hat to make with Raffia?
7. What type of straw is Rush Straw, and how is it sold and treated?
8. What type of straw is Paper Pulp? How is it treated and sold?
9. What is Straw Cloth?
10. How is Crinoline Braid and Horse Hair Braids sold, and to what types of hats are they best suited?

LESSON 26.

The Correct Edge Finishes

These are important. The wired edge of a brim must be neatly covered. There are several methods of covering the edges of brims.

1. **Fabric Folds.** The edge may be finished with a bias fold of satin or velvet. These folds may be neatly slip-stitched on both edges, or the fabric may be worked over a wire.

2. **Ribbon Binding.** Narrow Grosgrain or fancy ribbons stretched over the edge make a perfect finish, giving that tailored look finish. The edges may be slip-stitched down or sewn with long embroidery thread stitches.

3. **Fancy Straw Braids** may be sewn over the edge of straw brims.

4. **Fancy or Plain Crinoline Braid** may be used as an edge finish on straw brims. This is ideal also for adding width to a straw brim.

5. **Chenille or Yarn Braids** are effective for felt hats. These may be caught down with embroidery silk, yarn, chenille, or slip-stitched.

6. **Blanket or Buttonhole Stitch Edges.** Suitable for felts and children's felts and bonnets.

◆　◆　◆

DO YOU KNOW THE ANSWERS TO THESE 10 QUESTIONS ?

1. How is straw prepared for working? Name three varieties of straw obtainable in hoods only, and two varieties obtainable by the yard or in bundles?

2. How is a Panama hat prepared for blocking?

3. What causes the outer edge of the straw to become fluted while working?

4. What stitch is used to sew straw together?

5. What is the correct method of pressing straw?

6. How is a ribbon binding prepared?

7. How is the edge of a brim wired?

8. How is the headline of a straw hat joined to the brim?

9. What is Tuscan braid?

10. What straw braids or hoods are suitable for sports wear and dressy hats?

Other Books Available. Write to the Secretary for List

LESSON 27.

Making a Small Cocktail Hat

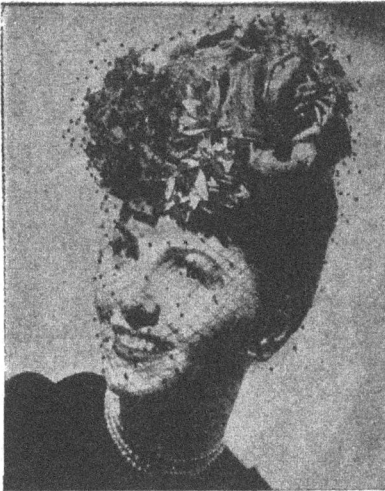

"CHARM," a Lovely Model Cocktail Hat.

This lovely model Cocktail Hat can be trimmed with flowers, feathers or lace and feather bows. The foundation of the hat is made of Espartra, or from ordinary canvas, whichever is desired. It is easily and quickly made.

Diagram 1 clearly illustrates how to cut out the foundation of the hat (the pattern). Rule an oblong, 12½ ins. long by 8½ ins., on brown paper. Rule a line as from 1 to 2 through the centre.

NOTE.—The centre is easily and quickly located by folding the paper (the oblong in half) and ruling a line down the crease centre line.

Measure from 4 to 3 and from 5 to 6 (4 ins.). Mark with a point; 7 is located half-way between 6 and 11; 8 is located 2 ins. from 7; 10 is located half-way between 4 and 14; 9 is also located 2 ins. from 10. Slit from 10 to 9 and 7 to 8. These slits are overlapped 1½ ins. at 7 and 10, tapering off to nothing.

When Espartra is cut out, curve from 5 around to 7 and from 3 around to 10. Curve from 7 around to 2 and from 2 around 10; 15 is located 1½ ins. above 2. Cut and overlap on Espartra ½ in. 12 and 13 are located 1½ ins. below 5 and 3, and these cuts are overlapped. This is the front of the crown. Position 2 is the centre back of the crown.

When pattern is completed, cut out; lay on Espartra, and mark around pattern. Remove pattern and cut out Espartra shape. Overlap slits where directed, and stitch firmly. The edge is then bound with wire (as previously explained Wiring Edges). The stitch used is the "button hole" stitch.

The edge of crown being wired, we must next cover the wire. This is done by folding over 1 in. or 2 in. wide velvet ribbon. The 2 in. width gives us 1 in. on the underside of crown edge. Bring the ribbon across the back and front to cover most of the shape. The remainder of shape is covered with flowers, bows, feathers or selected trimmings. If you do not want to spend time cutting and making the Espartra shape, various Espartra shapes can be bought from department stores cheaply and can be cut to the desired shape. Also, if you want a smart cocktail hat and you must make it in a few minutes, the crown of a lightweight felt or straw hat may be used as a foundation for the flowers or feathers, or bows of ribbon, which will completely hide the under part. This is inexpensive, as only the flowers or ribbon or feathers or bows would have to be purchased, and if you have already learned the art of making French hand-made flowers, your hat for this and any other occasion will cost you very little. Cocktail hats are expensive to buy ready made; and are the easiest of all hats to make. Select with care the trimmings, as that is the important touch for your cocktail hat.

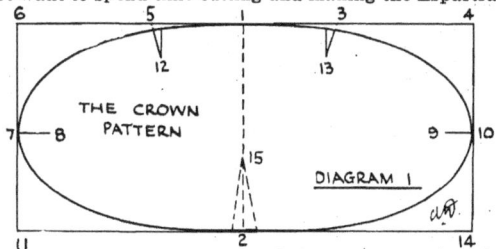

LESSON 28.

A DAINTY DUTCH BONNET
(Or CORONET)

Cut an Espartra Foundation the length of side to side measurement required (15 ins. is the usual). The straw is sewn to this foundation, and the Petersham ribbon is placed at the inner headline.

THE CORRECT METHOD OF COVERING THE BONNET SHAPE WITH STRAW.

The Making. You know how to treat the straw before commencing the working of the straw; you know how to wire the edge. Commence to cover the Espartra shape by sewing on the straw braid in rows. Commence the braid 4 ins. inwards from the sides of the Espartra on the underneath of the Espartra, continuing the straw over the edge of the bonnet and over to the under part, finishing up each row of the straw braid 4 ins. on the other side of the underneath of Espartra. The straw braid is cut off as each row is completed. It takes several rows of straw braid to cover this part of the Espartra shape. Then begin by sewing another row of braid (you know the stitch to use), lapping the braid over the wired edge to neatly bind the edge and conceal the wire. Next the two short pieces of straw must be neatly sewn across the raw edges, on the underneath of the bonnet. If any straw over, make two circular frills, one for each side, and add sprays of flowers or clusters of ribbon to the centre of each.

A band of velvet ribbon can be brought over the top of bonnet, out through the centres of the frills of straw, and looped into several small loops. Both are smart trimmings. Attach the elastic in the usual way. A variety of colours may be selected; all white or two-toned; pastel or dark shades to suit a special frock.

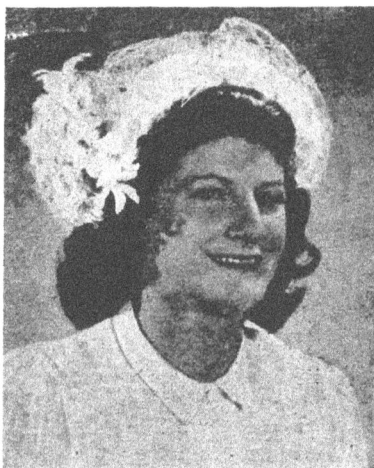

●

"MARG." A Smart Coronet featuring Mesh Veiling and Flower Trimming.

●

COST OF MATERIALS.

The Shape	1	6
2½ yards Braid	7	3½
¾ yard Mesh Veiling	2	2
Flowers	7	6
Inner Head Band and Elastic ..	0	10½
Total	19	4

Materials supplied by Courtesy of
ROCKMANS PTY. LTD.
Brisbane, Melbourne, and Branches.

LESSON 29.

THE LARGE BRIM MODEL

Fashion's
Favourite
for Summer Wear

★

(A Test Lesson)

To make this becoming model hat a "Sailor" shape block will be necessary and a large brim board. These are available from the Academy at a reasonable price.

The trimmings of veiling, flowers and velvet ribbon are a feature of this model. Coarse straw in any colour to suit, or fine straw if desired.

Note: The veiling is used on crown of hat, tying under chin of wearer.

You can picture this lovely model made in cream, coarse or fine straw, chip straw, or Baku straw bound at edge with ribbon, especially tonings of brown, or a white model trimmed with contrasting flowers or all white.

"SALLY," A SPECIAL MODEL.
Straw, Flower and Mesh Veiling Trimmed.

There are many colour schemes that can be introduced in this smart model.

This lesson is given as a test lesson, as at this stage a simple "Sailor" shape will not be difficult to make and trim. Gardenias and veiling are always popular trimmings.

The quantity of straw required to make this model:—

9 yards of 1 in. straw; 5 yards of 2 in. straw; ¼ yard of Espartra.
¾ yard of ribbon for headline; 1 coil of wire (colour to suit).
(Have a few spare coils of wire in your work box.)
3½ yards to 4 yards of veiling; 1½ yards of 1 in. velvet ribbon; flowers.

Follow directions for making as detailed in straw hat making. Trim hat as design illustrated.

Note: If you do not want to make the hat with straw braid, buy a large hat ready to block and trim. These hoods are available in a variety of straws, large or small sizes.

This model is illustrated to teach you to copy models. You will thus gain confidence when you attempt to do things without detailed instructions.

LESSON 30.

SHADY STRAWS

The larger Shady Straw Hat, showing front and side view, is made on a dome block the size of head fitting required, the brim on the larger brim board. If no blocks, use a substitute and the pattern of the Lady's Brim of Material Hat, as a working basis for the straw.

Pin firmly to a board with drawing pins and follow same directions given for making straw brims in another lesson. Complete the hat by same directions.

The trimming is contrasting velvet ribbon and small flowers.

The smart flower trimmed Sailor Model can be made in a variety of straws. Flower trimmed. Veiling may be added.

This is a test lesson, as at this stage you will know how to make several different shapes. You must try and copy different models and in this way gain confidence in yourself. You can vary the trimmings and practice trimming hats in this way.

MAKING A STRAW BRAID CROWN ON A DOME SHAPED HEAD BLOCK.

The wooden dome shape hat block is used. The correct size head fitting is necessary. Buckram crowns will serve as shapes to sew braid on, but will not stand the repeated heat of the iron. They soften when straw crowns are blocked on them, even over a wooden block. It is advisable to have the wooden block as it is used so often.

When sewing together a straw braid crown, pull up the draw thread at one side of the braid. Ease it gradually till the tip of crown will curve around. (If there is no draw thread in the type of braid you are using, run one in the edge of straw braid). When the braid is curved into a small circle, turn back the end for a neat finish. Each row of braid slightly overlaps the last row. (This has been previously explained.) Continue working the braid around to fit the block until the base of the crown is reached.

❖ ❖ ❖

LESSON 32.

OFF THE FACE MODEL

"CLASSIC" is a charming flower and veiled trimmed model. The shape is the Halo, a smart turned-up brim off the face. The crown can be made on a dome block, or if you make this model hat in Grosgrain you can make a crown with side-band and tip, using this pattern of the style of crown given in another lesson.

This model can also be made in velvet, straw, etc. A variety of flowers can be used; mesh veiling of self or contrasting colour is smart. This is another model for you to copy and is given as a test lesson.

Make it with a bonnet brim and trim it with velvet ribbon and flowers. Make it with a side band crown and no tip and another brim. Several different styles will result, and you will improve as you make each model.

You can make the model with feathers instead of flowers and veiling. This would be smart and tailored looking. Navy and white, black and white, grey and navy, blue and navy, brown and gold, and ever so many different colours are suitable for this model.

"CLASSIC," a smart Flower and Veiling Trimmed Model.

HERE ARE SMART NEW HATS YOU AND YOUR CUSTOMERS WILL BE LOOKING FOR.

Hats designed to express the Individual Characteristics of the wearer. Inexpensive, too, yet smart. Fashion's highlight is the Straw Ribboned Bonnet, the flower or feather trimmed model. All fashion's favourites. Large check Taffeta bows, small bows; large ostrich plumes; small feathers, all add to the beauty of the design. Women are very responsive indeed to new fashion. Try always to introduce something new, something different. Many large millinery businesses are built on individuality. Something out of the ordinary—styles and trimmings that catch the eye—bonnets made of Grosgrain—feather trimmed Chipped Straw and Baku Straw make excellent hats and bonnets. Practically all varieties are used, a combination of deep pink velvet ribbon and Fuchsia veiling trimmed, a Lavender or Mauve Straw. A Sun-baked Baku Straw trimmed with velvet ribbon and sprays of daisies are suggestions of spring bonnets and hats.

LESSON 33.

The Making of this Lovely Feather Trimmed Bridesmaid's Model Bonnet

"SELECT." A DAINTY MODEL BONNET.

The Making of this Lovely Feather Trimmed
Bridesmaid's Model Bonnet

The Materials required:—

6 yards of 1 in. straw.

There are endless varieties to choose from—Rapal Braid, Glossy Rapal Braid, Crinoline Braid, Baku Straw, or a hood of fine Tagel Straw.

¾ yard of Petersham ribbon for the inner head band.

3 yards of 4 ins. wide ribbon.

Taffeta picot edged ribbon or Satin ribbon, whichever is desired for the occasion (velvet is too heavy for this bonnet).

2 large ostrich feathers (use the pattern given for another bonnet in this section).

Hat wire and Espartra, as the shape is made of Espartra covered with straw, or the straw can be tacked on the shape (using pattern sections) and then removed from the pattern sections wired in the usual manner and the brim underlined with shirred georgette lace or net.

If making the bonnet over the Espartra or leno shape; cut out the shape; commence by covering the brim of bonnet (the under-brim first). Commence half an inch from the wired edge. Ease in the draw thread on one edge of the straw, pinning one row around on the Espartra shape, leaving ¾ in. at each end to turn into crown of bonnet. Cut off the straw and commence another row; repeat as last, and another row until the brim is covered. Then sew the straw firmly to the shape with neat stitches, avoiding any bulges in the straw. The upper brim is then covered (directions given in another lesson), then the crown section is covered (also dealt with in another lesson) and bonnet made up. If a transparent bonnet is to be made, such as crinoline straw, the brim must be wired. The straw is not made over an Espartra shape. The feathers are placed over the Taffeta ribbon, which is taken around the crown of bonnet and tied at side under the chin. Flowers may be used as a trimming instead of the ostrich plumes, as these are expensive, yet can be used for many years.

This bonnet can also be made in fabric, such as Organdi, Satin, Grosgrain, or material to match the frock. The ribbon could also be made of same material as the frock, having the edges picoted. This would save the cost of the ribbon, also would be an exact matching colour for the frock.

A few suggestions for colour schemes: Blue Taffeta, trimmed pale pink straw with deep pink ostrich plumes; all white bonnet, with plumes of white; pale pink bonnet, with white plumes and pale pink Taffeta ties; a variety of pastel shades combined or all self are the most suitable for this model.

♦ ♦ ♦

LESSON 34.

The Quantity of Straw Required for Making the Bonnet

5 yards of $1\frac{1}{2}$ ins. wide straw or $7\frac{1}{2}$ yards of 1 in. straw; 23 or 24 ins. of head band ribbon (usually 1 in. more than around head measure is required for neatening; 1 coil of hat wire (colour to suit); $\frac{1}{2}$ yard of Espartra. Dampen straw before using. Have all equipment required for working at hand. Choose correct shades of cotton for sewing the straw. Neatness is essential.

To make a Smart Straw Bonnet—to cut the pattern—the brim section.

Diagram 1. Rule an oblong $6\frac{1}{2}$ ins. by $7\frac{1}{4}$ ins. on brown paper. Measure as from 1 to 2 ($3\frac{1}{4}$ ins.). Mark all points clearly. Measure from 5 down to 3 (3 ins.). Measure from 3 to 4 ($3\frac{1}{2}$ ins.). Rule line from 5 through 3 to 4 as clearly shown in Diagram 1. Measure from 7 up to 6 (1 in.) and from 6 to 8 (3 ins.). Rule line on angle shown from 6 to 8. Curve from 8 through 4 to 2 and from 1 through 3 to 6. This completes half of the brim pattern. The line 1 to 2 must be placed on folded paper to cut out the whole brim pattern. Then the brim pattern is placed on the Espartra on the "bias" or cross of the Espartra. This is very important as it must be cut correctly to obtain the perfect fit. Pin pattern firmly on Espartra and pencil or chalk around pattern. Remove pattern and then cut out the Espartra shape of brim.

To cut the crown section referred to as a crown band—there is no tip or crown in this bonnet, but small flowers can be placed over veiling or net if desired to give the effect of a crown. The crown band is cut from the Espartra, also on the "bias," and is cut 3 ins. wide by $22\frac{1}{2}$ ins. for a $21\frac{1}{2}$ ins. head measure, or 24 ins. for a 23 ins. head measure. The inch is for joining allowance. Note: The ends must be cut as shown in diagram.

DIAGRAM 1

To cut the crown section referred to as a crown band—there is no tip or crown in this bonnet, but small flowers can be placed over veiling or net if desired to give the effect of a crown. The crown band is cut from the Espartra, also on the "bias," and is cut 3 ins. wide by $22\frac{1}{2}$ ins. for a $21\frac{1}{2}$ ins. head measure, or 24 ins. for a 23 ins. head measure. The inch is for joining allowance.

Note.—The ends must be cut as shown in diagram.

THE CROWN BAND CUT ON THE BIAS   DIAGRAM 2

3" WIDE $22\frac{1}{2}$"

LESSON 35.

Correct Method of Wiring Brim of Bonnet

Measure from point 3 to 6 and from 6 to 1 on the first paper (half of pattern) and double the amount. Cut off length of wire required. Attach the wire to edge of Espartra securely by buttonhole stitch. Next make ½ in. cuts in the Espartra about ¾ in. apart around the headline (8 through 4 to 2). These are bent over to attach to the crown band.

The Correct Method of Sewing the Straw to the wired Espartra Brim: The straw is damped and folded over double. This is placed over the wired edge, commencing at point 8 and sewn on around brim. Do you know the stitch to use? It has been explained before. You will at this stage know the correct stitches and their uses. Cut off straw and neaten the cut edge. Next sew a row of straw under the brim next to the half width of straw on the edge of the brim, and another row until the under brim is covered; also on the top until the top Espartra is covered, leaving only the small snipped pieces of Espartra around the headline to attach to the crown band. The 3rd row of straw, if 1½ ins. in width, will cover the Espartra brim. If 1 in. wide straw is being used more rows will be required to cover brim.

If covering bonnet with velvet or material (see this section of course). **The correct method of making the crown of bonnet:** Join the 3 in. strip of Espartra to size required for headband. Wire the upper and lower edges as previous directions on wiring the brim; attach wire securely. Join wire together first, which has been explained in course. The straw is next sewn to the crown band. This is commenced at wired edge at the centre front of the bonnet (as the joins in straw will be covered with flowers and will not be seen). The join in the Espartra is placed at the back of the crown. This is covered with the straw. Sew the straw plait flat on the Espartra, tapering off slightly at the beginning of the straw so as to hide the ends of the straw. Proceed sewing on the straw until the other wire is reached. Fold the last row of straw over to cover the top wire and stitch firmly. Do you know the correct stitch? Sew the edge of straw inside the crown. Make a strip of material similar to Espartra and join for the head lining. Taffeta is best. Have the head lining ready and pressed.

The Correct Method of Joining the Crown to the Brim. First mark with a pin the centre of the brim and centre front of crown. Pin them together, fitting the snipped pieces of Espartra inside of the crown band. Each piece must be sewn firmly. The head lining is finally attached to the inside of the crown band, neatly sewing same in. The edges of the brim are bent on each side to give a bonnet shape. Important—the trimming. A variety of trimmings may be used, ribbon feathers or flowers, veiling and flowers combined. The ribbon in a mass of loops is effective, or large bows. Ornaments also may be used as a trimming.

◆ ◆ ◆

"Modern Tailoring" teaches all Ladies Tailoring, fully illustrated. Write to *"The New Art Publishers"* for lists of all Trade Publications.

D

LESSON 36.

A SMART SAILOR SHAPE HAT

(RIBBON TRIMMED)

This smart Ever Popular Style can be made in straw, fabric or felt. The model illustrated is simple to make. The shape can be bought ready blocked in straw. The trimming is pleated, Petersham ribbon finished with a narrow ribbon and small bow and veiling, or an old hat can be cleaned, re-blocked and trimmed with the ribbon, as illustrated.

This hat can also be made in materials and stitched and trimmed two-tone. The trimming is suggested to also add height to the wearer. A navy and white, tan and white, brown and beige, or grey and white are suggested as two tones.

Feathers or loops of straw may be added to give height to the crown. A large taffeta bow across the front or back of hat will also add height to this crown, or the crown can be raised as previously described in another section.

If straw cannot be matched, insert Buckram or Espartra and cover the inset piece with ribbon.

If you desire to make this hat, use a sailor block or an upturned saucepan of the correct around head measure required. (See the Making of Straw Hats. Full directions are given.)

You can make the pattern of the brim by laying the hat block on paper and pencilling around the headline and measuring from headline out the width of brim required and pencil around in a circle. Practice this in your spare time.

These short cuts are always helpful in the making of patterns. Make both plain and scalloped brim edges and uneven brims. You can create new designs.

* * *

DO YOU KNOW THE ANSWERS TO THESE 10 QUESTIONS?

1. What material is used for the making of small shapes, with brim and crown in one piece?
2. What is the correct method of fixing a piped edge?
3. What material is suited best for head linings?
4. What trimmings are suitable for sports hats?
5. What is the correct method of joining a crown to a brim?
6. What is a hood?
7. How is Petersham ribbon prepared to bind a brim edge?
8. What is the correct method of varnishing straws?
9. Which are the easier types of straw to handle?
10. What quantities of 1 in. straw would be required to make a Sailor shape and a large Garden hat? What quantities of 2 in. straw would be required to make the same hats?

LESSON 37.

MODELS FOR ANY OCCASION

The three attractive hats illustrated will appeal to any Girl or Woman. The first smart model is made in a crisp straw any colour desired. The quantity of straw required is 6 yards of 1 in. wide straw, 4 yards of 1¾ in. wide straw; a coil of hat wire; 1¼ yards of 1 in. to 1½ ins. ribbon; ¾ yard Petersham ribbon for inner-head line; and a small spray of flowers for under brim or bow of ribbon may be used instead of the flowers.

A Sailor hat block is the shape required. Head size required must be used. A medium size brim board, or you can use a paper pattern given for brim in another section of Course, and tack straw on this flat on a table, thus avoiding having to purchase a brim board.

However, if you are constantly making hats, all the necessary blocks save time and worry and they last for many years. They are a good investment, as time saved will pay for them in the end. A list of shapes and prices is given; you can select your requirements from this list if you desire.

NOTE: The edges of this model are fluted at both sides. This effect is easily obtained when hat is completed by bending the wire as in the design illustrated. The straw can be pressed over a round object, such as a wooden rolling pin. Trim hat as model illustrated.

NOTE: A large variety of types of straws may be used for any of these models illustrated.

The second model has a very small brim. It is trimmed with narrow loops of plain crinoline or any narrow straw braid can be used. Bows of veiling or spotted net are made, with the straw supporting each bow.

The quantity of material required for this model is 4½ yards of 1 in. straw; less if straw is wider. The Sailor crown block is used. The brim can be made by pinning the straw around a basin, taking care that the first row measures the head line measurement to fit the crown of hat. The brim is a small drooped brim. It can also be made slightly wider and reversed the other way as a turn-up semi-roll brim. The same narrow straw supporting the net or veiling bows is sewn in several rows around the outer headline of hat. A two-tone contrasting colour would be smart for this hat. Navy and white, red and white, brown and lemon, or all self colouring.

MODELS FOR ANY OCCASION

The third model illustrated is made in Crinoline Straw. The quantity of material required for this model is 4½ yards of 1½ in. wide crinoline straw, 2½ yards of 3 in. wide taffeta ribbon, plain or check design.

The ends of ribbon are fringed and made into a circle till all the ribbon is used except sufficient to place around the crown. The fringed end is pulled through the gathered centre of the ribbon. Crinoline plain may be used instead of the ribbon or loops of velvet ribbon, and flowers may be preferred as trimming for this smart model.

The Sailor block shape or Dome crown block shape may be used to make the crown of this model. If you do not wish to purchase blocks, the bottom of a saucepan may be used, but it is harder to work on as the straw cannot be pinned to the substitute block with drawing pins.

A variety of colours may be chosen for either straws or the trimmings.

These models will assist you to learn to copy models and a variety of styles from fashion plates and shop windows. Try also to create models and ideas of your own. This will make the work more interesting and assist you to gain confidence as you progress with each step of millinery.

Practice alone makes perfect, and on this your success depends. You cannot possibly learn everything in a few weeks; it takes months and great patience to master each important detail. It may even take years, but when millinery is learnt thoroughly it will be worth every minute of the time you have given to the subject of millinery.

Whatever you do, do it thoroughly. Do not skip important details. Learn to understand each subject, and as one subject is mastered the next will become easier, and you will progress much quicker.

* * *

LESSON 38.

DO YOU KNOW THE ANSWERS TO THESE 10 QUESTIONS ?

1. What is Lisere Braid, Cellophane, Hair Braid, and Milan Braid?

2. What Straw Braids can be used in combination with other braids?

3. What type of braids are suitable for Bridesmaids' Hats?

4. What types of Straw Hoods and Braids must be soaked in water for several hours or days?

5. What is the tip?

6. How is fine straw joined?

7. When must the hat stiffener be applied to the straw?

8. How is it applied to the straw?

9. When is the head lining placed in the hat?

10. Why is it necessary to insert a head lining or ribbon at the inner head line of a hat?

LESSON 39.

A SAILOR STRAW

THE MAKING OF THIS EVER POPULAR SAILOR STRAW RIBBON TRIMMED HAT.

Materials required: 6 yards of 1 in. wide straw (Rapal or any desired straw); hat wire; ¾ yard Petersham ribbon for head line; silk Petersham or Moire ribbon 2 in. wide for trimming; a sailor hat block the head measurement required, or as a substitute the upturned saucepan of the same circumference as the around head measure required. A block is best, as you are able to pin the straw with drawing pins to the block as you work, making it easier and quicker.

The Correct Method of making the Crown Section of the Hat. Commence the straw crown by treating the straw as previously detailed. Commence by drawing the draw thread on one side of the straw braid till the braid forms a small closed circle of straw. Next press this circle of straw flat, placing it in the centre of the block and holding it in place with drawing pins. Continue with the drawing up of the straw, forming a circle, and pin in position with edge slightly overlapping last row of straw until the top of the block is completely covered with the straw braid.

If you are using a saucepan in place of the wooden block, it is best to make the top circle on the table and block it on the saucepan.

When the circle of braid is completed tack, and then sew firmly. You know the stitch to use. Then press flat with a warm iron and damp cloth on the wrong side of the braid. When completed and pressed, place straw tip of crown back on the block, pinning in place with the drawing pins.

Commence the side crown section by pinning a row of the straw braid around the top of the block and at the side of block. This straw must not be eased on the side of the block. Pin another row around and another till the last row is on the side crown section. (See further details in lesson "Making of Straw Hats.") Any of the detailed instructions you cannot remember will be found in the section dealing with Straw Hat Making. Allow straw to dry thoroughly, then brush over with the hat stiffening.

◆ ◆ ◆

"Exclusive Lingerie" **teaches all Model Lingerie, Sports Wear, etc., Trousseau Wear, etc., fully illustrated.** *Write for full details.*

Correct Method of Making the Sailor Brim

If you have not purchased a small brim board to work all small brims on, you can easily make the Sailor brim on a flat table. Commence by placing the crown on a sheet of brown paper and pencil around the headline of crown. This determines the correct size of the inner headline of the brim. Measure out from this line 2 ins. or 3 ins. all the way around in a circle, or wider if desired. Circle around, forming the outer edge of the paper pattern of the brim. Cut pattern out.

Commence the straw from the outer edge of the circle. Begin by pinning the first row of straw overlapping the edge of paper about ¼ in. (This is turned in over the wire to hide the wire.) Ease up the draw thread in the straw as you work, giving the straw a semi-circular effect, enabling it to lie straight and flat on the paper pattern.

When the first row is completed around the brim, next cross over the straw to commence the shaping of the 2nd row of straw. Pinning the straw securely to the paper pattern, finally cross the straw over again to work in the third row. It is necessary to slope the last cross over of the straw so that the straw lies flat.

The last row of straw placed on brim will allow sufficient to be pressed back, enabling it to stand up a little to sew the crown to. The rows of straw must be sewn neatly edge to edge. (You know the stitch to use.) Press the outer edge of brim over into a small fold to cover the wire (the wire must be prepared and made ready to slip in the finished brim). This has been dealt with in another lesson. Slip the wire under a folded edge of the straw and hem neatly.

NOTE.—The edge of the straw brim can be finished with the wire edge and Petersham ribbon binding. This has been explained also in another lesson. The centre front and centre back of the crown section is now joined to the centre front and centre back of the brim section.

The trimming can be varied. Velvet ribbon can be used if desired. The brim section will require a coat of hat stiffening.

LESSON 41.

THE CORRECT HEAD LININGS

THE MAIN USE FOR A HEAD LINING IS—

(1) To neaten the inner crown of the hat.

(2) To give longer wear to the hat.

(3) To keep the inner head of hat clean.

(4) For comfort in wear.

The Correct Materials for Head Linings are important. These must be light in weight and different qualities are used. The most suitable materials for Head Linings:

(1) **Taffeta—White or Black.** The white is used for light coloured materials. The black for dark materials.

(2) **Jap Silk.** Very light in weight; obtainable in a variety of colours.

(3) **Muslin or Fine Voile.** A variety of linings and their widths are dealt with in suitable millinery material section. Refer to this section.

The Head Lining made with a Draw String. To make this type of hat lining, it is necessary to cut the material on the "exact cross" or "bias," making it the head measurement in length, adding 1 in. for joining seams. The width must equal the depth of the side band of the crown it is required for, adding 3 ins. for turnings and freedom of movement in the finished lining.

NOTE.—The directions how to cut on the "cross" or "bias" is detailed and illustrated in another lesson. Follow this lesson carefully.

The tip of crown is cut out in a square of material 6 ins. by 6 ins. folded over like a handkerchief into four and the ends rounded. The side band of the lining is joined up and pressed and a running thread placed on one edge, easing it up to fit around the tip just cut out. Press on wrong side when finished.

When inserting the lining in the crown of hat, the wrong side of lining must face the inside of the crown. The right side is facing outwards so that when viewed inside the hat the right side of lining is facing you, the seams being hidden on the inside.

Pin first in position, then sew neatly into the hat. NOTE: You know the stitch to use for sewing in the lining. This has been dealt with elsewhere in the lessons. It is important to place the line of stitches so that the stitches or the edge of the lining do not show when the hat is on the head of the wearer. If the head lining is stretched at the headline or is too large to fit around the headline, small tucks may be placed on the wrong side of the lining or pleats as the lining is tacked into the crown of the hat.

The clearly illustrated diagrams show step by step, the correct method of making the head lining.

Another method of cutting a fitted lining using the pieced crown hat pattern, cut the lining allowing usual turnings and seams. This lining is also made for fabric hats.

NOTE.—Special Headlinings can be bought ready made. They are not highly priced; you can buy them for practically the price of the material. They save time and are ready to use whenever required. They are usually obtainable from department stores or millinery supply departments.

LESSON 42.

For Sports Hats Head Linings

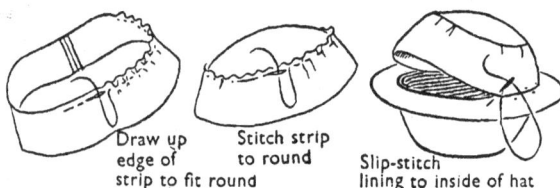

Draw up edge of strip to fit round   Stitch strip to round   Slip-stitch lining to inside of hat

If only a part of the crown is required to be lined, this type of lining is most suitable; also a strengthening piece in one can be used for the inner head line. This is excellent for Felt Hats or the smoother varieties of Straw Hats.

Using a piece of Espartra, Double Leno or Canvas, cut on the "bias" or cross. Cut the length of the around head measure required, adding 1 in. for joining. The width requires to be 2 ins. Cut the headlining also on the cross to same measurements and about 2½ ins. deep.

Join the strip into a circle, which must fit neatly inside the crown of the hat. Press the seams open. Machine a small hem along one edge. Next tack in the strengthening piece 2 ins. in from the raw edge overlapping for the join at the back. Turn the raw edge to enclose the strengthening piece.

Next machine through the three thicknesses or neatly hand sew same. Run a strong thread through the small hem at top of head lining and ease up. Insert the finished lining in same way as previously detailed.

Neatness even in headlinings is essential and just as important as all neatness in millinery.

"Advanced Modern Dress-cutting to Measure by Tape Measure." Teaching the Cutting of Perfect Fitting Garments for all Figures including abnormal and disproportionate Figures. Write for Particulars.

LESSON 43.

THE CUTTING OF THE HALO (2 Shapes)

SUITABLE FOR BRIDAL WEAR
One Plain, the other Scalloped in Centre

Rule an oblong 12¼ ins. by 9½ ins. on brown paper.

Measure as from 1 to 2 (3¾ ins.), also from 4 to 3 (3¾ ins.).

Mark with points.

The line 5 to 6 is the centre line; 5 to located half way between 1 and 4, and 6 is located half way between 7 and 8.

Rule the line from 5 to 6.

Measure from 5 up to 9 (6 ins.).

From 1 to 10 measure up 3½ ins., and from 4 to 11 feasure up 3½ ins.

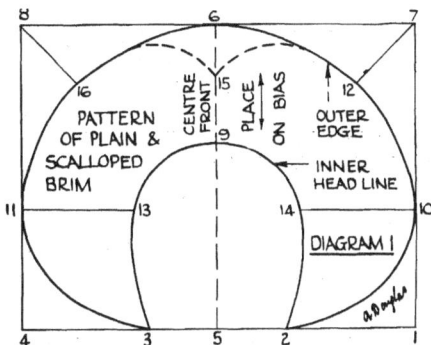

DIAGRAM 1.

Measure from 7 to 12 and 8 to 16 on angle shown 2¼ ins.

14 is located in line with 10. From 10 to 14, measure 3¼ ins.

Measure from 11 to 13, also 3¼ ins.

Shape from 3 through 13 and 9 and 14 to 2 for the inner head line.

Shape from 3 through 11 and 16 to 6 and through 12 and 10 to 2 for the outer headline.

Cut out pattern.

To cut the Heart or Scalloped-shaped Front Halo, re-cut another pattern from the one cut out.

Measure down from 6 to 15 (1½ ins.). Mark with point.

Curve from 15 as shown in diagram to form the scallop.

Fold pattern over on the centre line and cut scallop even; if required deeper, cut a little more out till the desired size is obtained.

Cut both Patterns on firm Cardboard or Paper.

LESSON 44.

The Making of the Bridal Veil

TO MAKE THIS BRIDAL VEIL.

4 yards of fine Brussels net, silk net or any suitable net or tulle will make a lovely veil.

The bridal nets are usually 2 yards to 2½ yards wide; also obtainable in 54 in. widths.

Hem the edges of the net, and with silk embroidery thread run two or three rows around the hem. Stitches about ¼ in. long. This hem will be made on the right side so as the stitching will show as a trimming.

Fold the net over double, marking the centre with cotton. This can then be placed over a stiffened net crown that the scalloped or plain halo has been attached to, and caught at each side with a spray of orange blossoms. If a longer veil is required 5 yards to 6 yards of net would be necessary.

The veil can be embroidered or have small sprays of the orange blossom sewn here and there on the veil. A heavy net is not suitable for bridal veils.

The veil can be arranged on a block, then tried on to test the correct hang of the veil, and if it is suitable to the wearer.

◆   ◆   ◆

LESSON 45.

The Making of a Lovely Bride's or Maid's Halo or Hat

This lovely headwear is easy to make, and can be made in a variety of materials. The most suitable materials are Lacy Crinoline Braid or All-over Lace. The lace to match the frock (12 ins. is sufficient). Wire for the edges.

Cut the lace out by the pattern, allowing 1 in. turnings. Sew the wire around the edge; turn the material once over the edge before sewing it. You know the stitch to use.

The heart shaped Halo, as illustrated, is a popular type and holds the lovely tulle veil in position. A pleated double narrow tulle frill around outer edge makes a nice finish to the Halo, or narrow gathered lace or ribbon may be used as a finish.

This lovely Halo, either heart shaped or plain, is inexpensive to make.

The lace can be shirred in the centre of the Halo and small sprays of orange blossoms catching the veil at the sides makes the loveliest bridal headwear. These Halos can be worn with long or short veils.

When you have completed the making of the Halo, stiffen the lace or crinoline with hat stiffening, using a clean brush. Allow to dry. Attach the elastic from side to side of Halo, tying a knot first in each end of elastic before sewing it in place. This avoids elastic.slipping. Special millinery elastic must be used to hold the Halo in place on the head of the wearer.

Fine Chiffon or Georgette or all Tulle may be used instead of Lace or Crinoline.

Important: Measure off the amount of wire required for wiring the edge of Halo. Cut off, allowing 1½ ins. for the joining. You know how to join the wire. The wire must be straightened out by running it between your thumb and finger before attempting to sew it to the Lace Halo.

The join in wire must be perfect, and the cut ends neatly concealed.

This has been thoroughly dealt with and fully detailed in another lesson. In all work neatness is essential.

◆   ◆   ◆

Write for Lists of 28 Trade Publications and Children's Fashion Books

LESSON 46.

Suggestions for Bridesmaids Head Wear

A Delightful Little "Coronet" made from Crinoline Braid and Flowers.

Inexpensive to make, but expensive to buy ready made. The materials required: 2 yards of plain Crinoline Braid, 3 ins. in width. Sprays or bunches of flowers to match frock.

First measure from side to side of head to obtain correct length of the band of Crinoline Braid.

(You know how to take this measurement. It is clearly illustrated in the lesson **"How to Take the Head Measurements."** Refer to this important subject if you are not quite sure.)

Cut off the piece of Crinoline Braid to the length required, leaving ½ in. each end for neatening. With the remaining piece of Crinoline Braid make it into four small loops, which you sew to each side of the head band. Finish with the flowers among the loops and around the head band, if desired, or at each side only.

NOTE: There are a variety of shades in Crinoline Braid. Pastel shades or white are best. There may be some spare pieces left over from a hat. These can be used up in this way. Tulle may be used in place of the Crinoline loops. These little coronets may be made up in spare time. They are always in demand and the choice of either fair or dark haired bridesmaids.

A VARIETY OF DESIGNS CAN BE USED IN CRINOLINE BRAID

◊   ◊   ◊

NOTE.—CHILDREN'S ROUND NECK SMOCKED BLOUSE OR FROCK PATTERNS, ALSO ADULTS' ROUND NECK SMOCKED BLOUSE PATTERNS, AND A VARIETY OF GIRLS' SMOCKED FROCK PATTERNS, AND BOYS' SMOCK SUIT PATTERNS AVAILABLE.
All with Free Instructions How to Smock.

LESSON 47.

The Correct Method of Cutting Velvet or Plush Covering for a Hat

Diagram 1.

THE CORRECT LAY-OUT.

Velvet and Plush or **Fur Fabric** materials all have a pile finish, giving the material a dark shade when viewed one way and a light shade when viewed another way. **Therefore caution must be taken** when cutting any material with a pile.

All Velvet for covering the shapes must be so placed that the darker shade runs from the front to the back of the hat. This shows up the rich beauty of the material when the hat is being worn.

Rich Pan Velvet. Pan Velvet has a pile which is flattened by steaming process. The pile runs smoothly from front to back.

To cut out the Upper Brim Covering in Velvet: Lay the Velvet on a table (with the top to right hand if Velvet or Plush is being used). The right side of Velvet down to table, the wrong side facing you. Mark the front and back on the Velvet with chalk, placing the pattern or the Espartra shape front on the cross, taking care to see that the dark shade of Velvet is going the right way.

Mark around the headline and cut out, leaving the usual turnings at headline. (Snip at headline.)

To Cut the Underbrim: It is essential also to have the underbrim running exactly the same way as the upper brim. Therefore it is necessary to place the upper brim piece of Velvet on the remaining Velvet, with pile to pile; check to see that pile on both runs the dark way (front to back of brim).

Cut out around the outer edge of brim. Do not cut out the inner headline. (See section "Covering Material and Velvet Shapes." This is clearly illustrated.) The Velvet at headline is cut when the brim is fixed securely.

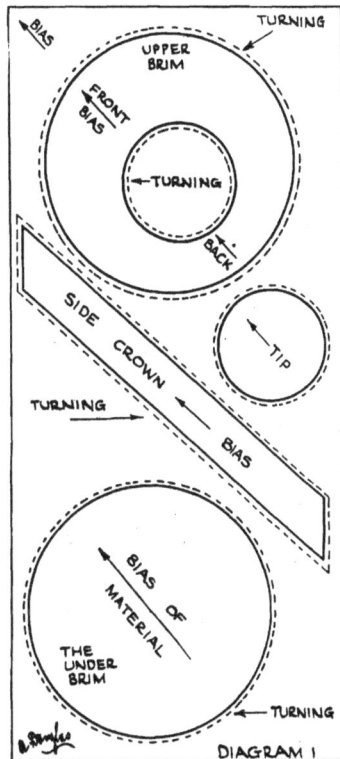

DIAGRAM 1
THE CORRECT LAYOUT ON THE MATERIAL

The Side Crown: This also must be cut on the cross or bias of the Velvet. The dark shade must be to the top, allowing ¼ in. to ¾ in. turnings on both sides and ends of side crown piece of Velvet.

The Tip of Crown. First mark the dark shade with chalk line. Place the tip pattern with front of pattern on Velvet so that the dark shade runs to the back (to match brim). Cut out, allowing ¾ in. turning all round, as some Velvets fray more than others.

To Cut a Covered Shape in Silk or Grosgrain. The silk not having a dark and light shade effect, the hat is cut out on the bias without regard to shade. The same care must be taken not to cut out the headline on the underbrim until the covering is securely fixed.

The Correct Method of Cutting Velvet or Plush for a Hat

Diagram 1 clearly illustrates the correct layout on material; the correct placement of the upper brim pattern; the correct placement of the tip pattern; the correct placement of the side crown pattern; the correct placement of the under brim pattern. The dotted lines represent the turning allowances on each pattern.

Note very carefully the correct layout. This is very important.

The illustrated diagram must be carefully followed. Failure is impossible if the directions given throughout this course of instruction are followed as set out.

Your success as a milliner depends entirely on you. Practice also is important to achieve the best results.

❖   ❖   ❖

LESSON 48.

The Covering of the Underbrim with a Piped Edge

(See Diagrams)

First pin up the back seam. Fit on for head fitting test, stitch, and then press. Next join up a ring of support wire, the measurement taken just inside the outer edge of the brim. Allow the usual 1½ ins. overlap on the wire.

You know the correct method of joining the wire neatly and securely. Damp the cotton; this avoids the cotton slipping off the wire while binding. Temporary ties every 4 ins. can hold the wire on the underbrim.

Next lay the underbrim in position on the shape. Note if the centre front and centre back and centre of each side is correctly placed. Stab here and there on the outer edge with pins. Always remember to draw in position in the same direction as the straight thread in the material.

The turnings at the outer edge are next trimmed off—a little at a time. Use the end of a bodkin to tuck in the material between the wire and the edge of the hat brim. Pin close to the wire through the mull or binding, but not through the upper covering.

To Fix the Piped Edge. Using strong thread, a knot must be made in the thread 1½ ins. from end of thread. You must pass the needle from between the two brims to the right side of the underbrim.

Next take a stitch ⅛ in. in length (you know this stitch) along under the wire piping and stab the needle through between the two brims. It is necessary to hold the cotton tight with the left hand.

Next pick up a very small stitch on the "mull." You then pull the cotton through and hold it tight again. Then pass the needle back again almost through the hole made by the needle, to come out just below the wire on the underbrim. Repeat till finished. See Diagram illustrating correct methods.

LESSON 49.

Making and Preparing the Shapes for Covered Fabric Hats and Bonnets

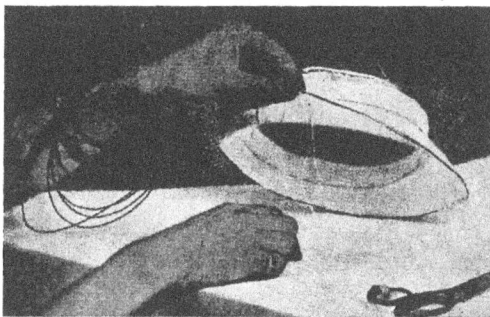

The diagram clearly illustrating the correct method of wiring a
brim edge of hat shape. The correct method of holding the wire
while working.

This section deals with the Shape Cutting and Making of Covered Hats and Bonnets. As these are many and varied and can be bought very cheaply in a large variety of shapes, only a few of the easy to make types are dealt with in these lessons on Hat Shape Making.

As styles change with every passing phase of fashion, only the plainer types are dealt with; those that are simple to make and understand. Many larger shapes moulded in Buckram can be bought and cut down to smaller uneven brim shapes and re-wired. A brim wide at front and back can be cut narrow at front and back and left wide at each side. The sides can be curved up or down with the use of a damp cloth and hot iron, or cut into a scalloped effect in front or one-sided effect as desired.

There are usually so many different shapes to select from that little if any alteration is necessary.

LESSON 50.

The Choice of Materials and Shapes

DIAGRAM 1.—THE LAYOUT.

These all play an important part in millinery. Fashion must be followed. Lightness and comfort in wear must be considered. The standard general methods of shape making are given, and they may be used in different materials and different ways.

The correct method of making a stiff Espartra or Buckram brim, ready for covering. Using a sheet of Espartra or Buckram, the layout of the pattern sections must be placed on the "crossways" or "bias" ways of the Espartra or Buckram. This applies to all shape cutting.

NOTE: This is very important—the Muslin finished side of the Espartra and the smooth side of the Buckram are kept next to the head for comfort in wear.

Note: The reason why in making all hat shapes the patterns must be placed on the "cross" or "bias" on the Espartra or Buckram.

When hats are placed on the head and pulled down on the forehead they would split and tear away easily. The reason for cutting on the "cross" or "bias" is for the material to give, and the "cross" cut material makes a better and more comfortable to wear shape.

When cutting out the shapes, always outline the pattern pieces with pencil or chalk, then allow all the necessary turnings.

1. To Join the Brim Section.

Overlap the pencil or chalk line of the centre back with the two lines meeting on the top of each other. Pin securely in position. Next thread your needle with strong cotton, making a knot 1½ ins. from end of cotton. Beginning at the headline, neatly join the back seam, using 2 rows of back stitching as strength is required here. Stitches may vary in length from ½ in. to ¾ in.

It is important to place the stitches on the side of the brim where they will least be noticed when the shape is covered.

2. If for a turned down brim, place the stitches on the inner side, and on the upper side if a turned up brim. When working, take care not to bend the material.

Stitches must be "Stab Stitch," which has been explained in the stitches used for millinery. Finish off at the headline by tying the two ends of thread—the one left when beginning, and the one when finishing the stitching. This avoids tearing the shape by double stitching.

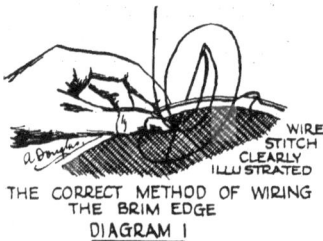

THE CORRECT METHOD OF WIRING
THE BRIM EDGE
DIAGRAM I

Avoid bulky seams as they will show through the material covering the shape. This can be done after considerable practice. Lift the Muslin covering from the Espartra at the raw edge and cut away the grass from the edge about one-sixth of an inch. Replace the Muslin by sewing or sticking it over the raw edge covering it.

The Choice of Materials and Shapes

To Correctly Wire the Head.

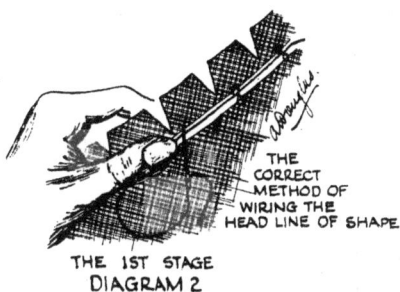

THE CORRECT METHOD OF WIRING THE HEAD LINE OF SHAPE

THE 1ST STAGE
DIAGRAM 2

Perfect fitting is essential. The shape must not be pulled in too tight, spoiling the fitting. This usually occurs with the beginner while sewing.

It is important to test the head measure very carefully on the pencil line of the Espartra or Buckram shape. To measure around the headline correctly, stand the tape measure on its edge, measuring very carefully. If the head measure is too big it is necessary to re-pencil the headline again, slightly inside the first pencil line.

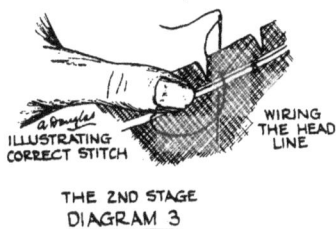

ILLUSTRATING CORRECT STITCH

WIRING THE HEAD LINE

THE 2ND STAGE
DIAGRAM 3

When correct, you must then snip the turnings as far as the correct headline. (Snips placed $\frac{1}{2}$ in. apart around the headline.)

Cut off a length of wire equal to the head measurement, adding $1\frac{1}{2}$ ins. for overlapping. Run wire between finger and thumb to smooth out any creases (forming a circle). Then overlap ends of wire and fasten as detailed previously.

NOTE:—The ends must be secure.

Next you must place the wire in position, beginning at the back. Avoid the Espartra join, as it will make hat bulky. (Two joins must not be placed one on the other.) After fixing the wire on the pencil line, fix securely with wire stitch. This is the correct stitch to use. Wire from right to left, holding the cotton parallel with the wire. Insert your needle on one side of the wire by stabbing. It is then brought up on one side of the wire and cotton to pass through the loop of cotton. When thread is used up in needle and fresh cotton has to be used, leave one end of the cotton, beginning the fresh cotton with a knot as previously described, and tie the old and the new end of the cotton securely in a knot.

It is necessary to work the stitches very closely together where the wire is joined. This will cover the points of the wire where they are overlapped.

E

LESSON 51.

To Wire the Outer Edge of Brim

Diagram 1.

For a turned up brim it is necessary to place the wire over slightly to the right side of the brim. **For a turned down brim,** it is necessary to place the wire over on the under side of the brim. This is very important.

Avoid cracking the Espartra or Buckram while working. Begin at the centre back of the brim.

Next, holding the wire on the edge of the hat brim, you must work from right to left, working on your knee (not the table). It is best to keep the hat in a position between the hands and the chest while working, as you will have more control over your work.

Diagram 2.

TO FASTEN THE WIRE ON THE BRIM.

You must begin with a millinery knot. This important stitch must be always used when beginning to attach the wire. Care must be taken not to allow the wire to slip between the stitches as you work. Hold the cotton tight in the left hand till the wire is firmly attached. (See Diagrams 2 and 3.)

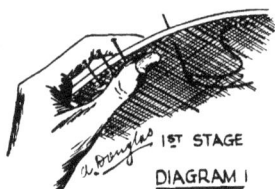

1ST STAGE
DIAGRAM 1

It is necessary to take particular notice of the model you are copying and watch this model as you work.

While working it is often necessary to hold the wire a little firmer, easing the brim edge to the wire. This will cause a more rounded turn up brim, and when you are more experienced in the making of hats you will be able to do more as you progress with the work. The headline is finished off as described above.

Next test the head measure. This is necessary as the work is proceeded with. If the headline requires to be strengthened, and an Espartra crown is not used, it is necessary to cut a crossways strip of Espartra at least 1 in. in width and the length of the around the head measurement, adding $\frac{1}{2}$ in. for joining. This strip of Espartra is placed above the head wire on the outside of the turnings and the snipped turnings are "stab stitched" to it.

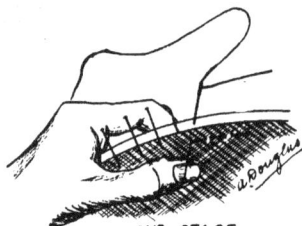

2ND STAGE
CLEARLY ILLUSTRATING THE BACK STITCH TO HOLD THE WIRE PIPING ON THE UNDERBRIM OF SHAPE
DIAGRAM 2

The stitches must be arranged, keeping the small snipped pieces of the headline of brim in position. (See Diagram 6, clearly illustrating the correct method of strengthening and attaching Espartra to the inner headline of brim.) Avoid drawing the Espartra strip around inner headline of brim in too much as you work. There is a tendency to do this while working; this must be avoided, as if the headline is drawn in the head fitting becomes too small for the wearer. Great care must be taken to avoid this. You must again test the head measure as you proceed with the work, as it is easier to rectify this at this stage than when the hat shape is completed.

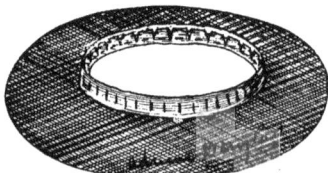

THE HAT SHAPE WITH STRENGTHENED STRIP AT HEAD LINE
DIAGRAM 6

LESSON 52.

THE MULL BINDING

AND THE CORRECT METHOD OF MULLING THE WIRED EDGE OF THE BRIM.

DIAGRAM 4

For softening edges of brims, the mulling is used also as a basis for the outer covering of material to be attached to. Mull Muslin is a special muslin manufactured especially for "mulling," but it is not always obtainable. A good substitute to use is soft Silk, Georgette, or Chiffon.

To Prepare the Mull or Material Binding. (Diagram 4.)

It is necessary to cut a strip on the bias or cross grain of material. (Note: Cutting on the bias is dealt with in another section.) As the mulling must be cut exactly on the bias, refer to "Cutting on the Bias." Cut the strip the measurement of around brim required, allowing 1 in. to spare. Cut this bias strip 1½ in. in width.

Diagram 4 clearly illustrates the 1st and 2nd stages of preparing the "Mull Binding."

The first stage clearly illustrates the mull or "material" folded over.

There are now two thicknesses of material at each end of the folded material and three thicknesses in the centre.

The second stage clearly illustrates the mull or material folded again in half and creased. (See illustration.)

The binding is now ready to place over the edge of the brim shape. Stitch the binding well. The binding is then fixed to the edge of the brim shape by means of "back stitch." It is necessary to use strong cotton, placing the long stitches where they will be less noticeable.

IMPORTANT: When joining the mull binding, to avoid a bulky join cut off the binding straight, allowing no turning for joins, as this is met together, not joined in usual manner with a seam. (As this is covered with material later, the edges are not seen.)

"Back-stitch" is used to hold firmly in shape. If using a thick covering, such as velvet, a row of **"back stitches"** can be worked ½ in. in from the outer edge of brim shape. These can be used when sewing the covering of material on shape, to sew the material to.

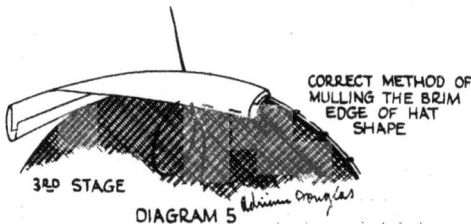

CORRECT METHOD OF MULLING THE BRIM EDGE OF HAT SHAPE

3RD STAGE

DIAGRAM 5

LESSON 53.

TO SHAPE A CURVED BRIM BY HAND

Using a hot iron, place the brim to be shaped over a rolled piece of blanket. Damp the brim slightly by dipping the fingers in water or dabbing with a wet cloth. Grip the shape firmly in the left hand, place the brim on the pad and press into the curved shape desired.

NOTE: A large variety of Buckram and Espartra brims and crowns are available ready blocked. These cost from 1/6 to 4/11, and a large variety are available.

When shaping curved brims, work by placing the centre of the iron on the brim over the pad, and work by rocking the iron backwards and forwards on the padded curve. Do not press hard.

NOTE: Special brim boards, large and small, are available. (See Price Lists.)

◆   ◆   ◆

LESSON 54.

Correct Methods of Crown Making

The Crown Foundations may be made of

1. The same type of material as used for the brim shape, such as Espartra or Buckram.

   Leno, etc., is ideal for Bridesmaids' Small Hats. They can be made in pieces shapes, or moulded on the block. This requires experience.

2. For Crowns of Cocktail Hats and Foundations for Crinoline Straw Hats, Feathers or Flowers, Lace, etc. The lighter materials are used for these crowns and are easier to block in one piece. **Leno, Book Muslin, Millinery Net, Light Canvas,** all are suitable for these crowns. The making of pieced crowns, used in stitched material hats, are dealt with in that section.

CROWNS MADE OF BUCKRAM OR ESPARTRA.

3. The side band of these crowns is cut on the "bias" or "cross" of the Espartra or Buckram. To prepare the crown, cut a bias strip of the Espartra or Buckram the length of the around head measure required, allowing ½ in. for overlapping.

The width or depth would depend upon the style of crown in fashion, 3 in. or deeper if required.

You can try the crown on and cut a little off if it is too deep for your requirements.

Avoid having to add a piece; this makes unnecessary work.

LESSON 55.

TO CUT THE TIP OF CROWN.

4. When you have sewn the side band together (you know the stitch to use), lay the band on a sheet of paper. Pencil around the band on the paper. Obtain the correct size of the tip of the crown. Then lay out the pattern. Pin firmly on the Espartra or Buckram. Pencil around pattern.

Remove pattern. Cut out ¾ in. outside the pencil mark, as the turnings are necessary here to attach tip of crown to side band section.

Snip around edge of crown to within ⅛ in. of pencil line. Bend the snipped pieces to overlap each other.

When the upper and lower edge of the side band of the crown is wired, place the tip with overlapped snipped edges inside the side-band.

First pin firmly in position. Then sew tip securely to side band. You know the stitch to use.

TO MOULD A CROWN IN ONE PIECE.

5. Wet the Buckram or Leno and, while wet, work it over a block to shape and size desired. Leave to dry. The shape is ready to cover. The crowns can be wired, or mulled, whichever is desired. When crown is completed, it is fixed to the brim in the usual way. This has been explained in another section, "Covering of Velvet or Material Hats."

LESSON 56.

The Correct Method of Making Crowns With Moulded Tips

Cut out the side band as previously described and crown section, leaving 1 in. to 1¼ in. extra on crown instead of the lesser amount, as on previous crown tip.

The tip is then placed on a dome or rounded top, blocked and pressed, to shape. This gives the "tip" a moulded effect, and it can be fitted to the side band in the same manner.

The **back** and **front** must be marked on the tip while on the block, and placed exactly in position on the brim. **Centre back and front.**

When marking the **crown tip** out on the Espartra, mark it on the smooth side of the Espartra.

Join the back seam of the Espartra. The smooth side outward.

The Espartra being non-transparent, it is necessary to take care to see that the outline of the tip is cut to perfect shape to commence with.

When pinning the tip to the side-band the pins must be placed in an upright position (not sideways).

While pinning, care must be taken not to get an uneven effect. Commence by pinning roughly at intervals all around the crown first, then going around again, making is perfectly even all around.

NOTE.—While the Espartra is still damp there is a tendency for the muslin to pull apart from the Espartra. The scraps of the grass can be trimmed away, allowing the muslin to lay over the raw edges. This can then be firmly fixed by rows of **backstitching**, placing one row close to each edge of the Espartra, and long stitches on the inside of the Espartra.

The rolled piece of blanket, or special pad, is then placed inside the crown and the crown moulded over this or the block, whichever is available.

If the covering material requires it, the seam around the tip can be mulled with fine material. A bias cut ¾ in. wide, stretched well, and placed single around the seam of tip, fastened securely with fine silk thread and very small stitches. The covering is then caught to this binding.

The lower edge of crown is finished as previously detailed.

LESSON 58.

Correct Method of Blocking Crowns in one Piece

Transparent types of Hats require semi-transparent foundations. These types of crowns can be made of **"Leno,"** **Book Muslin, blocked Millinery Net** and even starched Organdi. The brims can be made of Espartra.

It is necessary when making up Crinoline, or Lace Straws, to make them over a transparent foundation; also small Cocktail Hats, Bridesmaids' Hats, or hats made entirely of flowers, ribbon or feathers.

There are many types of straws that do not require whole crown foundations.

For Soft Straws, a foundation in the crown of hat not only helps to keep the shape of the crown, but avoids the head stretching the crown of hat.

◆ ◆ ◆

LESSON 59.

MILLINERY NET

TO PREPARE THE NET FOR BLOCKING.

Cut two squares 18 ins. If using Leno, these are used double. Rub bees wax over the block to avoid net sticking to the block.

Place the two squares together. Dip in water.

Place on the block, placing a corner of the Leno or net to the centre front and back, and each of the sides of the block. Then tie firmly around the head line position on the block with string.

The fullness in net or Leno is removed by pulling down on the corners. All the fullness can be removed in this manner, leaving the net or Leno above the string a perfect fitting shape of the block.

When net is dry, cut off below the string ¼ in.

Remove net shape to see if it is right size and shape. Cut the Espartra band and attach as previously directed. **Try on to see if fitting is correct.**

Book Muslin sticks easily when wet owing to the large amount of starch or stiffening used in the making.

It is used for making hard crowns, and is more suitable for heavier types of straw or cloth coverings.

Crowns can also be blocked in Tulle.

These are ideal for bridal wear, and are used also as a lining for lace straw, a foundation for Bridal Veils, Bridesmaids' Caps, and Lace Hats.

Waterproof Tulle is the correct type to use, as the other types will not stand blocking at all.

The block is prepared the same as for millinery net. Fold the Tulle into layers (about 6 to 10 layers would be necessary), each 18 in. to 20 in. square.

Place on the block, tying with string the corners in same position as previously described.

Pull down on block, then hold in front of the steam from your kettle, steaming all around and pulling down on block till free of all fullness. When finished, leave to dry.

Cut off any Tulle below the string, allowing ¼ in. to attach to the Espartra head band. Attach head band. **Try on for correct head fitting.**

Any soft type of Straw Hat is greatly improved with a blocked Leno or Net Inner Crown. The shape of the hat is preserved.

A head lining also is essential to protect the inner head line of the hat.

(SEE SECTION — THE MAKING OF HEAD LININGS.)

LESSON 60.

The Correct Method of Copying a Model Bonnet or Hat

The inside around head measurement must be taken.

The outer edge of around brim measurement.

The headline measurement.

The width of the brim at centre front, back and sides.

The side to side measurement also must be taken.

The measurement around the tip.

The depth of the crown measurement.

The width across the tip.

If copying a hat shape, it is necessary to carefully note all details. The placement of the wiring of the shape. The measurement between the wires.

The pattern must be tested and any measurements not just right must be corrected. **Do not forget to allow all turnings when cutting out the covering for the shape.**

Do not forget to snip the inner head line of covering.

Do you know where the joins of crowns and brims are placed? Refer always to the smallest detail if you are not sure and avoid unnecessary mistakes.

TO OBTAIN EXPERIENCE IN THE MAKING OF ALL MILLINERY

Make for others, even if you only charge for the materials used in the models you are making. This is excellent practice, and your ideas can be shown in the many models you will learn to create, and in this way you will obtain many orders for which you will be able to charge for the making. It is important, too, that you study the various styles in millinery showing in shops; you can then keep your models up to date. The styles and trimmings change from year to year. All good millinery must be modern and up to date.

LESSON 61. .

The Cutting of Hat Brim Shapes Without Cutting Patterns

Place your brim board on a sheet of brown paper. Pencil around the outline of the brim board. (Note all sizes of brim boards are available. See price lists of blocks and brim boards.)

When the outline of brim board is pencilled around, remove board from the paper.

Place the crown hat block of head measure and shape required in the centre of the pencilled circle, placing it either exact in centre for a brim even all around, or more to the back for a wider brim in front.

Pencil around the crown block, remove from paper, cut out pattern around outer edge, then around pencilled edge of the headline.

To adjust this pattern to different shapes, cut off several patterns from the one just made (retaining the original for future pattern making).

Fold one of the patterns over side to side and trim off where required, either making brim narrower in front and wider at sides, narrow at back or one-sided, whichever is desired.

A large variety of different shaped brims can quickly be made in this manner, the crowns being blocked to any shape to suit.

Patterns of crowns are not necessary. These can all be made direct on the various shapes of head blocks.

All Shapes and Sizes are Obtainable from "MODERN DESIGNERS ACADEMY,"
77 Queen Street, Brisbane, Q'land., at Lowest Prices.

These hat blocks are all first quality and latest styles. A price list and photos of all blocks and brim boards are illustrated for your selection. Any special designs will be made to your order and measurement.

Many hours of work are saved when you have the correct hat blocks and brim boards to create the numerous shapes, sizes and designs demanded in modern millinery.

Practice pattern making by the above method. You will appreciate the quick results obtained.

LESSON 62.

· Test Your Progress   .

The following are of vital importance to your progress. Can you answer these?

1. What is the procedure for cutting a true bias?
2. What is the procedure for cutting a long bias?
3. When is each necessary?
4. What are the rules for measuring materials for a stitched bias fold?
5. What is the correct way to shade velvet?
6. What is meant by line in millinery?

7. Do the general principles of line in hats change with the fashions?
8. What is the object to be attained in choosing the lines of a hat for an individual?
9. What are the general rules in selecting a hat for a person with an oval face, a round face, and a narrow face oval?
10. What are the essential qualities of a sports hat?

LESSON 63.

The Making of Velvet, Grosgrain, Silk or Fabric Hats

Boaters'

All Fabric Hats are made on an Espartra Shape, Canvas, Leno or Book Muslin.

Either the shape is cut out or the Espartra is blocked to the required shape. Buckram also is used.

TO BLOCK AND MAKE AN ESPARTRA OR BUCKRAM SHAPE.

First cut out the Espartra or Buckram shape of the circumference required, wet well, then place over the block (the shape and the size required), and mould to the shape.

The material is easily worked to the shape by the hands while damp. The strands are forced together without overlapping. The shape must be left on the block until perfectly dry.

This is difficult work for a beginner, and until you have had considerable experience and practice it is advisable to buy your Espartra shapes ready made. These are obtainable from 1/6 each, so are not expensive, and by the time Espartra is bought you do not save much by making your own shapes.

The bought ones are correctly shaped and some can be bought ready wired, saving much time and work.

When covering a shape with velvet or any material that has a pile or nap which gives a dark shade one way and a light shade another way, when cutting out velvet for a hat the velvet must be cut with the dark shade going from the front to the back, showing all the richness of the material when the hat is on the head of the wearer.

> **FOR VELVET USE A GOOD FINE QUALITY (NOT VELVETEEN, IT IS TOO HEAVY FOR MILLINERY PURPOSES.)**

LESSON 64.

Moulded Buckram or Espartra Hat Shapes Ready Made

ADJUSTMENTS, IF ANY, CAN VERY QUICKLY AND EASILY BE MADE.

1. The Correct Method of Adjusting the Head Size of Shape.

The head size may be made larger by slashing the brim from the edge to the headline and inserting a piece of Buckram or Espartra.

Rip off the edge binding and the wire where it is lapped, pin in the necessary piece of material; try on the shape for correct head fitting and adjust the size to suit.

Sew firmly in position with a tight "**back stitch.**" Replace the edge wire with binding.

To Make the Head Size Smaller.

Rip the binding and edge wire joining, slash from edge to headline and overlap the Buckram until the correct head fitting is obtained.

If the moulded shape is much too large, two slashes may be necessary, one at the back and one at the front.

NOTE: Too much overlapping will throw the moulded shape entirely out of shape.

To Make a Drooped Brim from a Sailor Brim.

Cut the brim from the back and the front from the edge to the headline, ripping off the edge binding and edge wire.

Overlap at the edge, running off to nothing at the headline.

The taking in of the brim edge and not at headline is what makes the brim droop. Trim a little off width of brim at back and front, making the brim slightly wider at sides than back and front.

A narrow back on this type of brim is better because it enables a fairly large brim to be worn without interfering with comfort in wear.

❖ ❖ ❖

LESSON 65.

Re-modelling for Poke or Bonnet Shape

To make a Poke or Bonnet Shape from the previous Type of Shape.

This process is much the same as the previous instructions, as the shape is already drooped.

Rip the binding and edge wire. Cut the back from edge to headline. Slant the seam so that the edge laps from 1 in. to 2 ins. and the head size laps only ¼ in.

To Use a Pattern on a Moulded Shape.

Many of the drooped shaped brims may be cut from any ordinary pressed Sailor or Drooped shape.

Cut off the head size slashes of the pattern on the headline. Pin the pattern into the drooped brim. Mark the correct edge and cut. This does away with the necessity of wiring a head size and saves the bother of looking for correct frame material.

The original edge binding may be replaced.

Poke or Bonnet patterns may be cut from drooped shapes in the same way.

Felt hats need not be cut; they are shaped by damping. The moulded frames will not shrink and shape, but must be treated as described.

◆ ◆ ◆

LESSON 66.

DO YOU KNOW THE ANSWERS TO THESE QUESTIONS ?

1. What stitch is used to join a seam in a Felt brim?
2. What material is used to strengthen the headline of a hat?
3. What stitch is used for joining two parts together where strength is not required and there is little, if any, strain?
4. What material is used for shape making?
5. What is the correct types of ribbon used in millinery?
6. How must Velvet be pressed?
7. Why is it the rule in all millinery that the centre front of all pieces must be placed on the "bias" or "cross" of materials?
8. What is the correct method of joining Straw Plait?
9. How can it be prevented showing an Espartra join through a thin hat covering?
10. How must stitching be finished off in all millinery?

LESSON 67.

The Thorough Professional Way of Teaching the Correct Method of Making Hat Shapes

FOR GROSGRAIN, VELVET AND FABRIC HATS.

Diagram 1 clearly illustrates the correct method of joining the side band. Do you know the correct stitch to use?

Diagram 2 clearly illustrates the correct method of wiring the side band. Do you know the correct stitch to use?

Diagram 3 clearly illustrates the correct method of stitching the Leno tip to crown section. Do you know the correct stitch to use?

Diagram 4 clearly illustrates the correct methods of attaching Espartra tip to side band. Do you know the correct stitch to use?

Diagram 5 clearly illustrates the Espartra crown being attached to the Espartra brim. Do you know the correct stitch to use?

NOTE.—As the stitches for millinery are all illustrated and fully detailed in the first part of the course, you will know each one and the use for each stitch.

 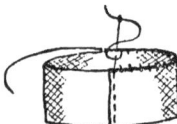 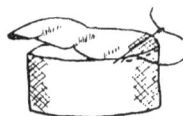

DIAGRAM 1   DIAGRAM 2   DIAGRAM 3

 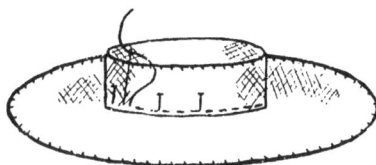

DIAGRAM 4   DIAGRAM 5
THE HAT SHAPE SHOWN IN THE VARIOUS STAGES OF MAKING.

THE CORRECT METHOD OF COVERING AN ESPARTA HAT SHAPE WITH VELVET OR MATERIAL.

Diagram 1 clearly illustrates the fitting and pinning in position of the velvet or material selected for the hat on the upper brim of the hat.

Diagram 2 clearly illustrates the correct method of the sewing of the inner wires in position.

Diagram 3 clearly illustrates the correct method of fixing of the velvet or material on the under brim of the hat.

NOTE.—The velvet or material must be in one piece; not even the head opening must be cut out at this stage. Note carefully how the pins are inserted, holding material in place.

Diagram 4 clearly illustrates the correct method of cutting out the headline of the hat, showing the basting or tacking stitch holding the material in place.

NOTE.—Before the headline is cut out, the outer edge of brim must be securely sewn in position, holding the material firmly.

Diagram 5 clearly illustrates the correct method of fixing of the tip of crown and the covered side band in position.

LESSON 68.

The Correct Method of Sewing the Velvet or Fabric Covering on the Shape

NOTE.—The edges of the sideband are turned in and placed over turned-in edges of the crown piece. When hat is completed all edges are concealed.

Do you know the correct stitches to use throughout the making and finishing of the hat?

The Upper Brim Section.

Fine steel pins must be used to fix the material in position. Do not tack Velvet if tacking can be avoided, as tacking threads mark the Velvet. (Other materials may be well tacked.)

If tacking Velvet is necessary, cut the threads at every tacking stitch when removing from the Velvet. Cut away any spare edges or turnings to avoid fullness and bulk.

DIAGRAM 1

When sewing Velvet, if you hold a small piece of Velvet in the left hand under the Velvet you are working on, this will avoid marking the Velvet.

Fit the straight parts of the Velvet. If any fullness in Velvet shows towards the headline, snip the Velvet around the headline a little deeper than previously. Then tack around the headline before commencing to sew the outer edge of brim. (Diagram 1.)

The Correct Method of Fitting the Upper Brim Section.

See **Diagram 2,** clearly illustrating step by step the correct methods.

Next slip the Velvet for the upper brim section over the crown section. The turnings left at headline must be carefully snipped.

Next fit very carefully and pin the outer edge in position. Take time and do the work well. If any fullness at crown, it is necessary

DIAGRAM 2

to snip the material a little deep to make it lie perfectly flat without fullness.

Next sew neatly around the headline of the hat. (You know the correct stitch to use.) Then, turning the brim to the wrong side, it is necessary to "catch stitch" the turnings to the inner wire or Buckram. Avoid showing stitches through to other side.

The Correct Method of Attaching the Under Brim Section.

Diagram 3 clearly illustrates the correct method. This requires much patience, and it is more difficult for a beginner to do. This must be very carefully pinned in position.

NOTE CAREFULLY.—The material must not frill or flute at the edge; there must be no bulges or ripples in the material at edge when attaching to shape.

If this trouble occurs the pins must be removed and the material drawn up firmer after fitting and pinning material correctly in position. It is then necessary to cut away any unwanted turnings. Then the edges of brim can be slip stitched neatly together.

DIAGRAM 3

NOTE.—Some materials are easier to handle than others. Velvet has more give or spring than firmer fabrics like Grosgrain and heavier silk; therefore is harder to handle and make up.

LESSON 69.

The Correct Method of Sewing the Velvet or Fabric Covering on the Shape

When you have fitted the edge correctly and neatly slip stitched it, next cut out the headline. (See **Diagram 4,** which clearly illustrates the correct method.)

It is necessary to leave $\frac{3}{4}$ in. for the turnings; the inside of the head can then be firmly stitched.

NOTE.—All brims for flat shapes, such as Sailor shapes, do not require to have a join in either the upper or under brim section of hat. This is unnecessary and would spoil the smartness of the hat.

DIAGRAM 4

Styles such as Bonnet brims, drooped brims, or brims curved downwards, must have a join in at centre back of brim, both in Buckram shape (unless you buy one without), and also in the upper and under brim of the material.

The joins must always be placed at back of hat unless they can be placed where they can be completely hidden by the trimming of the hat.

◇ ◇ ◇

LESSON 70.

The Correct Method of Fitting Tip of Crown

Diagram 5 clearly illustrates the correct methods. Note all details carefully. Practice is necessary for better results.

The Fitting of the Tip of the Crown Section.

First mark the front and back of the material and pin correctly in position. Then fit material over Espartra or Buckram shape, and pin firmly and evenly in position.

Either snip the turnings, so that the material will overlap, or pleat it around evenly in small pleats.

DIAGRAM 5

Next sew firmly around the top of the side crown section.

The Correct Method of Fitting the Side Crown Section.

Diagram 5 clearly illustrates the correct method. First turn down and tack the turnings around top and bottom of side crown. Turn the turnings inside the band of side crown next.

The side crown must be carefully pinned to the brim and tip of crown section, then neatly slip stitched.

The side band of crown is then lined with a Leno band. A separate head lining is advised, as a hat will wear and keep its shape longer and has a professional finish.

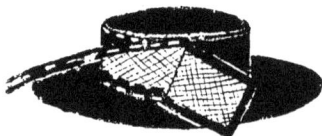

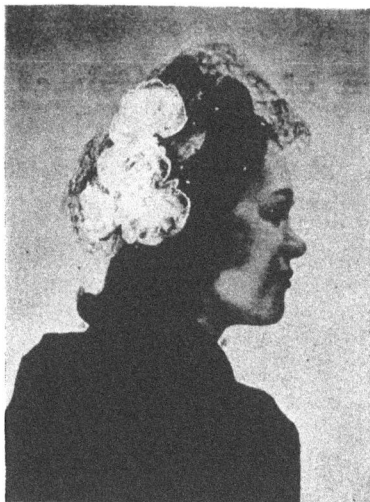

"CAPTIVITY," a lovely Model Hat in Black Grosgrain, trimmed Pink Flowers and Black Mesh Veiling with Pink Chenille Spots.

THE COST OF MATERIALS—

The Buckram Shape	2	11
½ yard Grosgrain	4	5
The Flowers	7	6
1 yard Veiling	3	11½
Inner Head Band and Elastic ..	0	10½
TOTAL COST ..	19	8

Materials supplied by courtesy of—
ROCKMANS PTY. LTD.
BRISBANE   and   MELBOURNE

♦ ♦ ♦

LESSON 71.

DO YOU KNOW THE ANSWERS TO THESE 10 QUESTIONS?

1. What materials are most suitable for making stitched Fabric Hats?

2. What materials are most suitable for interlinings?

3. What materials are most suitable for head linings?

4. How must the materials be treated before using?

5. What is the correct order of work in making up of Fabric Hats and Caps?

6. How must the centre front and centre back of crown and brim be marked?

7. Why must they be marked?

8. What is the correct method of making the brim of a Fabric Hat? What is the correct method of making the crown?

9. What interlining is used? How is it treated?

10. What is the best method of attaching the crown to the brim?

LESSON 72.

The Cutting of Pattern of Smart Misses or Women's Stitched Material, Felt or Straw Hats

The Materials required for Stitched Fabric Hat.

¾ yard of 36 in. material.

1 yard of 28 in. Canvas.

2 reels of Cotton to match.

Materials for Straw:

6¼ yards of 1 in Straw, or 5 yards of 1¼ in. Straw.   Hat wire.

1 yard of 1 in. Silk Petersham Ribbon for trimming.

Espartra for inner headlining.

¾ yard Cotton Petersham Ribbon if no headlining.

Material for Felt: 1 Felt Hood and the Trimmings.

NOTE.—There are two pieces of pattern: (1) The Half Brim Pattern.

(2) The Half Crown Pattern.

The crown is a novelty crown; the three peaks button or tie, or are stitched together in centre top of crown.

This model is ideal for tennis wear, made in Pique, Linen, Cesarine, or any firm Cotton material, as it can be opened out flat for laundering.

Important: When the half pattern has been cut out, it is necessary to lay the half pattern section on another folded piece of paper and cut the whole pattern of brim out. Then the crown section.

NOTE: The reason for this is all explained in the lay-out and making-up section. Study each important detail carefully.

NOTE: 20 in. head measurement is the size of pattern. It can be adjusted smaller or larger as detailed elsewhere.

LESSON 73. Diagram 1.

The Cutting to Measure of Half the Brim Section of Hat

20 in. Head Measurement.

Diagram 1 clearly illustrates the cutting to measure of the hat brim— half pattern.

Rule an oblong on brown paper 13 in. by 7½ in.

Measure as from 1 to 2 (the brim width in front) 4 ins.

Measure from 2 to 15 (2½ ins.).

Rule the construction lines 15 to 7, 15 to 5 and 15 to 8 as clearly shown.

NOTE: 15 and 7 can quickly be located by folding oblong in half, as 15 to 7 is the centre construction line.

Measure from 15 to 10 up 2¼ ins.

Measure from 15 to 11 up 3¾ ins.

Measure from 15 to 12 up 4½ ins. Mark all clearly with points.

Measure from 15 to 14 along 4½ ins.

Measure from 14 to 13 up 2¼ ins.

Shape from 2 through 10, 11, 12, to 13. This is half the inner head line of brim.

Measure from 3 up to 4 (3¾ ins.).

Rule line from 4 to 13. This is back edge of brim line.

Measure from 5 to 6 on angle shown 2½ ins.

Measure from 8 to 9 on angle shown 2¾ ins.

Shape from 4 through 6 and 7 and 9 and 1. This line is half the outer brim edge line.

Half of brim pattern is now completed.

Cut out pattern.

Fold another sheet of paper and place line 1 to 2 (the centre front) to the fold, cutting the whole pattern of the brim on paper.

Why? Because the brim must be cut in the material and interlining on the bias or cross of the material.

See layout in another section, "The Cutting and Making of Stitched or Material Hats."

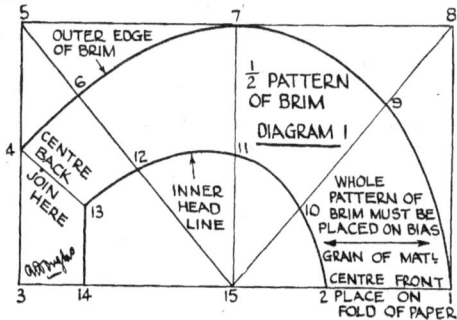

OUTER EDGE OF BRIM

CENTRE BACK JOIN HERE

½ PATTERN OF BRIM

DIAGRAM I

INNER HEAD LINE

WHOLE PATTERN OF BRIM MUST BE PLACED ON BIAS

GRAIN OF MAT'L

CENTRE FRONT

2 PLACE ON FOLD OF PAPER

LESSON 74.   Diagram 2.

The Cutting of the Three Peaked Crown

HALF PATTERN OF HAT.

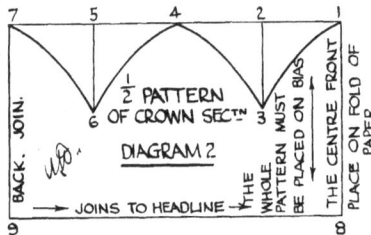

Diagram 2 clearly illustrates the cutting of Half Pattern of Crown Section.

Rule an oblong 10 ins. by 5 ins. on a sheet of brown paper.

Measure from 1 to 2 along 2½ ins.

Measure from 2 to 3 down 2½ ins.

Mark with points.

Measure from 2 to 4 along 2½ ins.

Measure from 4 to 5 along 2½ ins.

Measure from 5 to 6 down 2½ ins.

Curve from 7 to 6, from 6 to 4, and from 4 to 3 and 3 to 1 to form the half of centre front and back and one whole peak of crown.

NOTE.—The line 1 to 8 is the centre front line. The line 7 to 9 is the back of crown line.

This completes half the pattern.

Cut whole pattern.

No seams or turnings are allowed for on pattern. Allow these when cutting out on material.

NOTE.—These patterns can be used with other patterns given for shaped Material Hats. They can also be used for working foundations for straw hats and patterns for felt hats.

The Scalloped Brim Pattern can be used with this crown.

A variety of different styles can be made up in this manner, also you can learn to design various brims from any of the patterns cut in this section.

Care must be taken when making fabric hats. I advise the shrinking of all materials, including çanvas used in the making, and you will avoid having a hat that, when washed or wet with rain, will not fit you.

LESSON 75.

The Cutting of Pattern for a Sports Hat and Large Beach Hat for Ladies

This large Beach Hat has a shady brim. It can be made with a smaller brim by cutting off 2 ins. or more, as desired, from the outer edge of the brim pattern.

It is ideal for sports and tennis if made smaller in the brim from plain white Pique or Linen.

The Beach Hat looks smart made in Floral Cretonne, Cambric, Linen, or any gay patterned or plain material.

It can also be made in light weight straw or millinery felt.

As previous lessons have taught you how to wire and join the crown to the brim, you will proceed to make up this hat by the directions given in other lessons. A cord or ribbon, or bands of self material are most suitable for the trimming if you have spare pieces of material to use up.

The centre crown strip can be of one colour, the sides of crown pieces another colour, and the brim (upper) one colour and the underbrim lined another colour. Try this effect with spare pieces.

If you have to purchase the Cretonne, which is usually 30 ins. wide, you will require 1¼ yds. Often nice remnants are procurable of this amount.

If the material selected is 36 ins. wide, 1¼ yards would be sufficient, and for a smaller brim only ¾ yard would be required.

An interlining of Leno or Canvas or firm Calico must be cut. This is placed between the 2 brims (upper and under brim) and the three are all stitched with rows of machine stitching.

There are two ways of making the brim:

(1) Seam up the back seam of upper and under brim and the interlining. Place the interlining between the two brims, pinning first in position, then tacking centre fronts together and centre back seams together. (Press well first so that seams lay flat.)

Then machine around brim, commencing at within ¼ in. of edge of brim and machine rows about ¼ in. apart till whole brim is evenly stitched. The edges are then trimmed as close to stitching without cutting first row of stitching.

Then the edge is bound neatly with coloured or self bias binding.

The brims and interlinings are joined at back and pressed, the upper brim is turned with right side facing the right side of the under brim with the interlining placed between the two brim sections.

Machine close around outer edge of the brim, trim off close to stitching, turn the brim inside out to the right side.

The interlining will be between the two brims. Press well. Tack firmly, then machine as previous directions.

The Head band of crown section also is treated in same way, then joined to brim, finished and trimmed.

NOTE.—Crown can be made single and lined with separate head lining.

LESSON 76.

The Cutting of the Large Beach Hat and Sports Hat

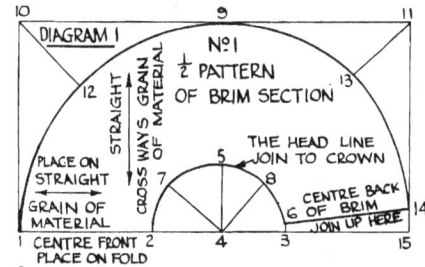

There are three sections of the pattern:

No. 1.—Half of the brim.

No. 2.—Half of the centre band of crown.

No. 3.—One side piece of crown.

NOTE.—Two of these are required, one each side of the centre strip of crown.

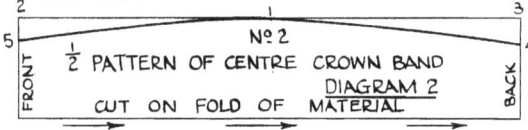

To cut section No. 1 (the half of brim), rule an oblong 23¼ ins. by 12 ins. on a sheet of paper.

Measure as from 1 to 2 (8¼ ins.).

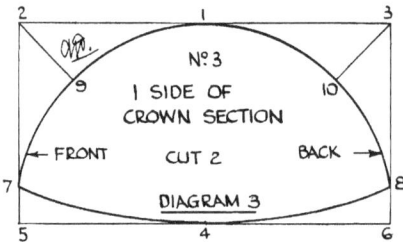

Measure from 2 to 3 (7¼ ins.).

Mark all with points.

4 is located half-way between 2 and 3. Measure from 4 up to 5 (3¾ ins.).

6 is located ½ in. above 3.

7 is located 3¾ ins. from 4 on an angle shown.

8 is located 3¾ ins. from 4 on an angle shown.

Curve from 2 through 7, 5 and 8 to 6. This line represents ½ of around head line.

9 is located half-way between 10 and 11. Measure from 11 to 13 on angle shown 4¾ ins.

Measure from 10 to 12 on angle shown, also 4¾ ins.

Measure from 15 up to 14 (1¼ in.).

Rule a line from 6 to 14. This is the centre of brim join line.

Curve from 1 through 12, through 9 to 13 and to 14; a complete semi-circle.

This completes half of the brim pattern. Cut the pattern out.

LESSON 77.

Cutting the Centre Crown Section

(Diagram 2.)

Half the pattern, No. 2.

Rule an oblong 11¼ ins. by 2 ins.

NOTE.—1 is located half-way between 2 and 3; 5 is located ½ in. below 2.

4 is also located ½ in. below 3.

Mark with points.

Curve from 5 through 1 to 4. This completes half the centre crown band.

NOTE.—Cut on fold of material as marked on Diagram 2. Cut out pattern. Mark pattern.

◆ ◆ ◆

DIAGRAM 3 (Lesson).

The Cutting of One Side Crown Section, No. 3

The pattern is for one piece; two pieces are necessary, one each side of centre crown band.

Rule an oblong on paper, 8½ ins. by 4¼ ins.

NOTE.—1 is located half-way between 2 and 3.

(This is quickly determined if the oblong is cut out and folded end to end. The crease mark locates the point 1 and also point 4, which is half-way between 5 and 6.)

Measure from 5 to 7 (¾ in.).

Measure from 6 to 8 (⅝ in.).

Measure from 2 to 9 and 3 to 10 on angle shown 1½ in.

Curve from 7 through 9 and 1 and through 10 to 8.

Curve from 7 through 4 to 8.

The line 7 through 4 to 8 is the head line and stitches to the brim head line.

Cut pattern out.

NOTE.—Cut two on material, one for each side of the centre band of crown. Mark pattern back and front and side crown.

(Copyright)

LESSON 78.

The Cutting and Making of a Smart Beret

Made with 1 in. Ribbon, Grosgrain or Felt or Straw.

The Diagram clearly illustrates the cutting of the Beret sections.

No block required for making. There are three pieces, namely:

(1) The Under Brim Section.

(2) The Crown Section.

(3) The Head Band Section.

NOTE carefully.—Only half of each piece of pattern is cut; therefore, when cutting out on material it is necessary to place the pattern sections on double material, and where marked on folds place on the fold of the material.

Joins where not necessary must be avoided.

For a Beret made of ribbon, first a foundation must be cut from the pattern and sewn together, then covered by the ribbon or the ribbon can be machined on each section and the sections afterwards joined.

Much care must be taken in the making. **(See the Making-up Section.)**

Write for list of other books available, to – *"The New Art Publishers"* – **77 Queen St., Brisbane, Queensland.**

The Cutting and Making of a Smart Beret

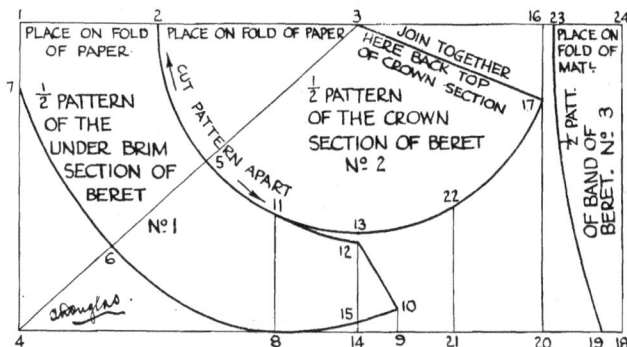

TO CUT THE PATTERN SECTIONS:

Rule an oblong 9 ins. by 18 ins. on a sheet of brown paper.

The diagram clearly illustrates, step by step, the quick way of cutting the patterns "by tape measure."

(1) Measure as from 1 to 2 (4 ins.).

(2) Measure as from 2 to 3 (6 ins.). Mark with points.

(3) Rule a line as from 3 to 4 on angle shown.

(4) Measure from 3 to 5 (6 ins.).

(5) Measure as from 4 to 6 ($3\frac{1}{4}$ ins.).

(6) Measure as from 1 to 7 ($1\frac{1}{2}$ ins.).

(7) Measure from 4 to 8 ($7\frac{3}{4}$ ins.).

(8) Measure from 8 to 9 ($3\frac{1}{2}$ ins.), and from 9 to 10 ($\frac{3}{4}$ in.).

Curve from 10 to 8 and from 8 along $\frac{3}{4}$ in., and then to 6, and from 6 to 7 to 1.

(9) NOTE: 11 is located 3 ins. above 8; 14 is located $1\frac{1}{4}$ in. from 8.

Rule a line from 14 through 15 to 12 ($2\frac{1}{4}$ ins. in length).

Rule a line from 12 to 10 on angle shown.

Curve from 12 through 11 and 5 to 2.

This completes half pattern of under section of Beret.

TO CUT UPPER CROWN SECTION:

Measure from 3 to 16 ($5\frac{1}{2}$ ins.) and from 16 down to 17 ($1\frac{3}{4}$ in.).

Shape slight curve from 3 to 17.

From 18 to 20 measures $2\frac{1}{4}$ ins.

From 20 up to 17 must measure $7\frac{1}{4}$ ins., and 21 is located $2\frac{1}{4}$ ins. from 20.

From 21 to 22 measure up 4 ins.

13 is located $\frac{1}{4}$ in. above 12.

Shape from 17 through 22 through 13 to 11.

NOTE.—The remainder of the line from 11 through 5 to 2 is cut through, forming both lines of two separate pattern sections.

TO CUT HALF SECTION OF BAND

SECTION.

Measure from 24 to 23 ($2\frac{1}{4}$ ins.). Measure from 18 to 19 ($\frac{1}{2}$ in.).

Curve from 23 to 19, as clearly shown in diagram. This completes the three sections of pattern. Cut patterns out on firm paper or cardboard, carefully marking each section on pattern pieces. They are then ready for immediate use and can be easily adjusted to various head sizes by cutting smaller or larger patterns. A full range of sizes from small to large head measurements can be made.

NOTE.—The under section of the Beret is referred to as the "halo" part of the Beret.

Work neatly as neatness is essential in all millinery.

LESSON 79.

THE MAKING OF THE BERET

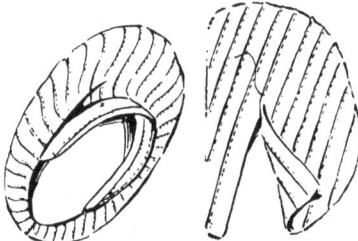

DIAGRAM 1.
Clearly illustrating Ribbon stitched on the
Foundation.

The Directions for making with a 1 in. Ribbon.

Ten yards of 1 in. Petersham ribbon is required to make the Beret. The inner head lining also requires a piece of Petersham Ribbon of same shade.

This Beret is attractive in navy and white, black and white, all white, or any colour desired to match a frock.

Diagram 1 clearly illustrates the ribbon stitched on foundation. The foundation can be made of canvas, as it is not too stiff looking, and the ribbon, when stitched on, helps to make it firmer.

Pique is excellent for a Beret.

Diagram 2 clearly illustrates the Beret joined together, with the head band attached.

When covering the canvas shape with ribbon, start by stitching each strip of ribbon slightly over the edge of the previous strip till the section is completely covered.

NOTE.—When crown section is covered, the line 3 to 17 is joined, as this forms the head shape in the Beret.

Cover the halo section in the Beret with ribbon to match, and when head band is attached finish with a bow of all self or two-tone ribbon as desired.

The head can be made from pieces of the ribbon stitched on canvas. When finishing each section, turn inside out and press well.

NOTE.—This Beret can be made in Straw; also in Felt. Two Felt hats can be made into this Beret.

Two-tone effects are smart—a brown and beige, grey and navy, black and white, blue and dusty pink, also navy and dusty pink.

A smart pin or ornament can be used as trimming.

There is no need to discard old hats. You can remodel and make them like new for just a few hours of your time and some new ribbon.

Try out some of your own ideas on trimmings and making; the results will surprise you, and confidence will be gained.

LESSON 80.

BERET MADE FROM ALLOVER FELT

This Smart Model can be made at little cost from an 18 in. by 18 in. square of Felt in any colour desired, using the same pattern as for the ribboned Beret.

Ribbon or self felt may be used for the head band and self felt trimming in form of leaves.

The same amount of canvas will be required to stiffen the Beret.

Pin the pattern sections firmly on the felt with quite a few pins to hold it in position.

Mark out around pattern shapes with chalk.

Allow any necessary turnings when cutting out.

Cut the canvas to shape of felt sections.

Make up by same directions as given in section dealing with stitched hats.

A few Suggestions are Given for Colour and Trimmings.

A nut-brown felt trimmed with self leaves veined in gold stitching, or trimmed with gold cord made into small circles about the size of a button, 1 in. across, and placed in groups with leaves.

A navy felt trimmed with white felt leaves bound with navy corded ribbon.

Black and white, grey and navy, pink and navy, green and brown, brown and lemon, all self or any colour scheme that will blend.

A smart ornament will add distinction to this useful Beret.

The Tailored Type of Beret Made in Grosgrain

Using the Pattern of the Ribbon-made Beret, cut out the shape on Leno; ½ yard of Leno is sufficient for this Beret. (Leno is 36 ins. wide.)

1 yard of Grosgrain will be required (Grosgrain is only 18 ins. wide).

Next cut out the pattern of the Beret on Grosgrain, only allow ¼ in. more all around the outline of pattern. This is seam allowance.

Next machine together the Leno shape, then next the Grosgrain shape. Place the two pieces together.

Next turn the Grosgrain inside out so that the seams will be inside; then slip in the Leno shape, which must fit exactly.

Place pins at different places to keep in place. Make slashes in the headline if fitting is too tight.

Either face the band to neaten or add 1 in. Petersham band to tone as a trimming, or trimmings can be made from the pieces of Grosgrain left over.

Add a smart ornament and a lovely Beret is yours.

◊ ◊ ◊

THE BERET MADE IN RAPAL STRAW BRAID.

Follow directions given for treating the Straw in section dealing with Straw Hat Making.

Preparing the Straw for the Making of the Beret. The Correct Method:

Commence by drawing in the draw thread on edge of straw about 2 yards.

Make a circle to start with, sewing it securely.

Next the straw must be pinned around until a piece large enough to cover the Leno round piece is made.

Sew the straw together, seeing that cotton matches; you know the stitch to use.

When finished, press on the wrong side, using warm iron over a damp cloth.

The straw must not be cut off.

Next pin before sewing, and when the straw is pressed nice and flat, pin on to the Leno shape; continue pinning around, easing as you work.

Pin and sew one row at a time, neatly and evenly.

When the headline edge is reached, half of the straw is folded over the headline edge and neatly sewn inside.

Try on the Beret and test the head fitting. It is easier to alter before sewing.

Rapal straw is easy to stretch, but must be stretched before sewing it to Leno.

When Beret is finished, insert a band of Petersham ribbon over the straw edge inside the headline of Beret.

This Beret can be trimmed with ribbon or feathers, or ornaments.

Materials Required to Make the Beret.

½ yard of Leno or Book Muslin, Rapal Braid or suitable Straw Braid. 1¼ in. wide will require 4½ yards. If 1½ ins. wide, 5¼ yards will be required.

If a straw is used that is 1 in. wide, 7 yards will be required, and ¾ yard of Petersham ribbon for the head-band.

Two large ornament pins may be used as a trimming, or ribbon if desired.

LESSON 81.

The Cutting and Making of this Charming Little Toque or Beret

In Grosgrain, Velvet, Felt for Day Wear, or Lame for Evening Wear.

The materials required:—

½ yard Grosgrain or Velvet, etc., as desired.

A strip of "Espartra" or "Buckram" for strengthening inner headline (if no interlining is used).

The inner lining of ¼ yard Canvas, "Buckham" or "Espartra."

The lining: ½ yard Taffeta, Silk, Muslin, etc.

A jewelled clip for evening wear. A feather ornament or velvet bow trimming for day wear.

The diagram clearly illustrates the three-cornered piece of material cut to make the Beret or Small Toque.

No paper pattern is necessary.

Fold the Grosgrain or material selected over into the shape of the three-cornered piece. The two side edges will measure 18 ins. The edge that swathes around the head and gathers will measure more than the sides.

Gather where shown by the dotted line. This is cut on the bias or cross of the material.

If you desire a higher Beret, cut it out on Velvet (which is wider than "Grosgrain," "Lame" or "Felt").

The Grosgrain, Velvet or Lame will require an interlining. Felt requires no interlining.

To make up the Beret or Toque, cut out the interlining and lining by shape of the piece of material being used to make the Beret.

Dart the interlining where gather line is shown. This is an easy matter by slashing the "Espartra" in the centre, cutting a slash about 2½ ins. in length, and another one each side of the centre one 2 ins. apart.

Then overlap the slashes at bottom, fitting Espartra when pinned up the size of head. (You know the stitch to use.)

The covering of material is gathered in centre where shown.

Bring the two ends around to back, the top point over meeting the two side points.

Pin first; then baste.

Next pin the material and edge of "Espartra" interlining together around headline, pinning the material ⅛ in. above the headline of the "Espartra."

Then baste. This gives a little extra height in crown.

THE HEAD BAND

Cut a bias strip of Grosgrain or material being used 3 ins. in width and length of around the head measure, adding 5 ins. for the two ends to overlap as showing.

Turn the edges in ¾ in. on each side, leaving the band 1½ in. wide when finished. (A 1 in. can be made if desired.)

Pin band on, covering the material and Espartra.

Try on to test head fitting. If correct, finish the Beret. You know the stitch to use.

Insert the headlining and neatly slip stitch the inside of the headline.

Trim as desired. A two-tone effect is also smart.

This Toque for day wear can be made in navy and white, navy and grey, tan and green, black and white, brown and beige, brown and pink, or all self trimmed with a contrasting coloured feather. For evening wear Velvet or Lame is most suitable. The Lame is obtainable in gold and silver and brocaded effects. All work must be neat. The stitches must not show.

(Copyright)

LESSON 82.

The Cutting and Making of a Smart Pill-box Hat

The measurements given here are for a 23 ins. head measurement.   The pattern can be adjusted smaller or larger, if desired.

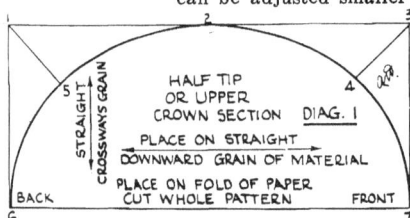

5 | STRAIGHT CROSSWAYS GRAIN

HALF TIP
OR UPPER
CROWN SECTION   DIAG. I
PLACE ON STRAIGHT
DOWNWARD GRAIN OF MATERIAL
PLACE ON FOLD OF PAPER
CUT WHOLE PATTERN

BACK   FRONT

There are two pieces of pattern:

(1) The Tip.

(2) The Crown Side Band.

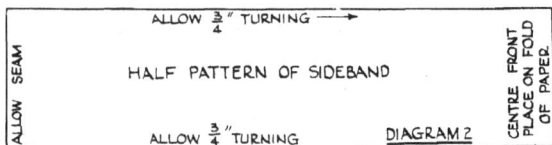

ALLOW ¾" TURNING →

ALLOW SEAM

HALF PATTERN OF SIDEBAND

CENTRE FRONT
PLACE ON FOLD
OF PAPER.

ALLOW ¾" TURNING   DIAGRAM 2

TO CUT PATTERN OF THE TIP   (Diagram 1).

Rule an oblong on brown paper, 9 ins. by 4 ins.

Measure from 1 to 2 along line 4½ ins. Mark with point.

Measure from 1 to 5 on angle shown 1¾ in.

Measure from 3 to 4 on angle shown 1¾ in.

Curve from 6 through 5 and 2 and 4 to 7 as shown in Diagram 1.

NOTE.—The line 6 to 7 is the centre line of tip.

POINT 7 is the CENTRE FRONT.

POINT 6 is the CENTRE BACK.

Cut half pattern out.

Place line 6 to 7 on folded paper and cut the whole pattern.

Diagram 2 clearly illustrates the cutting of the ½ side band section of crown. Rule an oblong on paper 11¼ ins. by 3 ins. Cut out around pencil line. This half pattern must be placed on fold of paper and the whole pattern of side band cut. Write on each piece of pattern as previously directed.

LESSON 83.

The Making of the Pill-box Hat in Velvet, Felt, Grosgrain or Straw Braid

MATERIAL REQUIRED: ⅜th yard 36 ins. wide. Straw braid, 4½ yards 1 in. wide. Interlining: Buckram, ¼ yard 18 ins. wide. Cotton to match. Hat wire.

This little model is quickly and easily made, and can be made from spare pieces of material, Felt, Straw, Ribbons, etc.

If making the hat in Velvet, you know the correct way the Velvet must lay. This is very important and has been thoroughly dealt with in another lesson.

If you have a Sailor crown hat block you can block this shape from the crown section of last season's felt hats or make a new one.

This charming little model is illustrated, trimmed in two different ways. One model features a feather trimming, a tall curled feather finished at side with a self bow.

A Suggestion of Colours for this Model: Tan Felt or Rust Velvet trimmed with a green feather and self bow; Black Velvet trimmed with a white feather and black and white bow; Navy Grosgrain trimmed with a grey or blue feather and self bow; a Brown Velvet or Felt trimmed with a honey shade feather and self bow or clip.

There are numerous colour schemes that can be used and a variety of trimmings.

The other model can be made in Rich Velvet, any shade desired, or Felt, Grosgrain, Astrachan, Ribbon or Straw.

The veiling is draped over the hat and caught at sides with ribbon or an ornament and tied under the chin.

TO MAKE THE HAT.

First cut out the Buckram or Espartra tip by pinning pattern on the Espartra. (Drawing pins are excellent to hold pattern in place.)

Pencil around the paper pattern, remove from Espartra. Cut ¼ in. outside the pencil line.

Pin pattern of side band of the crown also on Espartra.

Mark and cut out, allowing ¼ in. each side of band for turnings and ½ in. on each end of band for joining. (You know how to join Espartra, avoiding bulky joins.) This has been previously explained.

Cut out the covering for shape by the same patterns, allowing also the turnings (a little more than allowed on Espartra).

Seam the side band. Join the Espartra neatly.

Cut another sideband in silk or lightweight material to underline the sideband for neatness.

To Attach Crown Section to Sideband (Material Covering).

Seam the sideband to crown, centre front to centre front, centre back to centre back.

Trim seam and press towards the side band. Trim off any surplus amount on seams.

NOTE.—Shape can be made by directions given for making Velvet hats.

Whip the crown edges Espartra to edges of sideband.

Slip the Espartra shape inside the crown, working the edge of crown of Espartra well down into seam of band

and facing. Baste firmly.

Next pin the lining (which is also cut and made by the same patterns) inside of the hat crown, covering the Espartra or Buckram.

Next turn under the edge of the side band facing, pinning first, then neatly hemming over edge of crown lining.

NOTE.—If under side band is faced with self material only the tip need be lined. Cut ¼ in. larger than Espartra tip to allow turning on lining.

This hat may also be made in Straw Braid by following directions given in Straw Hat making section.

LESSON 84.

Cutting Material on the "Cross" or "Bias"

All materials being used for millinery purposes must be cut on the "cross" or the "bias," as a more artistic finish is obtained; also the material will lay better.

Every care must be taken when joining materials on the "cross" or "bias".

First pin the right sides together and pin the selvedges, letting the cut edges of the lengths meet.

Open out to see if correct, then join neatly by backstitch.

To Cut Velvet on the Cross or Bias.

Lay the Velvet on the table, right side upwards, and the selvedge towards you, and begin by turning the bottom right hand corner up and the dark shade running to the cut edge.

See **diagram clearly illustrating the correct method of cutting on the "bias" or "cross."**

THESE ARE IMPORTANT.

Diagram 16 — Bias Bindings. Bias bands should be cut on the exact bias, otherwise a twisted band will result in the finished work. To cut the band, commence by levelling up the material edge by tearing across or cutting in a drawn thread mark, and then fold the end of the material towards the selvedge to form a diagonal fold edge which is the true bias. The bias should be cut on this fold edge, marked off the width required. Follow the fold edge accurately.

When seaming bias bands for increased length, cut diagonally across the end of the bands and machine together on the straight of the material. The diagram shows the right way to machine bias bands, with the grain of each band agreeing. With diagonal stripes, match the bias bands so that the pattern runs the same way when machined together.

Bias bands shape themselves to curves if they are not too acute, but care should be taken to ensure that the seam of the material is notched to prevent twisting.

Bindings are cut to varying widths, depending on the material required to be bound. For velvets, a single-width band cut to four times the finished binding width is required. For thin materials, such as silks and transparent fabrics, a double band cut on the fold edge should be used so that less difficulty will be experienced in turning back and hemming down to a regular width.

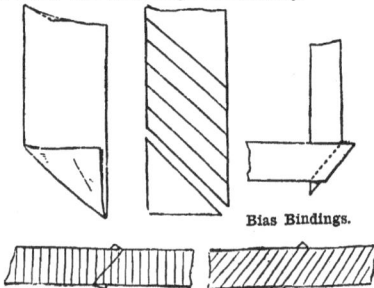

Bias Bindings.

Diagram 16.

Diagram 16 clearly illustrates the correct method of joining and cutting bias binding.

LESSON 85.

The Correct Table of Bias Measures

The measurement given may be on the selvedge or through the strip of bias. Always note which measure is given. The following table is of help in determining the amount of material necessary for a hat.

6 inches on the selvedge of a bias	=	$4\frac{1}{2}$ inches through the bias.		
9 ,,	,,	,,	,,	,,	=	$6\frac{1}{4}$,,	,,	,,
10 ,,	,,	,,	,,	,,	=	$7\frac{1}{4}$,,	,,	,,
12 ,,	,,	,,	,,	,,	=	$8\frac{1}{4}$,,	,,	,,
18 ,,	,,	,,	,,	,,	=	$13\frac{1}{4}$,,	,,	,,
24 ,,	,,	,,	,,	,,	=	18 ,,	,,	,,

RULES FOR MEASURING MATERIAL FOR A BIAS WHICH IS TO BE STRETCHED.

Folds.

In measuring the length of either bias flange or fold, stretch the bias strip (with correct width measure as given below) tightly around the edge of the hat and allow one-half inch on each end for a seam.

Stretch and pin the material to the form as it will be when finished. That is, down the centre lengthwise for a fold; on one edge for a flange.

In measuring for a stretched bias fold of not more than $1\frac{1}{2}$ inch finished, allow $\frac{3}{4}$ inch to be taken up in stretching and 1 inch for turning under the edges. That is, $1\frac{3}{4}$ inch in all.

For a fold more than $1\frac{1}{2}$ inch, allow $\frac{1}{4}$ inch more stretch for each inch added in width.

Measure only with a tape measure and not a ruler.

When a True Bias is Necessary.

An absolutely true bias is necessary when material is to be stretched and fitted on a frame as for a bias flange, a bias-stretched fold, a fitted side crown, a milliner's fold.

Importance of Stretching.

The fullness at the inner edge (inner circumference) of a bias flange or fold can be worked out only in exact proportion to the amount of stretching done to the outer edge of the flange or fold. The more fullness that it stretched out of the edge the less there will be to work out on the inner circumference.

Important Matching Seams.

Seams on a stretched bias must always run with the warp or selvedge. To make a seam on the cross threads or woof is to have a lumpy-looking seam, because the seam stitching runs counter to the heavier warp threads. On striped or figured materials the pattern may be made to match just as on a straight seam.

Seam Placement.

In hats, all seams should come at the back unless they will be hidden by trimming. When two seams are required (as for velvet folds or flanges on a large-brim edge), place one on each side of the back. Keep them far enough apart so that the extra length does not look like a patch.

To Cut a Correct Bias on Lyons Velvet.

In draping hats, it is important that bias runs the same way. The following rule has been evolved and is uniformly observed by careful workers. **Rule:** Place the velvet flat on a table in front of you, so that the nap is rough to the left. In turning the bias, throw the selvedge from you.

Greatest Economy of Materials.

By proper placing of the pattern a great deal of material may be saved. Because of the swing of the brim in fitting, one pattern may be made to fit into the curve of the other. If the material is merely fitted on the brim without making patterns, this advantage is lost.

LESSON 86.

DO YOU KNOW THE ANSWERS TO THESE 10 QUESTION?

1. How is the correct head size obtained?

2. What stitches are used in wiring a shape or hat brim?

3. What stitch is used for sewing the headline band in crown of hat?

4. What stitch is used to fix two parts temporarily together?

5. What stitch is used to finish headlinings?

6. What stitch is used to prevent materials ravelling or fraying or for drawing up edges of lace and fine materials?

7. What stitch is used for fixing down edges or folds of materials such as velvet and heavy types of materials?

8. What stitch is used for fixing trimmings that require strength?

9. What stitch must be used for fixing material over Buckram, Espartra or stiff net?

10. What stitch is used for fixing and attaching feather tips, lace or light trimmings?

◊ ◊ ◊

A FEW SUGGESTIONS FOR COLOUR.

Colours, as we all know, plays an important part in dress. A pale mauve straw bonnet trimmed with bunches of deep purple violets and a bow of Velvet ribbon to tone; a dusty pink straw trimmed with deeper pink and blue flowers; a red straw trimmed with white flowers, and all white straw trimmed with white flowers; a navy straw trimmed with blue flowers or pink flowers; a pale lemon straw trimmed with white daisies with lemon centres. Remember, when choosing colours, to see that they blend and harmonise. Pastel shades are youthful; dark shades are old looking. Choose flowers and trimmings carefully. Flowers are expensive. You can learn to make all types of beautiful flowers—paper, fabric, felt, wax, etc.—orange blossoms, orchids, roses, daisies, carnations, pansies, etc.—all popular varieties.

LESSON 87.

This Section deals with Hat Trimmings

1.—TRIMMINGS FOR WHICH THE HAT IS A BACKGROUND.

When choosing a Picture Hat it must be remembered always that there are two outstanding qualities for which millinery designers strive in making this type of millinery. One is beauty; the other style or smartness. To attain both is the designer's ambition.

If you are really going to learn millinery you must decide in your mind whether you or your customer wants a sweet hat or a smart hat. Strive to design both. Have both qualities when it is possible, and be sure that you know in your own mind exactly what you want; you are then more likely to attain it.

Dress Hat Trimmings may be Divided into Two Classes.

A trimming which uses the hat as a background only, and trimming which is part of the design of the model.

There are many times when a hat must be chosen for the trimmings rather than the trimmings for the hat. Flowers are usually the choice for garden type party hats; the large Picture Hat trimmed with flowers and velvet ribbon will always be the choice for garden party wear, also for dressy day wear hats and evening wear hats.

Flowers, Ribbon, Veiling Combined.

These must not be over-trimmed. Many beautiful flowers can be purchased ready made. These, of course, are expensive. If you have learnt to make "Beautiful French Flowers" (this course is available at moderate fee to all who desire to learn the art to save money), you can make your own trimmings at a moderate cost.

Flowers and colours chosen to match or harmonise with both hat and frock make a much more pleasing ensemble than flowers just selected at random.

There is no more picturesque hat to wear with organdi, lace, etc., than the Garden Hat. This lovely hat is one that lends colour and atmosphere to summer frocks.

Large hoods may be purchased to block and trim. (See sections of Straw Hat making.)

G

LESSON 88.

General Trimmings used in Millinery

THEIR WIDTHS AND TEXTURES.

TULLE: Obtainable in various colours, 30 ins. to 40 ins. in width, a fine, light stiffened net used for Bridal Veils and Hat Trimmings.

NINON: Obtainable in a variety of shades, 36 ins. to 42 ins. in width, a fine, closely woven, very transparent light material. Used generally for the linings of Hats, Bonnets, Bridesmaids' Hats and Veils.

BRUSSELS NET: 36 ins. to 72 ins. wide; a strong, coarse mesh net resembling Tulle, but stronger; mainly used for Confirmation and Bridal Veils.

BRETON NET (usually 18 ins. to 36 ins. wide). Similar to Brussels Net. Used mainly for ruching, pleating, Veils and trimmings under brims of Bonnets and Hats.

SILK GAUZE (36 ins. to 42 ins. wide): A very fine transparent gauze used for trimmings and veils.

JAP. SILK (27 ins. to 36 ins. wide): Used for head linings and children's bonnets; a fine lightweight silk.

CREPE DE CHENE (36 ins to 42 ins. wide): Used for Baby's Bonnets and trimmings; a lightweight silk.

CHINA SILK: Used for Head Linings, Small Hats and Bonnets. Usually 27 ins. to 36 ins. wide.

SATIN: Usually 18 ins. wide, referred to as millinery Satin; a bright shiny surface, usually cotton or silk back. Used for hats and trimmings.

TAFFETA (36 ins. to 42 ins. wide): Used for bows, under brims of adult's and children's bonnets, head linings, etc.; has a dull silk finish. Also obtainable in a large range of colours, plains, florals, spots and checks, and black and white.

RIBBONS: A variety of colours, obtainable in widths ranging from $\frac{1}{4}$ in. to 10 ins. and 12 ins. in width. Corded, Moire, Cire Satin, Plain Satin, Silk, Taffeta and Velvet are the most popular for millinery, including Cotton and Silk Petersham Ribbon.

FLOWERS: Endless varieties and types. Fabric is the best for millinery.

ORNAMENTS: A large variety; Silver, Gilt, Pearl, etc. Smart for Matron's Hats.

MILLINERY ELASTIC in Black and White, round and fine, used for keeping the hat on head of wearer.

NOTE.—When attaching millinery elastic to the hat, after cutting off the correct length required tie a knot in each end. It is easier to sew to the inner headline of hat. The knots will avoid the elastic slipping undone from the stitching.

LESSON 89.

DO YOU KNOW THE ANSWERS TO THESE 10 QUESTIONS?

1. What is the most important point in seam placement?
2. How is Hat Stiffening made?
3. What is the Correct Method of cleaning dyed Milan Straw?
4. What is the Correct Method of Cleaning Light Felt Hats?
5. What is the Correct Method of Cutting Hat Wire?
6. What type of hat is best suited to a Short Figure?
7. What type of hat is best suited to a large Stout Figure?
8. What is the Correct Method of Blocking a Felt Hood.
9. How are Creases Removed from Velvet or Velvet Ribbon?
10. What is "Mulling," and for what purpose is it used?

LESSON 90.

RIBBON TRIMMINGS

THE CORRECT TYPE OF RIBBONS FOR MILLINERY.

PETERSHAM RIBBON, especially Silk Petersham, can be purchased in a variety of colours and widths from ¼ in. wide to 6 ins. wide.

NOTE.—Berets and small hats and bonnets can be made from the 6 in. width. For shrinking, Silk Petersham is the correct ribbon to purchase.

Artificial Silk or Mercerised Cotton Petersham Ribbon will split when wet, but is suitable for bows, not binding.

Petersham Ribbon is hard wearing and is always an attractive, neat trimming for millinery. As Petersham ribbon can be shaped and shrunk, it is ideal for binding the outer edges of hat brims.

SATIN RIBBON is used for Infants' and Children's Millinery. This is also obtainable in a large variety of colours and various widths. A Satin ribbon, 1 in. or 1¼ in. wide made up with insertion and lace makes lovely infants and small girls' bonnets. Also ribbon stitched together makes small Bonnets or Hats for young children.

There are many varieties of ribbon, some ribbed and plain.

The **SILK RIBBON** used as ties on Infants' Bonnets is obtainable in all widths, also narrow Baby Ribbon for trimmings.

For Ladies' and Misses' Hats there is a large variety; Plain and beautiful check Taffeta Ribbon, Striped Satin, Taffeta and Silk Ribbon for large bows. Velvet Ribbon, both Silk and Cotton Velvet, in a variety of colours and widths. There are numerous ribbons that can be used for trimming.

The **COTTON PETERSHAM** is suitable for head lining (for hats that are not lined with head lining).

CIRE SATIN in all colours and widths.

The **MOIRE RIBBON,** also obtainable in various colours and widths, is smart for matrons and women's hats. A pleated trimming of ribbon is smart on felt or straws. The ribbon must blend with the hat.

Choose the correct colours. This is important for successful results.

Do not make large bows for big figure types; small dainty trimmings are best. The slim figure type can wear a hat with large bows of ribbon.

LESSON 91.

Smart Ribbon Trimmings for Modern Millinery

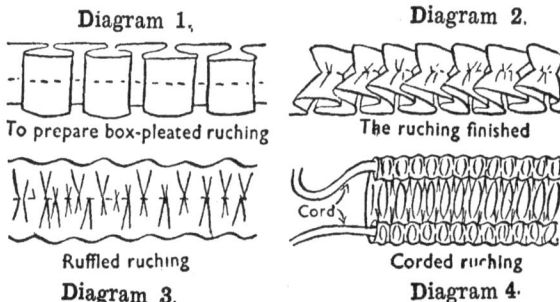

Diagram 1.

Diagram 2.

To prepare box-pleated ruching

The ruching finished

Ruffled ruching

Diagram 3.

Corded ruching

Diagram 4.

Diagram 1 clearly illustrates a Box Pleated Ruching.

This trimming can be made of Silk Petersham Ribbon, Taffeta, Satin, etc., and is ideal as a hat trimming or for underbrims of children's hats and bonnets. It can also be made from Taffeta picoted edged.

It is necessary to allow three times the length required, as when pleated the ribbon will be one-third of the original length.

For 1 yard of box pleated ruching you would require 3 yards of ribbon.

Fold the ribbon in half lengthways and pleat into box pleats. (Practice this on paper first.)

Fold a 2 ins. wide strip of paper, 6 ins. long, in half. Measure from the fold 1 in., stitch across paper. Fold the crease line of the fold over on row of stitching and you have a box pleat.

NOTE.—When all the pleats are tacked firmly in the ribbon, run a line of machine gathers through centre as shown clearly in **Diagram 2,** or you can leave the pleating plain.

Diagram 3 clearly illustrates a plain ruffled ruching. This is made by running a machine row of stitching down the centre of the ribbon. It is also very effective with 3 rows (shirring) down the centre, and makes an excellent trimming for hats or children's bonnets.

Diagram 4 clearly illustrates the corded ruching. Using straight pieces of material, 2 ins. wide, and three times the length required, hem the edges and insert with a bodkin two strands of wool.

Gather the material up along each edge by easing the wool. This gives the edges a raised appearance.

This trimming can also be used for cushions and bedspreads, etc., besides millinery, and makes a fine trimming on the inside brims of children's bonnets or hats. This ruching is not suitable in heavy types of material. Georgette, Mariette, Voile, Net, Ninon, Chiffon or Silk and any soft fine material is suitable.

Practice this on a scrap of material.

LESSON 92.

RIBBON LOOPS AS TRIMMINGS

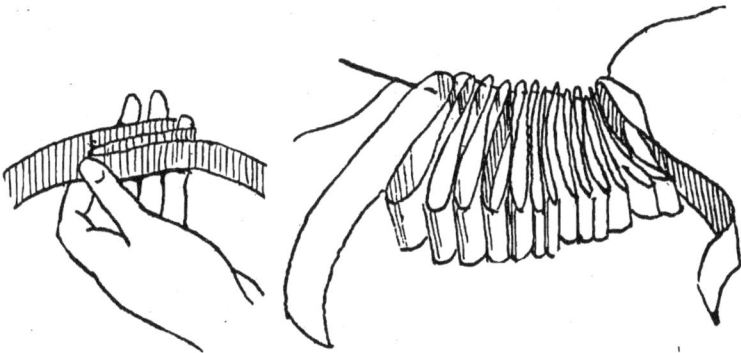

The illustrated diagram shows how the loops are made, then caught to hold in position. Large or small loops may be made, whichever is desired.

Narrow or wide ribbon may be used.

The Gathered Ribbon Rosette is easy to make. The edge of ribbon is gathered up and the gathered ribbon is stitched firmly on to a small circular piece of muslin or canvas.

The Pleated Rosette is ribbon pleated instead of being gathered and sewn on a small firm piece of material.

Follow the diagrams showing how easy it is to make these popular and useful ribbon trimmings.

❖ ❖ ❖

LESSON 93.

THE MAKING OF RIBBON TRIMMINGS

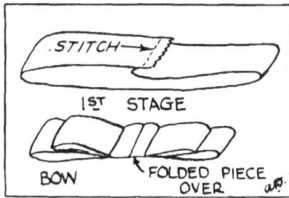

STITCH →

1ST STAGE

BOW   FOLDED PIECE OVER

If a smart tailored ribbon bow is required to finish a Sports Hat or plain tailored type, Petersham ribbon is used for the trimming.

Cut off a length of ribbon about 8 ins., fold the ends to meet in the middle, secure with a stitch.

Fold a small piece over the join and stitch neatly at back.

This is the easiest bow made and can be made in many sizes to suit. Ends may be attached and fringed or cut plain.

To Make Ribbon Rosettes for Trimming Felt or Straw Hats.

There are two varieties illustrated, and directions are given for making. The loop Rosette is made of a bunch of looped ribbon, the loops being of equal size.

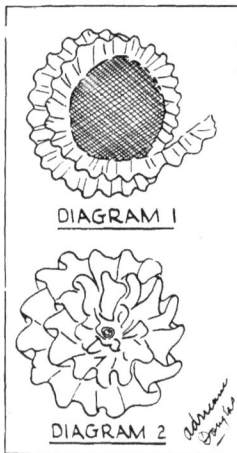

DIAGRAM 1

DIAGRAM 2

Start with the length of ribbon by making a loop of size desired, pleat as clearly shown, and catch with a stitch at the bottom of the loop, leaving $\frac{1}{2}$ in. at the end as shown. Wind the cotton around the $\frac{1}{2}$ in. at end to keep the loop firm.

Make as many loops as desired, as large or small rosettes can be made. This rosette is used mainly on Children's or Maids' Hats and Bonnets.

A tiny flower can be sewn to the centre, which is an attractive trimming.

A Gathered Rosette.

Run a gathered thread along one edge of the ribbon, draw up the thread. Tack ribbon to a round piece of net or ribbon of same colour. Tack each layer in place until a rosette is made the size required.

To Make a Smart Lace Bow.

Make 2 loops of wire and fasten each at ends. Fold lace over each loop and stitch securely.

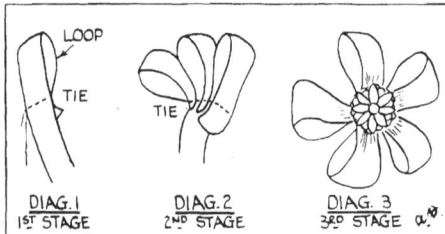

LOOP

TIE

TIE

DIAG. 1
1ST STAGE

DIAG. 2
2ND STAGE

DIAG. 3
3RD STAGE

Make two smaller loops and repeat. Stitch all together in bow.

Fold lace of centre to hide the joins. A smart, inexpensive trimming for a summer hat.

Even a whole hat can be made of lace, using a wire shape.

Lace hats are ideal for Bridesmaids' and Picture Hats.

LESSON 94.

BOW TRIMMINGS

A smart finish, excellent in striped, check or plain Taffeta, Velvet or any Millinery material.

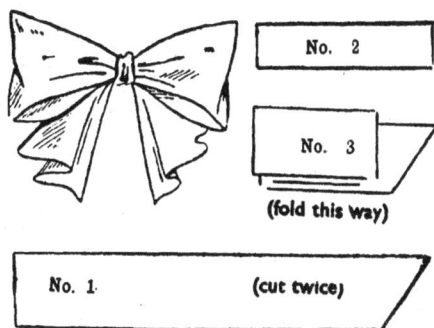

No. 2

No. 3

(fold this way)

No. 1.   **(cut twice)**

TO MAKE THE BOW.

DIAGRAM 1.

Cut two pieces of ribbon 6 ins. in length.

DIAGRAM 2.

Cut another piece 3 ins. long. Fold this strip with the two raw edges to the centre. This piece is for the centre of the bow.

Press and fold the other two pieces as clearly shown in **Diagram 3.**

Catch together, stitch the centre piece securely around the middle. The bow is then complete.

For bow made from material, underline with contrasting material. Bow can be made smaller or larger if desired. Also narrow or wide ribbon may be used. Only ½ yard of ribbon is necessary for this bow.

If made in wide ribbon, the edges can be stiffened by very narrow crinoline braid, making a smart trimming.

LESSON 95.

ATTRACTIVE CORDED SHIRRING

AND CORDED OR PADDED TUCKING

This Corded Shirring is easy to do. It is an attractive trimming for Infants' and Girls' Bonnets and Hats.

Soft, fine materials are best for shirring; Georgette, Satin, Net, Crepe de Chene, Silk, Taffeta and Allover Fine Lace or Chiffon.

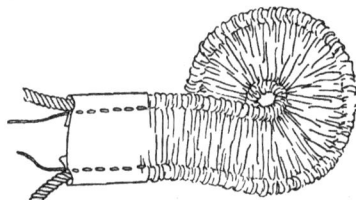

Trimming band with cord at each edge. Use a running stitch to hold the cord and shirr the fabric by pushing it back.

DIAGRAM 5.

Diagram 5 Clearly Illustrates the Corded Shirring.

To prepare the material for shirring, cut the strips of material the width desired, 1 in. or 2 ins., or as wide as required, allowing $\frac{1}{2}$ in. on each side of strip for turning of a narrow hem. The strips must be three times the finished length.

For instance, if you require 1 yard of corded shirring, the strip of material being used must be 3 yards in length.

The material strip is cut on the straight grain of material. The sides hemmed with $\frac{1}{4}$ in. hem.

To Gather up the Shirring.

Thread a bodkin with three strands of wool same colour as material being used. Thread the wool through the narrow hems on each side of the hemmed strip.

Gather up as clearly illustrated in the Diagram 5.

Corded or padded trucking, used mainly on brims of Children's Organdi and Fabric Bonnets and Hats, both as a trimming and to aid in supporting the brims. This padded tucking is easy to do.

The brim, when made double, is stitched around close to the outer edge of the brim, then another row of stitching following around $\frac{1}{8}$ in. apart from the first row. Then two more rows and another two rows.

Leave a space of 1 in. and machine

another two rows $\frac{1}{8}$ in. apart, and repeat two more rows and another two rows.

There are now six double rows of stitching, the three on outer edge of brim and three spaced 1 in. apart from first three double rows.

The fine cord is threaded through these with bodkin, or wool of same colour which has previously been shrunk.

The small opening where bodkin is inserted between each row of stitching is hand neatened when all tucks are finished. The tucks have a distinct raised finish.

Practice these on a spare piece of material.

You will be delighted with this lovely trimming.

NOTE.—A fine wire can be used with the wool or cording, giving a better support to the brim. The corded tucks give the Bonnet or Hat a tailored finish.

LESSON 96.

FLOWERS FOR MILLINERY PURPOSES

A large variety of Flowers are suitable for Millinery. The main ones
I have dealt with here. Single Roses, Sprays of Roses, Rosettes,
Cabachons, Sprays of Mixed Flowers.

1. **Silk Flowers,** such as Violets, Rose-buds, large Roses and Sprays are the main varieties under this heading.

2. **Linen and Lawn Flowers.** A large variety are made of Linen, Lawn, Organdi, Forget-me-nots, Sweet Peas, Lily of the Valley, Roses, Wheat, Grasses, Berries, Lilies, etc., all come under this classification. These are all effective trimmings.

3. **Metal, Lame Flowers.** Tinsel, Sequin Sprays, Leaves and Sprays are usually featured in the metal class.

4. **Velvet.** Many of the better type of flowers — Pansies, Roses, Nasturtiums, Orchids, etc. These are more expensive, but add beauty to all millinery.

5. **Hand-made Flowers.** These are in endless variety and all types of material. They are very satisfactory for many reasons, and furnish the most beautiful trimmings for anyone who will take the trouble to learn to make them for a small outlay for the materials. The colours can always be blended to give the desired colour scheme desired.

The really finished hand-made flower is never common. Beautiful workmanship is one thing cheap manufacturers cannot copy.

Georgette is excellent for hand-made flowers, because it is available in all attractive shades, easy to handle and realistic made into flowers.

Try making a Georgette flower over thin wire. Twist three different size loops of fine tie wire, or electrician's fine wire, 2 ins. for the smallest, 2½ ins. for the next size, and 3 ins. for the larger size.

When the three loops are formed and the ends twisted together to hold them in position, hold each loop in left hand one at a time, frill Georgette double over it to cover it.

Sew Georgette securely at end of the wire (ends of loops). Cut off any surplus material.

Make four groups of petals of loops

covered, six medium and eight large ones.

Assemble them into a daisy shape, the larger petals on outside, the medium, and then the small ones.

Finish the centre with a covered button (Velvet), beads, or roll the Georgette.

Cover a cord with Georgette for stem. Attach the flower and the leaves.

This makes a lovely frock or hat spray for lace hats or soft large straw hats. Silk or Organdi may be used instead of the Georgette.

There are all varieties of hand-made flowers—Orchids, Roses, Carnations, Chrysanthemums, Sweet Peas, Wild Briar Roses, Daisies, Sunflowers, Wax Orange Blossoms, etc., Felt, Paper Fabric Flowers, Fruit, etc.

All throughly taught in a special course, "French Flower Making," obtainable from "Modern Designers Academy." Write to Secretary for full details. You can learn immediately to make beautiful hand-made flowers.

LESSON 97.

Lovely Flower Trimmings Made in Lace, Chiffon, Organdi or Georgette

Such smart Hand-made Trimmings will really go to your head. You can change the plainest hat into a new creation.

The space at my disposal here will not permit all the many varieties of flowers to be dealt with. The types detailed in these lessons are suitable for Spring, Summer, Autumn and Winter wear, also for Cocktail hats.

The little lace or Chiffon, etc., ones are lovely for Bridesmaids' wear or large Picture Hats. Also sprays can be made to match the spray on the hat, to wear as a posy; these also are excellent for girls' Hats and Bonnets.

A large range of beautiful Flowers for all Millinery and Home Decorations made in paper, Fabric, Velvet, Wax Flowers, etc. . . . Gorgeous life-like Orchids, Wax Orange Blossom, Sweet Peas, Daisies, Ranunculus, Frangipani, Roses, Briar Roses, etc., etc. . . . Sunflowers, Pansies, Carnations, and many more, including Holly, Cherries, Felt work for Cushions and Home Decorations and all types of beautiful flowers are contained in a special thorough course of instruction in "French Flower Making" by the same author.

Particulars will be sent on application to—

THE SECRETARY,

"MODERN DESIGNERS ACADEMY,"

77 QUEEN ST., BRISBANE, Q'LD.

We all know how very expensive Hand-made and even Factory-made Flowers are to buy. Sometimes they cost as much as the hat itself; often more.

◆ ◆ ◆

LESSON 98.

FLOWER MAKING FOR TRIMMINGS

To make the Little Roses in Chiffon, Organdi, Velvet, Voile, Lace, Georgette, etc.

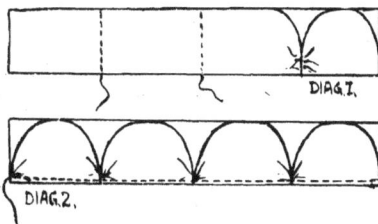

DIAG.1.

DIAG.2.

Diagram 1 clearly illustrates the Way to Begin.

For each rose required cut a bias strip of material 1 in. wide and 3 ins. in length.

Next fold this strip lengthways in half, making the width ¼ in., with the two raw edges meeting together.

Mark with pins into four even sections.

Gather down from folded edge of the material on divisions marked with pins.

Draw thread up as clearly shown in Diagram 1.

Repeat till the three lines and the ends are drawn up, forming four petals; tie off firmly.

DIAG.3

DIAG 4

Diagram 2 clearly illustrates the petals drawn up between each one and at the corners.

Next a gathering thread is run along the raw edges (keeping the two edges together). Run the thread as close to edge as possible.

Gather up tight till rose is formed. Stitch securely.

Diagram 3 clearly illustrates the finished flower, with the stamens in the centre.

Diagram 4. To Make the Stamens. If you cannot obtain them ready made, it is an easy matter to make them.

Cut off five or six pieces of stiff yellow cotton 1 in. in length. Tie knots on each end or dip the ends in seccotine or any cement glue.

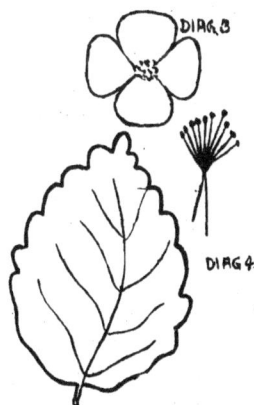

FLOWER MAKING FOR TRIMMINGS

TO MAKE THE STAMENS (Continued).

Then crush a piece of yellow chalk finely and dip the glued ends of the cotton into the chalk.

Allow to dry well. Double the cotton over, cut off 2 or 3 ins. of fine wire. (Fuse wire will do if no other is obtainable.)

Place the wire through the looped ends of cotton.

Insert wire through centre of flower and pull down till only a portion of the cotton with yellow tips is showing.

Sew flower securely to wire; leave the wire to attach to others for a spray.

Repeat till as many flowers are made as required—about seven makes a nice spray.

They can be bunched together and the wires bound with fine bias-cut strips of green Georgette, Organdi or Chiffon.

THE LEAVES.

To make these, trace off a pattern from leaf illustrated, using tissue or grease-proof paper.

Cut the leaf out in velvet or firm green material.

Lay a fine wire on back down centre of leaf, leaving 1½ in. end.

Paste another leaf, same size, cut from Organdi or green Silk or Taffeta, over the wire. Use millinery solution or strong glue.

The wire is now between the two leaves. Bind end of wire to match stems of flowers; about three leaves is sufficient, or the roses can be used without leaves if desired.

NOTE.—The material used to make the roses can also be treated with stiffening before being made up. It is necessary to allow the material to dry thoroughly before making the flowers.

These small Roses can be made up in a bunch or a spray. The Roses can be made in white with lemon centres, pink with lemon centres, yellow with white centres, pale blue with white or yellow centres.

Pastel shades are the most suitable.

The fine wire for stems is obtainable at all Hardware Departments of leading stores. Fine electrician's wire can also be used. Millinery wire is too heavy and must not be used for flower making.

These roses, being very small, are ideal for Children's Hats and Bonnets.

Larger Roses can be made by doubling the length and width of the material in directions given for these small ones. They are exclusive for Bridesmaids' wear.

A whole crown covered with tiny roses and veiling makes a charming little Cocktail Hat.

Pieces from your scrap bag can be used up making lovely flowers. Save them all; you will find a use for those little pieces.

LESSON 99.

CAN YOU ANSWER THESE QUESTIONS ?

1. What is the difference between a "Flange" and a "Fold," and for what purpose is a "Flange" used?

2. What is the correct procedure of putting on a "Flange"?

3. What makes of Straw Braids are the best qualities, and where are they made?

4. What are the correct colours for Brunettes to wear?

5. What are the correct colours for Blonde types to wear?

6. What are the correct colours for Red-headed types to wear?

7. Why must colour harmony be considered and applied to the individual?

8. Is colour harmony essential in millinery?

9. How can a low crown be raised higher?

10. How can a high crown be lowered?

LESSON 100.

EXQUISITE HAND-MADE FLOWERS

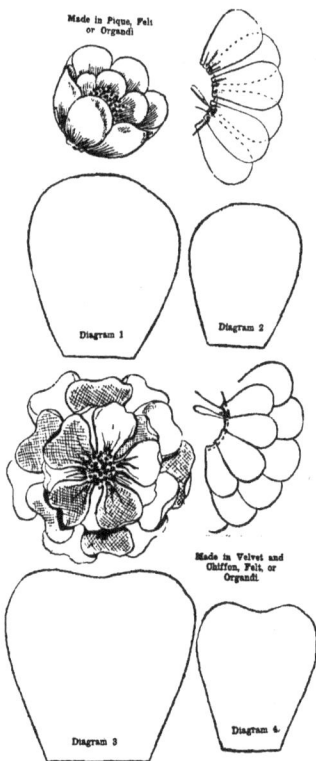

Made in Pique, Felt
or Organdi

Diagram 1

Diagram 2

Made in Velvet and
Chiffon, Felt, or
Organdi

Diagram 3

Diagram 4.

Dainty Flowers in Pique, Organdi, Lace, Georgette, Chiffon, Patent Leather or Felt. Easy to follow diagrams, and fully detailed instructions, teach step by step the art of making these flowers.

To Prepare the Materials for Flower Making.

If using Fabric, the material must first be stiffened. Use hat stiffener for this purpose.

Cover the material with the stiffener, using a clean brush; then allow the material to dry thoroughly.

Trace off the patterns of each size of the petals, using grease-proof paper or tissue paper. Cut patterns out. Re-cut on thin firm cardboard or thick brown paper.

Diagram 1.—The Larger Petal.

Diagram 2.—The Smaller Petal of the First Flower design.

Diagram 3.—The Larger Petal.

Diagram 4.—The Smaller Petal of the Second Design of Flower.

Velvet and Georgette are ideal for making this lovely flower. A variety of materials can be used as previously mentioned.

When cutting out the petals on the material, fold the material over in four layers, enabling four petals to be cut at the one time. Place the pattern of the petals on the folded material. Cut out around the pattern of each size petal. Gather the petals at base as clearly illustrated.

Note how the petals are overlapped.

It is necessary to complete the large row of petals, then the smaller row which is placed inside the larger row of petals.

NOTE.—Only half circle of petals is shown; the whole circles are necessary. This is described in another lesson (How to Make the Flower Centres).

The edges of the petals in the larger flower are stretched by using the head of a large nail or any round metal object which can be heated. Use a small cushion filled with sand and heat the end of the nail.

Press at corners and around edges of the petals on the cushion, giving the edges of petals a natural cupped effect. The tool must not be too hot.

(A full range of beautiful flowers are thoroughly taught in the Flower Making Course.)

NOTE.—These patterns of petals can be used for Felt, Leather or any materials. The flowers illustrated can also be made in white or a variety of colours, and are suitable for general millinery purposes. Practice these flowers in your spare time. They can be made from scraps of material and Lace or Felt.

Cutting Patterns and Making Stitched Hats

This Section deals with the Cutting of Patterns and Making Girls' Stitched Hats and Bonnets and Infants' Bonnets.

You no doubt have some lovely pieces of Organdi and Lace, also left-over pieces from frocks. These can all be used in the making of Children's Hats and Bonnets.

There is always a demand for dainty Infants' and Children's Bonnets, and your spare time can be turned into a profitable hobby.

Children's Hats and Bonnets are not difficult to cut and make, and once you have thoroughly learnt all the thorough lessons given in this course, you will be able to create various designs of your own. You may see a dainty model in a shop window. Try to copy it. This is all excellent practice.

You will no doubt see remnants of Lace and Ribbons, small sprays of flowers that all would make lovely bonnets.

If you decide to make hats and bonnets to sell, it is wise to obtain your materials from a warehouse; this allows you a fair margin of profit, and you can create the model much cheaper than if you purchased the materials retail.

A Smart Hat for Teen-age Wear—a Flower and Ribbon Trimmed Model.

If you are making for your family or friends you will find lots of materials to suit you in any department store. Select colours that blend. Do not buy useless colours because they are cheap. Colour plays an important part in millinery.

This subject has been dealt with in another part of the course. Study it carefully. All details have been carefully detailed; each is important to your success.

You can also take an old bonnet or hat apart and cut a pattern from it. Some styles are more in demand than others. I have seen a model made and thousands of others made from it. It sold on sight, and was made in a large variety of colours and different materials because the style was popular.

(Copyright)

You may also create or design a style that takes the eye immediately. The same style can be trimmed differently, and different colour schemes used in the making.

A few of the materials suitable for Children's Hats and Bonnets: Pique, Organdi (Plain and Floral), Haircord, Tobralco, Indian Head, Cesarine, Voile, Satin, Velvet, Fur Fabric, Wool Jersey, Millinery Felt, Eyelet Embroidery, Floral and Plain Linens, Felt Hoods, Straw Hoods, or Straw Braid by the yard, Crinoline Straw for Party Hats and Bonnets, or Flower Girls.

Ribbon stitched on to an Espartra shape, and many other fabrics will be found suitable. For small infants, Vyella, Flannel and Silks are best. Often an adult hat can be made like new and remodelled for a school girl. **Do not discard old hats.** If you do not need them, clean them and place in a calico bag away from moths and silverfish. They are excellent for practice purposes.

◆ ◇ ◆

LESSON 102.

Trimmings for Children's Millinery

Small Rosettes of Lace and Ribbon are smart and soft for children's millinery. A rosette of lace with a tiny flower in centre placed around the headline of the brim makes a dainty trimming. Small loops in a bunch of narrow ribbon also is attractive. Select very small flowers for tiny girls; larger for the older girl or teen-ager.

I have illustrated a simple straw hat for a teen-ager. **No block required.** You can use any brim pattern and crown pattern to suit; or the crown can be made on a pudding basin—the brim on a larger basin.

The straw can be fine or coarse. You can make it in Felt or Straw. There is no tip in the crown. The trimming is simple.

I have designed this smart Teen-age Model as a Test Lesson, as after completing the section of the course dealing with the making of Straw Hats, you will not find it at all difficult to make this simple model or any others you may desire to make.

Remember, neatness is essential. On this your success depends.

Do not hurry the work. If you are not in the mood, place the work aside and begin when you really will enjoy making hats for all occasions.

(Copyright)

LESSON 103.

CHILDREN'S MILLINERY

The general styles of Infants' and Girls' Bonnets and Hats are clearly detailed and illustrated in this section. All Children's Millinery must have simplicity of style, daintiness and neatness. The materials, too, must be suitable and dainty.

For infants' wear soft lightweight materials must be selected for summer wear. Warmer and heavier materials and Felts for winter wear.

It is necessary to shrink all materials, including interlining and lining, before making up bonnets. A brief list of materials most suitable for Infants' and small Girls' Bonnets is given:—

THE OUTER MATERIALS		THE INTERLINING	THE LINING
Pique	Muslin	Taffeta	Silk
Silk Pique	Voile	Book Muslin	Jap Silk
Tobralco	Crepe de Chene	Cambric	Crepe de Chene
Haircord	Fugi Silk	Leno	Lawn
Plain Organdi	Flannel	Canvas	Net
Floral Organdi	Fur Fabric	Heavy Calico	Muslin
Broderie Anglaise	Velvet		Voile
Eyelet Linen	Corded Velvet		
Allover Lace	Velour		
Lace Insertion	Straw		
Astrachan	Felt		
Georgette			
Silk Petersham			

THE QUANTITY OF MATERIALS REQUIRED

These, of course, would vary according to the style of Bonnet and size of Bonnet being made. To make an Infant's size Bonnet, $\frac{1}{4}$ yard of outer material, interlining and lining would be necessary, and trimming, and for the ribbon ties $1\frac{1}{4}$ to $1\frac{1}{2}$ yards of 1 in. to $1\frac{1}{4}$ in. would be necessary.

If rosettes of ribbon are added, about 3 to 4 yards of $\frac{1}{4}$ in. ribbon would be required.

Age cannot be considered for size. The head measurement varies and therefore must be measured.

❖   ❖   ❖

H

LESSON 104.

The Correct Methods of Taking Measurements for Infants and Children's Millinery

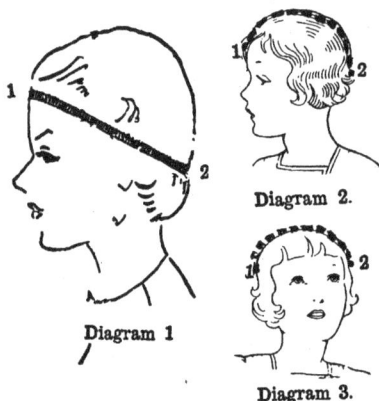

Diagram 1

Diagram 2.

Diagram 3.

Exclusive Children's Millinery

CLEARLY ILLUSTRATING THE CORRECT WAY TO TAKE CHILDREN'S HEAD MEASUREMENTS.

Note carefully the positions.

Your success will depend on accuracy. The measurements must be correct. Illustrated diagrams clearly show the correct positions that the head measurements must be taken in. Three measurements are necessary.

Diagram 1.—Place the tape measure around the head in position shown. This is around the head measurement.

Diagram 2 clearly illustrates the back to front measurement. Note carefully the position.

Diagram 3 clearly illustrates the side to side measurement. Note carefully the correct positions as illustrated. Check all measurements carefully.

Avoid unnecessary work. The measurements must be right or the hat will not fit the wearer. It is necessary to fit the hat as the making is proceeded with. This also avoids unnecessary work and the best results are assured.

It is necessary to take the children's measurements each time a hat is being made as the measurements alter slightly as the child grows.

The Hat Block can be padded with cloth or paper to make it slightly larger for various head fittings.

A scale of stock size measurements are given. These will enable you to check measurements, and they can also be used to make up Ready-to-wear Bonnets, and for general practice purposes.

LESSON 105.

The Correct Table of Sizes of Infants and Children's Bonnets

Age.	Size Around the Face	Ear to Ear Back Measurement	Front to Back Measurement
Infants (1st size)	12 ins.	9¼ ins.	9 ins.
Infants (2nd size)	14½ ins.	9½ ins.	10 ins.
2 years of age (small face) ..	15½ ins.	9¾ ins.	10½ ins.
3 years of age	16 ins.	10 ins.	11 ins.
4 years of age	15½ in. to 16½ in.	10 ins.	11 ins.
5 years of age	15½ in. to 16½ in.	11 ins.	11½ ins.
6 years of age	15½ in. to 16½ in.	12 ins.	12 ins.
7 years of age	16 in. to 16½ in.	13 ins.	13 ins.

Full directions and diagrams clearly illustrate the correct methods of taking the head measurements. These must be carefully studied. The average head size for a 5 to 6 years of age boy will be about 20 ins. around the head.

Send for list of Beautiful Model Fashion Books for Infants, Small Children, Girls and Misses' Model Frock Fashions in Colour

LESSON 106.

The Cutting of Pattern of Infant's Bonnet

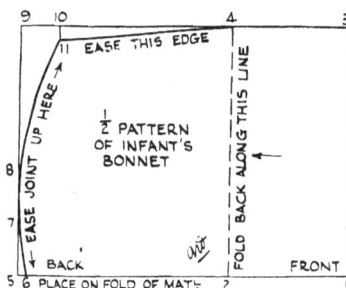

Rule an oblong 12¼ ins. by 9 ins. on paper.

Measure from 1 to 2 (4½ ins.).

Measure from 3 to 4 (4½ ins.).

Rule a line from 2 to 4. This represents the turn back line.

Measure from 5 to 6 (⅝ in.).

Measure from 5 to 7 (2 ins.).

Measure from 7 to 8 (2 ins.).

Measure from 9 to 10 (1¼ in.).

Measure from 10 to 11 (⅝ in.).

Rule line from 11 to 4.

Curve from 11 to 8 along line to 7.

Curve from 7 to 6. This completes half the pattern.

The rounded end is back, which is eased and joined, also the edge 11 to 4 is eased up and attached to ribbon.

THE MAKING OF THE "EASY TO MAKE" LITTLE INFANT'S BONNET AND HOOD

Material Required: ¼ yard of summer or winter material or a small piece of left-over material. Ribbon and lace to trim bonnet, or 1 in. Satin ribbon and lace. Insertion joined together makes a lovely bonnet.

The edges can also be finished with a corded ruching. (See this lovely ruching and how to make it in the Trimming Section.) This ruching is not suitable for heavy materials.

You can make this Bonnet in two designs. The one with the back seamed up as a Hood effect.

To make this style, fold material when cut out over on centre and seam from fold edge to bottom at back of hood.

Face the front to turn back as marked on pattern.

Gather a narrow row, or several rows of lace, and whip to edge of under front edge of bonnet.

Gather the lower edges and attach ribbon for ties.

The small Rosette of ribbon illustrated in the Trimming Section is excellent for trimming Bonnets and Children's Millinery.

Make two Rosettes of narrow ribbon. Make more loops and smaller ones for Infants' Bonnets.

Attach a Rosette to each side of Bonnet when the ribbon ties are sewn on.

INFANT'S BONNET and HOOD

NOTE.—This little Hood can be made for Toddlers and attached to a Cape.

To cut for older child, increase size of pattern 1½ ins. longer and 1 in. wider, or even larger if desired. It is also suitable made in All-over Felt and worked with Wool Blanket Stitch around edges.

To make the Bonnet design with small circle in back, cut a circle out on paper 3 ins. across. (A circle can be obtained by using a cup and pencilling around the edge of cup placed on paper.)

Cut the circle out and place on material.

Cut out, allowing ¼ in. seams.

Gather the back of the Bonnet and ease it evenly around circle, keeping the seam of back exactly at back.

Join up the seam.

This is the usual type of Infant's Bonnet, as it is designed to cover the head and for comfort in wear. It must be lined with soft Silk or Flannelette or Vyella. It requires no interlining other than the lining. White or Cream Vyella or Flannel makes a cosy Infant's Bonnet.

Cut both patterns out on tissue paper first and pin Bonnets (both designs) together; it is then easy to see how the completed Bonnet will look when finished.

NOTE.—When making up the Bonnet, baste the outer material, the interlining and the lining together, treating as one piece, or the lining can be added when the Bonnet is completed.

For fine materials it can be made with the outer and interlining as one.

For thick materials it is advisable to line it separately, slip stitching the lining into finished Bonnet.

◆ ◆ ◆

(Copyright)

The Cutting and Making of a Delightful Backless Bonnet

FINISHED WITH EMBROIDERY

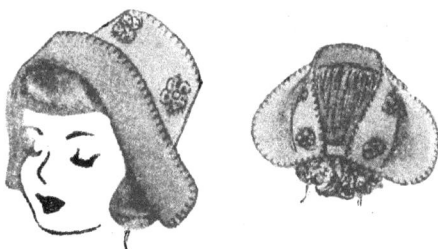

Material required: ¼ yard of 36 in. material; Canvas interlining ¼ yard 28 ins.

Materials suitable: Corduroy Velvet, Velvet, Wool Felt, Felt, Pique, Linen, Indian Head, Cesarine, or any firm material.

TO CUT THE PATTERN

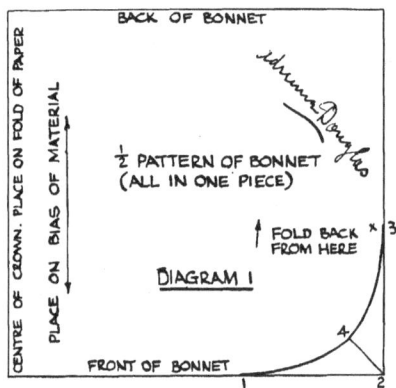

Rule an oblong 8½ ins. by 8 ins. on paper.

Measure from 2 to 1 (3¼ ins.).

Measure from 2 to 3, also 3¼ ins.

Measure from 2 to 4 on angle shown 1 inch.

Curve from 1 through 4 to 3 to shape corner. This completes simple pattern.

NOTE.—Cut pattern out. The curved ends are the front of Bonnet. Fold back from 3 as the brim turn back and crown are all in one piece.

NOTE.—The back of Bonnet is caught together with small tab. (See design.)

The Bonnet can be made from spare pieces of material, two-tone or all self.

The Making Up of the Little Bonnet

(QUICK AND EASY TO MAKE)

If Embroidery is to be used as a trimming, it is necessary to stamp your transfer on the Bonnet before making up.

Wool Embroidery on Felt is smart for Winter wear. Silk or Cotton Embroidery on Velvet or Cotton materials all add distinction to this useful, easy to make Bonnet.

For Felt, a lining is not necessary.

For a lined Bonnet, cut the lining to fit only to the turn-back ($\frac{1}{2}$ in. inside turn back line).

For Winter wear a warm material can be used for lining, such as Flannel or a scrap of Woollen dress material.

This Bonnet is smart made in plain and Tartan material. The lining of Tartan is cut to the whole pattern. The brim, when turned back, shows the Tartan. The remainder of Bonnet is plain.

Turn Bonnet inside out and there is a plain brim and Tartan crown. A variety of colour schemes can be used in the making, and this model can also be made in Straw Braid, Stitched Material, or Lace and Satin.

To make Bonnet with the canvas interlining, cut the canvas to shape of pattern and follow same directions as given in making up of stitched pieced hats. Ties of self material, or ribbon, may be used. The edges are blanket or buttonhole stitched.

To finish this Bonnet, piping or binding can be used, or edges left plain and stitched or ruched ribbon used as a trimming.

There is so little material required to make this Bonnet that it is an ideal pattern to use up those spare pieces of material.

LESSON 108.

The Cutting of the Patterns for the Two Designs of Girl's Bonnets and Making

The first model is a dainty Bonnet with scalloped brim and buttoned crown at back. This model is excellent made up in Pique or any material previously suggested.

TO CUT THE PATTERN SECTIONS.

There are only two pieces of pattern for this Bonnet—half the crown, No. 1 (clearly illustrated in Diagram 1) and the half brim pattern (clearly illustrated in Diagram 2).

Use 18 ins. side to side head measurement, commencing with the crown pattern, rule an oblong as 1 to 6 and 8 to 7 (8 ins. by 5¼ ins.).

For a 16 ins. side to side measurement. Note: The length of oblong 8 ins. represents half of side to side head measure required. The 8 ins. is given for practice.

It is best to measure head of wearer, or if making for stock, consult the table of sizes. This is given on page "How to take Children's Measurements" and is included in that lesson.

Measure from 1 to 2, 3¼ ins. This is half of width of back buttoned section of crown.

Measure from 2 to 3 up 1 in. (This is slit on pattern and material from 2 to 3.)

Measure from 2 to 5 and 1 to 4, one inch more than the measurement from 2 to 6, which is 4¾ ins., making the measurement 1 in. more from 2 to 5 and 1 to 4 would be 5¾ ins.

The distance from 2 to 5 must be divided into three scallops as shown. If the distance was 6 ins., fold a strip of paper 6 ins. in length and about 3 ins. wide; fold over into 2 in. pieces, cut out a scallop, open out the paper and three even scallops are obtained. Or cut a row of scallops out by using a line ruled on paper and the edge of a glass or lid to pencil out the scallops.

NOTE.—The measurement from 8 to 7 must be the same as from 1 to 6, and 4 to 5 must measure the same width as at 1 to 2.

Cut out the pattern. Do not cut across line 1 to 2 for this style.

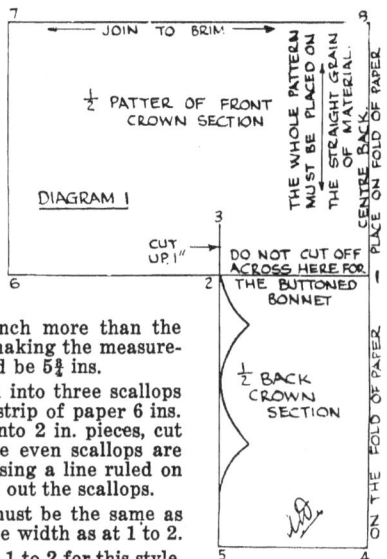

DIAGRAM 1

7   ← JOIN TO BRIM →   8

½ PATTER OF FRONT CROWN SECTION

THE WHOLE PATTERN MUST BE PLACED ON THE STRAIGHT GRAIN OF MATERIAL.

CENTRE BACK, PLACE ON FOLD OF PAPER

3

CUT UP 1"

DO NOT CUT OFF ACROSS HERE FOR THE BUTTONED BONNET

6   2

½ BACK CROWN SECTION

ON THE FOLD OF PAPER

5   4

LESSON 109.

TO CUT THE BRIM SECTION

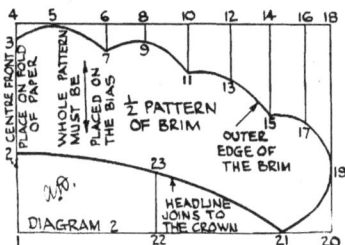

(DIAGRAM 2.)

Rule an oblong on paper 9¾ ins. by 6¼ ins.

Measure from 1 to 2 (2¼ ins.). Mark with points.

Measure from 4 to 3 (½ in.).

Measure from 4 to 5 (1¼ in.).

Measure from 5 to 6 (1½ in.).

Measure from 6 to 7 (down ¾ in.).

Measure from 6 to 8 (1 in.), and from 8 to 9 (½ in.).

Measure from 8 to 10 (1½ in.).

Measure from 10 to 11 (1¼ in.).

Measure from 10 to 12 (1¼ in.).

Measure from 12 to 13 (1¾ in.).

Measure from 12 to 14 (1⅛ in.).

Measure from 14 to 15 (2½ ins.).

Measure from 14 to 16 (1¼ in.).

Measure from 16 to 17 (2¾ ins.).

Measure from 18 to 19 (4 ins.).

Measure from 20 to 21 (1 in.).

22 is located half way between 1 and 21.

Measure from 22 to 23 (1¾ in.).

Curve from 2 through 23 to 21. This is half the headline of brim.

Scallop from point 3 to 5, 7, 9, 11, 13, 15, 17, 19 to 21.

This completes half the brim pattern.

When cutting on material the line 2 to 3 is centre front and is placed on fold, as there must not be a seam in centre front.

This brim is also used for the other Bonnet design.

LESSON 110.

THE CROWN SECTION OF DIAGRAM 2

Cut off a pattern from the Crown Pattern cut in the previous lesson. Re-cut another pattern. Cut pattern off along line 1 to 2. (Do not split at 2 to 3.) The crown section for back of crown is the same pattern as in another design with a plain brim. Use this pattern for back of crown.

When making up this Bonnet the scalloped sides are faced or bound or the whole crown section may be made double. Pique one side or lawn or thin calico on the inside, and turned out and pressed.

Worked or bound button holes can be used or buttons can be sewn on a fixture to trim the Bonnet. The brim is also underlined and wired or corded to hold firm. Close rows of stitching will hold firmly.

The scallops can be followed with several rows of stitching, and the remainder of the brim and crown with straight rows of machining.

If made in Organdi or Silk, a ruched row of lace can be added on the underbrim. This can be made of self material. Press well as the making is proceeded with.

The directions given for making a stitched hat are followed for making of all Fabric Hats and Bonnets. A narrow band of ribbon and bow can finish the outer headline and the lining can be neatly turned over to finish the inner head lining.

As these Bonnets are washing types, I do not recommend Espartra or Petersham ribbon in the inner headline. If requiring Bonnet very firm, an inner lining of canvas or book muslin can be used. All materials used in the making must be shrunk first, especially Linens.

These Bonnets can be made with plain crowns and floral brims or vice versa. Small flowers can be used for trimming, but these would have to be removed each time Bonnet was laundered.

This design also makes an ideal Beach Bonnet in Cretonne or gay patterned material. Make one up as a sample.

They are ideal Christmas or Birthday gifts, and will delight any little girl.

Wee Bonnet.

DELIGHTFUL
BONNETS

The two model Bonnets are illustrated showing the Bonnets made in Organdi with scalloped brim and two-tone Felt or any material desired.

The patterns use the same patterns as given in another lesson.

The cutting of these patterns is fully detailed.

The brims can be made by different brim patterns, varying the style of the Bonnet.

★

The Organdi Model will look attractive if you finish the brim with the corded tucking.

Stitching is also effective.

A variety of materials may be used to make these Bonnets. They can also be made in Straw and trimmed differently.

Practice making them on spare pieces of material.

The edges can be piped, bound or stitched.

★

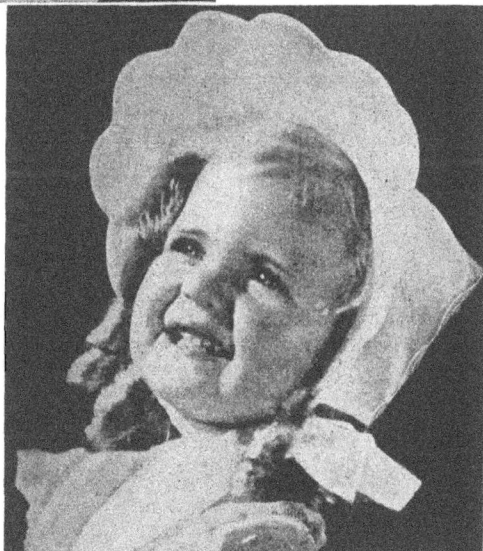

LESSON 112.

Bonnets in Embroidered and Plain Linen

**These two attractive little Bonnets feature Embroidered Linen and
Plain Linen—one with a lace trimmed edge of brim, the other with
Rick Rack Braid edge or Folded Ribbon edge.**

These two models are given as a Test Lesson. The cutting of the patterns has
been dealt with in another lesson.

These Bonnets are illustrated to show a variety of materials and trimmings.
They are easy to make and have been selected to show how spare pieces of material
may be used up.

An embroidered material for crown, a plain material for the brim.

You can make these in all-over Felt or from last season's Felt Hat. Pique, Cesarine,
Linen, Haircord, all are suitable for these Bonnets. Make them in material to match
the frock.

◆   ◆   ◆

Bonnets for the Well Dressed Child

Delightful Bonnets for the Well-Dressed Child, typified by the charming styles illustrated for you to make.

Bonnets can be made in a variety of materials, Straws or Felts. For Spring and Summer wear Pique, Dotted Swiss Muslin, Organdi, Eyelet Linen, Broderie Anglaise, Batiste, Plain or Floral materials and straws.

For Winter wear Felt or brushed Wool Velour, All-over Felt and Velvet.

Among the many models shown you will find a pattern to suit a special type of Bonnet you require. The brims can be made wider or narrower as desired, and different crown patterns used with different brim patterns. Variety is obtained in this way.

Also trimmings play an important part in the making of Bonnets. Take particular notice of the many Bonnets similar in shape but differently trimmed (showing in shops). From these ideas can be obtained. Notice the variety of colour combinations and the many different types of trimmings.

A FEW SUGGESTIONS FOR TRIMMING BONNETS AND HATS.

A Deep Cream Straw with Rosettes of Val. Lace and Velvet Ribbon. Pale Pink Straw with Velvet Ribbon of Deep Pink around the crown, with added sprays of tiny Forget-me-nots or Rosebuds.

The under brim finished with two rows of narrow Cream Val. Lace or shirred ribbon.

For Washing Bonnets the buttoned or clipped together type are easy to launder as they can be opened out flat. It is advisable to shrink the material before making it up, as most cotton materials will shrink, leaving the Bonnet smaller when laundered. Avoid this by shrinking materials before making.

◆ ◆ ◆

DO YOU KNOW THE ANSWERS TO THESE 10 QUESTIONS?

1. What are the most suitable materials for Infants' and Children's Bonnets?
2. What are the most suitable trimmings for Children's Hats and Bonnets?
3. What are the correct methods of measuring a Child's head?
4. How many measurements must be taken?
5. What are the correct materials to use in the making of Children's and Misses Fabric Hats?
6. How many yards of 1 in. Straw Braid is required to make a smart Straw Bonnet?
7. What are the correct Straws for Children's wear?
8. How must materials be treated for the making of Stitched Fabric Hats and Bonnets?
9. What are the most suitable colours for Children's Millinery?
10. Which Hat or Bonnet given in the Children's Millinery Section requires the smallest quantity of material?

LESSON 113.

The Cutting and Making of Two Smart Bonnets

These can be made in a variety of materials—Pique, Linen, Organdi, Felt and Straw. The pattern directions given here are for a head measurement of 21 ins., but can be increased or decreased when cutting out on material. Allow larger or smaller as desired.

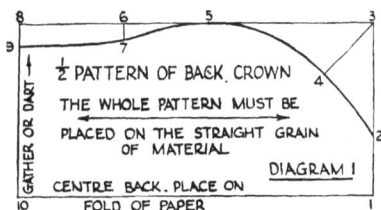

DIAGRAM I

½ PATTERN OF BACK CROWN
THE WHOLE PATTERN MUST BE PLACED ON THE STRAIGHT GRAIN OF MATERIAL
CENTRE BACK. PLACE ON FOLD OF PAPER

½ PATTERN OF SIDE CROWN SECTION
THE WHOLE PATTERN MUST BE PLACED ON THE STRAIGHT GRAIN OF MATERIAL
PLACE ON FOLD OF PAPER
DIAGRAM 2

THE OUTER EDGE OF BRIMS
SQUARE BRIM
½ PATTERN OF 2 BRIMS
POINTED BRIM
THE INNER HEADLINE OF BRIMS
THE WHOLE PATTERN MUST BE PLACED ON BIAS OF MATERIAL
C.F. FOLD OF PAPER
DIAGRAM 3

Diagram 1.—To Cut the Upper Crown Section.

Cut an oblong of brown paper 8¼ ins. by 3½ ins. Measure from 1 up to 2 (1 in.). Mark with point. Measure from 3 to 4 on an angle shown 1½ ins. 5 is located 3½ ins. from 3. Mark with point. 6 is located half-way between 5 and 8. 7 is located ½ in. below 6. 9 is located ½ in. below 8. Curve from 9 to 7 and 5 and from 5 through 4 and 2 to 1. This completes ½ pattern of upper crown section. The line 1 to 10 place on fold of material, as crown is double.

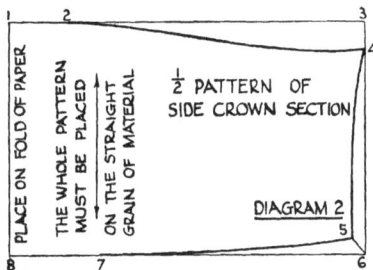

Diagram 2.—To Cut the Lower Crown Section.

Cut an oblong of paper 5¼ ins. by 8¼ ins. Measure from 1 to 2 (1 in.). Measure from 3 to 4 (¾ in.). Measure from 6 to 5 (¼ in.). Curve from 4 to 5. Measure from 8 to 7 (2 ins.). Shape from 7 to 5. Curve from 2 to 4, as clearly shown in Diagram 2. This completes half pattern of Lower Crown section. Place line 1 to 8 on fold of material, when cutting. Cut two Lower Crown sections as this is double in material, single in Felt.

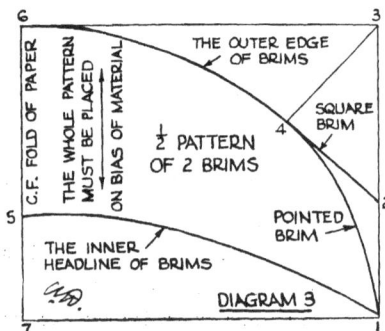

Diagram 3.—The two Brim Sections, Square Ends and Pointed Ends.

To cut the patterns. Cut an oblong of paper 8 ins. by 6½ ins. Measure from 1 up to 2 (2¾ ins.). Measure from 3 to 4 on angle shown 2¾ ins. From 7 to 5 measure 2½ ins. Mark with point. Curve from 6 through 4 to 2, and curve from 5 to 1. Note.—For pointed brim, curve from 4 to 1 as clearly shown. Cut both patterns. They are then ready for use. The line 5 to 6 is placed on fold of material. Cut two brims as the brim must be double in material, single in Felt.

LESSON 114.

The Cutting of Pattern of these Charming Buttoned Crown Bonnets with Different Brims

Front

Back

NOTE.—THE CUTTING OF THE BRIMS IS GIVEN IN ANOTHER LESSON.

The lesson teaches the cutting of the crown. The edges can be trimmed with Lace or left plain. Material required to make these Bonnets: ¾ yard of 36 in. material for each Bonnet.

TO CUT THE CROWN.

Rule an oblong 16 ins. by 12 ins. on a sheet of paper. Fold paper down centre and lay out flat. Rule a line down the crease line (the centre of oblong) 1 to 2. This line represents the centre back line of the crown.

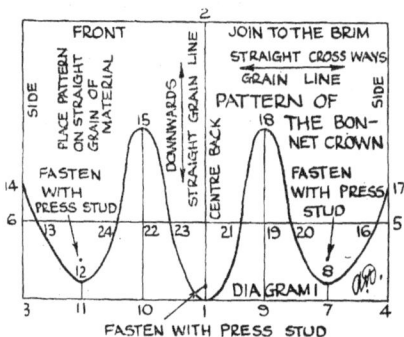
DIAGRAM 1

Measure from 4 up to 5 (3½ ins.). Measure from 3 up to 6 (3½ ins.). Rule a line across from 6 to 5. Measure from 4 to 7 (2½ ins.). Measure from 7 to 8 (¾ in.). Measure from 1 to 9 (3 ins.). Measure from 1 to 10 (3 ins.). Measure from 3 to 11 (2½ ins.). Measure from 5 to 17 (1½ ins.). Measure from 6 to 14 (1½ ins.). Measure from 5 to 16 (⅝ in.). Measure from 6 to 13 (⅝ in.). Measure from 11 to 12 (¾ in.). Measure from 9 to 18 (7½ in.). Measure from 10 to 15 (7½ in.). Measure from 19 to 20 across (1 in.). Measure from 19 to 21 across (1 in.). Measure from 22 to 23 across (1 in.). Measure from 22 to 24 across (1 in.).

Curve from 14 through 13, 12, 24 to 15. From 15 through 23 to 1 and around through 21 to 18, and through 20 and 8 and 16 to 17, shaping the rounded ends of peaks. This completes pattern of crown.

NOTE.—The centre peak is ¾ in. longer than the two side peaks.

No seams are necessary; they have been allowed for this size. For a larger size than 15 ins. side to side measurement, allow ½ in. seams front and sides. The oblong would then be increased 1 in. longer and ½ in. wider. Cut out pattern.

NOTE.—The centre peak clips over the other two, or buttons can be used.

This lovely model Bonnet is smart made in Pique, Linen, Organdi, or any Silk or Cotton material.

LESSON 115.

Sectional Fabric Hats and Caps

Sectional Fabric Hats and Caps are hats which receive their form from the fitting together of shapes, pieces or sections of material.

The majority of these hats are made with wedge-shaped pieces in the crown section, the apex of the sections forming the top centre of the crown.

VARIOUS SECTIONAL HATS.

There are several:—

(1) Three piece sectional crowns with a centre band and the two side sections of crown.

(2) Four section crowns.

(3) Six section crowns.

(4) Eight section hats have the same characteristics as six section hats.

(5) The side band and tip type, if made in fabric, is referred to as a 2 sectional crown having the two pieces in crown.

All Sectional Crowns are made up and finished in the same manner. The making of Sectional Hats is dealt with in the Children's Section, clearly illustrating step by step the making of a six-piece sectional Fabric Hat.

All sectional Fabric Hats, 2, 3, 4 and 6 pieced crowns, are made in the same manner. The type of style may vary, but the procedure of making up does not alter.

The Sectional Hats dealt with are the most popular types, and the ones in demand. Suitable materials for making have been detailed.

❖ ❖ ❖

LESSON 116.

The Cutting of Patterns of these Lovely Girl's Bonnets and Making

This dainty model can be made with either a scalloped or plain brim.

The directions are given for both.   •

This model can be made in a variety of materials: Pique, Organdi and Lace, All-over Lace, Floral Dimity, Tobralco, Haircord, Linen, Velvet, All-over Felt (bought by the yard).

A Felt Hood or Capeline, Straw Braid or a Straw Hood to the nearest shape and size required, or two last season's Felt Hats can be cleaned and successfully remodelled into this becoming style.

Small scallops of Lace or gathered ribbon around the headline can be added as trimming, also Felt can be cut out in three layers of different size scallops to trim this model.

A girl's bonnet-shaped head block is advised to be used for Straw or Felt, as it is easier to work the Straw or block the Felt to the shape, thus avoiding joining the top crown section of Bonnet.

This Bonnet is easily made, and the wire to hold a Fabric Bonnet in shape can be inserted through the brim (1¼ ins. back from the edge of the brim).

When the two layers of brim are stitched and carefully pressed, two rows of stitching are machined 1½ ins. back from the edge of brim. The two rows are placed ⅛ in. apart. The wire or a cord can be threaded through. The cord gives a raised tucked effect, and several rows can be used as a trimming if desired.

If the Bonnet is made of Organdi, this is an ideal trimming; also it can be used around the edge of a plain brim.

A bodkin threaded through with double thick knitting cotton and pulled through between the rows of stitching is ideal for padded tucking. I advise you to try this in your spare time on any scrap of material to match the frock.

The crown and lower crown section can be made in floral. The scalloped section can be made or underlined in white or a contrasting shade.

You can make this model for very little cost. When you compare the prices of the lovely ready-made Bonnets you can see the vast difference in the cost when you learn to make dainty, attractive models for just the cost of the materials.

J

LESSON 116 (continued).

DAINTY BONNET IN STRAW

**You can picture this little Bonnet made in soft
pink Straw Braid trimmed with Cream Lace,
Pale Blue Forget-me-nots, and velvet ribbon
to match.**

It would look attractive, too, made in Pale Blue,
White, Pink, Lemon, Pale Green, Red or Navy Felt.

•

You can use the pattern of the Bonnet and cut it
out in Espartra or Leno, and cover it with ribbon or
straw if you do not have a bonnet head block. These,
however, are not expensive and can be obtained quite
reasonably from the Academy.

A price list is given of all blocks obtainable.

The quantity of material required to make this Bonnet is ⅜ in. of a yard of 36
in. material, a little more if you are making it in Velvet. As Velvet must be cut to
run all the one way, it is necessary to have a little more material.

Ribbon 2 ins. to 2¼ ins. wide for the bows; 1¼ yards to 2 yards makes a nice bow
and ends.

It is necessary to cut a head lining and make it up in Muslin or Voile or
Taffeta. Allow ½ in. seams on lining, ¾ in. on the Bonnet pieces.

♦ ♦ ♦

LESSON 117.

The Cutting of the Pattern Pieces

NOTE.—There are three sections of patterns:—

(1) The half pattern of the tip or top crown section.

(2) The half pattern of the lower crown section.

(3) The half pattern of the brim section with scalloped and plain brim.

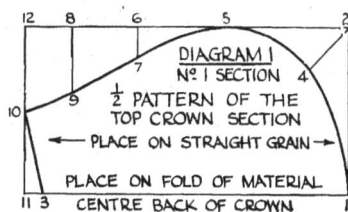

To Cut the Half Pattern of No. 1 Section
(The Tip)

Rule an oblong 3 ins. by 6½ ins. on a sheet of brown paper.

The line 1 to 3 is the centre of back crown section; 3 is located ½ in. from 11. Mark with point.

10 is located 1½ in. from 11. Rule a line as 10 to 3 on angle shown.

8 is located 1 in. from 12. From 8 down to 9 measure 1⅛ in.

6 is located 1½ in. from 8. From 6 down to 7 measure ⅝ in.

5 is located 1½ in. from 6.

Rule a line from 2 down to 4 on angle shown, 1 in. Curve from 1 to 4 and to 5, through 7 and 9 to 10.

This completes half the pattern. Cut pattern out. Mark on it half of crown. It is then ready for use.

◆ ◆ ◆

LESSON 118.

To Cut Half the Lower Crown Section

Pattern No. 2.

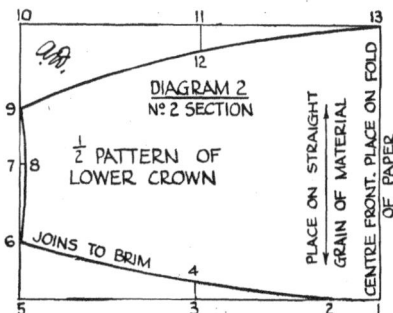

Rule an oblong 8¼ ins. by 6¼ ins. on brown paper.

Measure as from 1 to 2 (1 in.). Mark with point.

3 is located half-way between 1 and 5 (4¼ in. from 5). From 3 to 4 measures ¼ in.

6 is located 1¼ in. from 5.

9 is located 1¾ in. from 10.

7 is located half-way between 6 and 9.

8 is located ¼ in. from 7.

Curve slightly from 9 through 8 to 6.

Curve from 6 through 4 through 2 to 1.

11 is located half-way between 10 and 13.

12 is located ⅝ in. below 11.

Shape from 9 through 12 to 13. The line 9 through 12 to 13 is the edge that sews to the upper crown edge. This completes half Pattern Piece No. 2.

The Cutting of Half the Brim Pattern

Diagram 3.

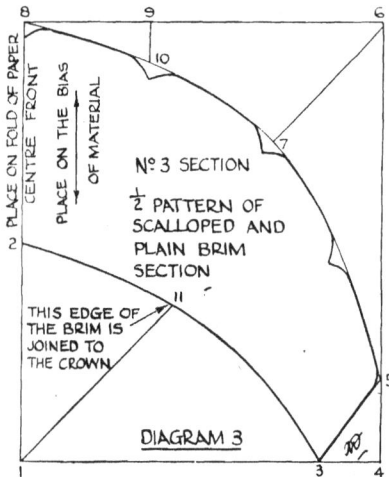

Rule an oblong 9¾ ins. by 8 ins. on brown paper.

Measure from 1 to 2 (5 ins.). Mark with point.

Measure from 1 to 3 (6 ins.).

Measure from 4 to 5 (1¾ ins.).

Measure from 6 to 7 on angle shown, 4 ins.

Measure from 8 to 9 (2¾ ins.).

Measure from 9 to 10 down ¾ in.

Measure from 1 to 11 on angle shown, 5 ins.

Curve from 2 through 11 to 3, shaping the inner edge of brim.

Curve from 8 through 10, 7 and 5, shaping the outer edge of brim.

Then rule a line from 3 to 5 as clearly shown (forming the end of brim).

This completes the plain brim pattern.

To cut the four scallops on half the pattern, cut out the pattern just completed. Re-cut another from it. Fold the outer edge into four even parts, and with the edges evenly together cut from the fold a scallop.

Open out flat. If scallop is not deep enough refold, and cut out only a little at a time. The edges of a glass or small tin lid can be used to mark out the scallop in pencil first if desired.

NOTE.—Only half of the pattern sections are cut. Place all sections on fold of material. Where marked, place on fold. Be sure to write on the pattern to avoid mistakes when cutting, as no joins must be placed in material where joins are not necessary.

You can cut the bonnet out on firm brown paper or any scraps of material, allowing seams, to test the shape and size.

If desiring a larger head fitting, cut more out around headline. If a smaller fitting is required, allow more turning at headline. This will make bonnet smaller.

The size given here is to fit a 20 in. to 21 in. head measurement. Seams must be allowed. You can use this brim with another crown pattern or this pattern of crown with another brim pattern and make a different shaped Bonnet. You can use this brim for a hat and make a dome-shaped crown.

Note.—All finishings must be neat. For Straw Bonnet making, follow same directions given in Straw Hat Making. For Felts, see section of Course dealing with Felts.

Study carefully each section. The answer to all your problems will be found in this thorough Course of Instruction in "Modern Millinery Made Easy."

You will find pleasure in making lovely hats for all occasions.

LESSON 119.

A Smart Fabric Bonnet and Hat for Girls and Misses

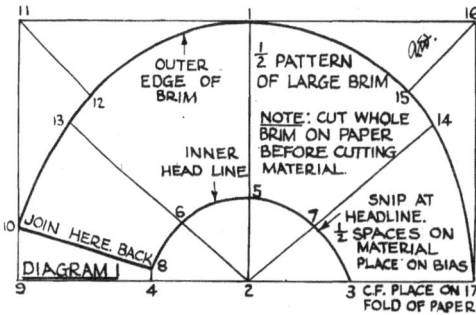

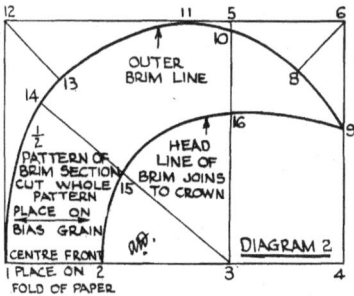

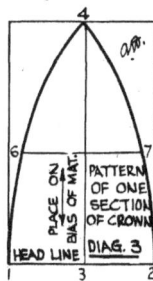

DIAGRAM 1

11
16
OUTER EDGE OF BRIM
½ PATTERN OF LARGE BRIM
12
13
15
14
NOTE: CUT WHOLE BRIM ON PAPER BEFORE CUTTING MATERIAL.
INNER HEAD LINE
6 5 7
SNIP AT HEADLINE. ½ SPACES ON MATERIAL PLACE ON BIAS
10 JOIN HERE BACK
8
9 4 2 3 C.F. PLACE ON FOLD OF PAPER 17

DIAGRAM 2

12 11 5 6
10
OUTER BRIM LINE
13 8
14
16
9
½ PATTERN OF BRIM SECTION CUT WHOLE PATTERN PLACE ON BIAS GRAIN
15
HEAD LINE OF BRIM JOINS TO CROWN
CENTRE FRONT
1 PLACE ON 2 3 4
FOLD OF PAPER

DIAG. 3

4
6 7
PLACE ON BIAS OF MAT.
PATTERN OF ONE SECTION OF CROWN
HEAD LINE
1 3 2

A Smart Fabric Bonnet and Hat for Girls and Misses

(Continued)

THESE USEFUL, EASY TO MAKE STYLES ARE EVER POPULAR.

Material Required: ½ yard 36 in. material; Interlining, ½ yard 36 in. material. Head lining, ⅝ yard 36 in. material for Bonnet style; ¼ yard more material is required for the hat.

To Cut the Brim Section (Large Brim) of these smart design Fabric Hats or Felts.

First Lesson.

Cut an oblong piece of paper 9¼ ins. by 17¼ ins.

Fold over and crease down centre.

Rule a line through crease mark as 1 to 2.

Measure from 2 to 3 and 2 to 4 (3¾ ins.). Mark with a point.

Measure from 2 up to 5 (3 ins.). Mark with a point.

Measure on an angle from 2 to 6 and 2 to 7, as shown by dotted line 3¼ ins.

Circle from 8 through 6, 5 and 7 to 3.

Measure from 4 up to 8 (½ in.). From 4 to 9 measures 5¼ ins.

From 9 up to 10 measures 2¼ ins.

Rule a line as from 10 to 8.

Measure from top corner 11 down to 12 on angle shown. Mark with point at 12.

Measure from 6 to 13 (5¾ ins.).

From 5 to 1 measures 6¼ ins., from 7 to 14 measures 5¾ ins,

From 16 to 15 measures 3¼ ins.

Curve from 10 through 13, 12, 1, 15 and 14 down to 17.

This completes half pattern of brim.

The line 3 to 17 is placed on fold.

The line 10 to 8 is the centre back and must be joined up.

TO CUT THE SMALL BRIM DESIGN.

Cut a piece of paper an oblong 7 ins. by 10¼ ins.

Measure as from 1 to 2 (3 ins.).

Measure from 4 to 3 (3½ ins.), and from 6 to 5 also (3¼ ins.). Mark with a point.

Rule a line down from 5 to 3.

Measure from 4 up to 9 (4½ ins.).

Measure from 6 down to 8 on angle as shown (1¾ ins.).

From 5 down to 10 (¼ in.).

Measure from 5 to 11 (1¼ ins.).

Measure from 12 down to 13 (2½ ins.).

Measure from 3 to 15 (4 ins.) and from 3 to 16 (4¼ ins.).

Curve from 2 through 15 and 16 to 9.

Curve from 1 through 14, 13, 11, 10, and 8 to 9.

This completes half pattern of brim.

The line 1 to 2 is centre front, and is cut on fold of material. The point 9 is back of the brim.

LESSON 120.

TO CUT THE CROWN SECTION

Rule a line across a sheet of paper as from 1 to 2 (4½ ins.) ; 3 is located half way between 1 and 2. Rule a line from 3 up to 4 (7½ ins. in length).

Measure from 3 half way up centre line and out to 7 (2 ins.), and out to 6 also (2 ins.).

Shape from 1 through 6 to 4 and from 4 through 7 to 2.

This completes one section of the crown pattern.

Re-cut all patterns on firm cardboard. They are then ready for immediate use and any necessary adjustments can be quickly made.

Suitable Materials: Linen, Cesarine, Pique, Haircord, Tobralco; also Felt and Straw. The crown would be blocked in one piece for Straw or Felt.

Make these models to match the Frocks; trim with contrasting materials. Follow same directions for making as detailed in the making of stitched pieced hats.

♦ ♦ ♦

LESSON 121.

The Cutting of Boy's Cap and Stitched Fabric Hat

These ever popular Hats and Caps are ideal for school or general wear.

The quantity of materials required are dealt with in the making-up section.

This section deals with the Cutting of the Hat and Cap patterns.

NOTE.—There are three pieces of pattern—(1) Half the brim section. (2) One section of the crown pattern which is used for both the Hat and the Cap. (3) The half pattern of the Cap peak.

TO CUT THE HALF BRIM PATTERN (Diagram 1).

Rule an oblong on a sheet of brown paper 14½ ins. by 7½ ins.

Measure from 1 to 2 (4 ins.). Mark with point.

Measure from 2 to 3 (7 ins.).

Measure from 3 to 4 (1¼ ins.).

Measure from 5 to 6 (3 ins.).

Measure from 2 to 7 (3½ ins.).

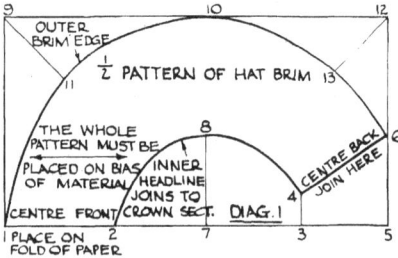

Measure from 7 to 8 (3½ ins.).

Rule line from 6 to 4.

Curve from 2 through 8 to 4.

This line represents half of around headline.

Measure from 9 to 10 (8 ins.).

Measure from 9 to 11 (3¼ ins.) on angle shown.

Measure from 12 to 13 (3¼ ins.) on angle shown.

Curve from 1 through 11, 10, 13 to 6. This completes the outer edge of half the brim pattern.

The half of brim pattern is now completed. Cut the pattern.

Place the line 1 to 2 on a folded sheet of paper and cut out the whole brim pattern..

There is no join in the centre front of brim.

The line 4 to 6 is the centre back; the brim is joined at the back.

Write on the pattern sections — Centre, Front and Back.

Rule the straight and crossways grain lines on pattern sections as clearly illustrated in diagrams.

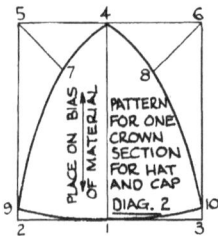

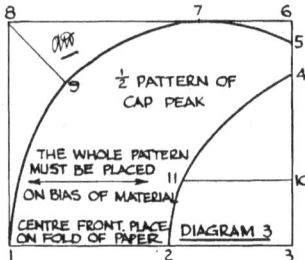

OUTER BRIM EDGE
½ PATTERN OF HAT BRIM
THE WHOLE PATTERN MUST BE PLACED ON BIAS OF MATERIAL
INNER HEADLINE JOINS TO CROWN SECT.
CENTRE BACK JOIN HERE
CENTRE FRONT
PLACE ON FOLD OF PAPER
DIAG. 1

PLACE ON BIAS OF MATERIAL
PATTERN FOR ONE CROWN SECTION FOR HAT AND CAP
DIAG. 2

½ PATTERN OF CAP PEAK
THE WHOLE PATTERN MUST BE PLACED ON BIAS OF MATERIAL
CENTRE FRONT. PLACE ON FOLD OF PAPER
DIAGRAM 3

The Cutting of Boy's Cap and Stitched Fabric Hat

(Continued.)

TO CUT THE CROWN PATTERN (Diagram 2).

Rule an oblong 5½ ins. by 5¾ ins. on paper.

Cut out oblong. Fold over in centre as line 1 to 4.

Lay out flat and rule line as 1 to 4.

Measure from 5 to 7 (2 ins.).

Measure from 6 to 8 (2 ins.).

Measure from 2 to 9 (¼ in.).

Measure from 3 to 10 (¼ in.).

Shape from 9 through 7 to 4 and from 4 through 8 to 10.

Curve from 9 through 1 to 10.

This completes one section of the pieced crown.

Cut out pattern.

TO CUT THE HALF OF PEAK PATTERN (Diagram 3).

Rule an oblong 5 ins. by 6¼ ins. on paper.

Measure from 1 to 2 (3¾ ins.).

Measure from 3 to 4 (3¾ ins.).

Measure from 4 to 5 (¾ in.).

Measure from 6 to 7 (2¼ ins.).

Measure from 8 to 9 (1¾ ins.).

Measure from 3 to 10 (1¼ ins.).

Measure from 10 to 11 (2½ ins.).

Shape from 2 through 11 to 4. This line is half of inner peak line and fits to crown of Cap.

Shape from 1 through 9 and 7 to 5. This line represents half of the outer edge of peak.

Cut pattern out.

Place line 1 to 2 on folded edge of paper, cutting the whole pattern of the peak.

Write on each pattern section so that they will be easily and quickly recognised. Cut all patterns out on firm cardboard. They are then ready for use.

The head measurement for this pattern is 20 ins. You can make a pattern of larger or smaller sizes. For smaller, allow no seams when cutting; for larger sizes allow a little on each pattern piece.

The brim half pattern, if placed ¼ in. back from the folded paper, will make the pattern 1 in. bigger around inner and outer edge of brim. If required smaller, overlap half pattern over the fold of paper ¼ inch, or as required.

Practice pattern adjustment in your spare time, and cut several different sizes. They are then ready for use.

❖   ❖   ❖

(Copyright)

LESSON 122.

The Correct Method of Making a Boy's Cap

The Material required: ¼ yard of 36 in. material. Interlining, ¼ yard of 36 in. material. Lining, ¼ yard of 36 in. material. Cotton to match. **Buckram for peak.**

Also pieces of suiting are useful for making the Cap. Flannel, Cotton Tweed, Drill or any firm material. Canvas is required for the interlining. Sateen or Cotton Lining or Italian Cloth is most serviceable for longest wear. Shrink all materials before making up.

CUTTING THE CAP.

Place the pattern of the crown on the bias of double material.

Chalk mark around edge of pattern.

Cut pieces. Allow ½ in. seams and turnings on all sections of the cap.

Cut a canvas stay 1¼ ins. wide on the bias. This must be the length of around head measure, adding 1 in. for seam.

Join this strip in a circle.

Next place the pattern of the Cap peak on the bias of Espartra.

Cut out twice as the peak must be made in double Espartra or Buckham.

Mull the edge of peak. (This has been dealt with previously.)

Cut the outer covering and the under covering by the peak pattern, allowing ¼ in. turning on the outer edge and ½ in. turning at the headline of peak.

The peak is made up as directed in brim making of Stitched Hats.

The head lining is cut by the crown sections and allowed ¾ in. longer at head line for turning.

The lining is neatly slip-stitched around headline of Cap.

TO MAKE UP THE CAP.

Join the seams of crown in pairs and press as machining is proceeded with.

Baste the bias cut stay inside the Cap ½ inch from the raw edge.

Next the peak must be pinned in correct position at the front of the Cap.

The upper side of the peak must be placed to the right side of the Cap.

Baste firmly. Test for correct fitting, then machine neatly.

Next the lower edge of the Cap is turned up ½ in. and caught on to the canvas stay. Press well by either placing cap on a hat block, the corner of a table or a pad.

Next insert the head lining and slip-stitch neatly.

NOTE.—If making a special School Cap and the School Emblem has to be embroidered on the Cap, this must be done before the Cap is made up.

SEE SECTION MAKING STITCHED HATS. FOLLOW SAME FOR CAP MAKING.

LESSON 123.

The Cutting of a Stitched Material Hat

These simplified easy lessons teach the Cutting of a (6-piece crown) Stitched Material Hat. Ideal for sports or general wear. Size 22 in. head measurement (adjustable to various sizes).

To Cut the Pattern of the Crown Section.

NOTE.—Only one piece of crown pattern is cut. Six sections are cut on material from the one pattern. (See section Making Stitched Hats.)

Rule an oblong on brown paper, 5½ ins. by 7 ins.

Cut out, fold over in half, creasing a centre line as 1 to 2.

Lay out flat again and rule the line as 1 to 2.

Measure from 4 to 6 (⅜ in.).

Measure from 3 to 5 (⅜ in.). Mark with points.

Measure from 7 to 10 on angle shown (2 ins.).

Measure from 8 to 9 on angle shown, also 2 ins.

Curve from 2 through 10 to 5.

Curve from 2 through 9 to 6.

Curve from 5 through 1 to 6.

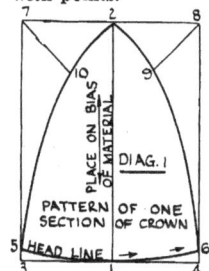

This completes one section of the crown, which is used as the pattern for the six sections of crown. Cut pattern out. Mark pattern.

LESSON 124.

To Cut the Brim Section (Half the Pattern of Brim).

Rule an oblong 13 ins. by 7¼ ins. on brown paper. Measure from 1 to 2 (3¼ ins.). Mark with points. Measure from 3 to 4 on angle shown (2¾ ins.). Measure from 3 to 5 along line 7 ins. Measure from 2 to 6 along line 3½ ins. Rule line from 5 to 6 as shown. Measure from 6 up to 7 (4¼ ins.). Measure from 6 to 8 along line 4 ins. Measure from 8 up to 9 (2¼ ins.). Measure from 10 up to 11 (5 ins.). Rule line 9 to 11 as shown. Measure from 12 to 13 on angle shown (2 ins.). Measure from 6 to 14 on angle shown (3¾ ins.). Shape from 1 through 4 to 5 through 13 to 11 (the outer edge of brim).

Shape from 2 through 14 and 7 to 9 (the inner headline of the brim).

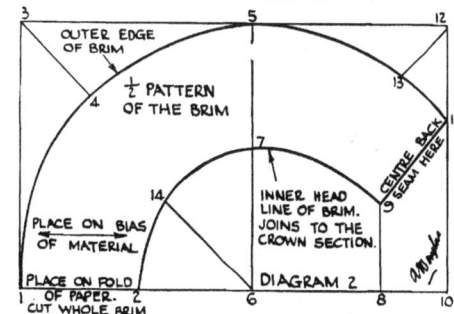

NOTE.—The line 1 to 2 is centre front of the brim and must be placed on the fold of the material when cutting out brim to avoid join. The line 9 to 11 is centre back line and is joined at the back. (See section on the Making of Stitched Hats.) The trimming band may be made of self material or a contrast.

(Copyright)

The Cutting of a Stitched Material Hat

TO CUT PATTERN FOR BACK BAND AND A BOW.

Cut a strip of brown paper 22 ins. in length for 22 ins. head measure (or the head measure desired).

The strip of paper must be 2 ins. in width.

This allows 1 in. band in width and turnings each side.

The turnings at end of band are allowed on material when cutting out.

The bow section piece is 1 in. wide by 10 ins. in length.

Cut a strip of brown paper 10 ins. in length and 1 in. in width for Bow Pattern piece.

Write on each section of the pattern pieces each part of the pattern. They are then always ready for use at any time, and time is saved cutting them again.

To make the pattern sections larger, add a small amount on the pattern sections; to make smaller, cut without seam allowance.

Check carefully all measurements.

NOTE.—Snip around the inner edge of the head line of the brim section of pattern. Make snips in the material of brim about $\frac{1}{2}$ in. apart and $\frac{1}{2}$ in. deep, to permit the brim to fit under the crown section.

Measure carefully with the tape measure. Accuracy is essential for the best results.

♦ ♦ ♦

LESSON 125.

THE MAKING OF STITCHED HATS

THE CORRECT LAYOUT ON MATERIAL OF THE PATTERN SECTIONS.

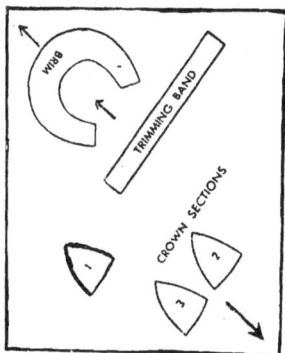

The clearly illustrated diagrams teach you step by step the making of Stitched Fabric Hats.

The design illustrated is the plain six-pieced crown type, the cutting of which is given in another lesson, dealing with the cutting of sectional or pieced Fabric Hats, Bonnets and Caps.

Clearly illustrated diagrams teach you step by step the correct layout of the pattern sections on the double material. Note carefully the correct placement of each of the pattern sections.

(1) **THE BRIM SECTION (centre front must be placed on the bias of the material), as clearly illustrated.**

(2) **THE CROWN SECTIONS are placed also on the bias.**

(3) **THE BAND AND BOW PIECES OF PATTERN are placed on the bias of the material.**

DIAGRAM 1.—CUTTING LAYOUT.

Bands and bows can be made double if there is sufficient material. The lay-out illustrates two of each being cut. If short of material, cut single and face with thin material.

The inner lining of hat—that is, the layer of stiffening material placed between the brim and crown— if desired, can be cut out of canvas. (Remember to shrink the canvas first.)

Place pattern sections in same manner on canvas as shown in the layout. Diagram 1.

Also the inner head lining must be cut to same shape as crown section of pattern. Allow all seams and turnings when cutting out on the material. This is important. This is illustrated in another lesson and is not repeated here.

Diagram 2 clearly illustrates the crown sections at two different stages.

First is shown the three pieces only of crown with canvas tacked firmly to each. All six pieces must be tacked firmly around and across each section so that the canvas will not slip.

The second stage shows the crown sections machine stitched. This must be neat and even. Commence by stitching one row around each crown section nearly $\frac{1}{2}$ in. from edge, then keeping all the other rows even, machine even distances apart from first row till each section of the crown is stitched neatly all over.

The edges of the canvas are then neatly pared away, leaving only the seam allowance on the outside of the material.

Diagram 3 clearly illustrates the six pieces of the crown tacked together, then neatly machined and the seams pressed open flat.

It is easier to join up three pieces of crown, then the other three pieces; then tack the two half sections of three pieces each together. Mark centre back and centre front with coloured cotton.

Diagram 3 also clearly shows the correct method of making the brim.

LESSON 126.

THE MAKING OF STITCHED HATS

1.—The two layers of material of the brim are first placed together flat on the table.

NOTE.—The right sides of material must be placed inwards together the wrong sides outwards. Then the canvas is first pinned, then tacked on and the three layers tacked firmly and machined around the outer edge.

2.—Cut away surplus material around edge, close to row of machining.

3.—Open out the brim sections from facing and sew the back seam of upper and under brim.

Press out flat. Do not sew the canvas. It will cause a bulky seam under the other seams. Overlap the canvas flat. You know the stitch to use to hold it firmly and securely in place. (See Diagram 3, showing brim sections turned out and stitched as detailed above.)

4.—The lower illustration in Diagram 3 illustrates the brim turned to the right side ready for machining.

Do press it well before you commence the machining. The machining must be even. The edge and outer and inner edge of brim must be firmly tacked before attempting to machine to avoid bubbles and a dragged look.

The brim must be smooth and free from all bubbles and unevenness. This type of hat is a tailored type, and must have a tailored appearance.

Diagram 4 clearly illustrates the brim stitched.

Commence by stitching as close to outer edge of the brim as possible, then continue stitching around brim same distance apart as on crown (usually $\frac{1}{4}$ in. apart, but closer or wider apart as desired).

Continue the machine stitching until the whole brim has been stitched up to the slits in brim edge at headline. Then press again.

Diagram 4 also clearly illustrates the band and bow section stitched in the same manner.

NOTE.—Corded Ribbon can be used for girls and women as a trimming. For boys the self material must be used; also for boys the crown section can be left plain and the brim stitched in groups 1 in. apart to hold canvas interlining firmly.

◆ ◆ ◆

LESSON 127.

THE MAKING OF STITCHED HATS

ATTACHING BRIM SECTIONS TO CROWNS.

5.—The Brim Section attached to Crown of Hat. Also clearly illustrated in Diagram 4.

Place the centre front of crown to centre front of brim. Likewise the centre back of crown to centre back of brim. Follow the diagrams carefully.

The hat is tacked firmly together. Then try the hat on wearer. Check the head fitting.

NOTE.—It is advisable to do this throughout the making of all hats.

If head fitting is correct, then machine the crown and brim together. Then press well. The inner headline can be finished with Cotton Petersham or a head lining inserted.

The final stages of the making are shown with the stitched band and bow attached to hat.

This hat can be made in materials to match a Coat or Frock. A variety of materials suitable: Linen, Cesarine, Tobralco, Indian Head, Lystav, Cotton Tweed and Woollen materials. **Any firm material is suitable.**

The Amount of Material required to make this Hat:

36 ins. to 42 ins. material ¾ yard. 52 ins. to 56 ins. material ⅝ of a yard. 28 ins. Canvas, ¼ of a yard. ¾ yard of Cotton Petersham. Ribbon for inner head line. 1½ yards of 1 in. Petersham for trimming hat if hat is being trimmed with ribbon instead of self material. Cotton to match the material, 3 small reels.

Take time to do all work. It must be neat. Your success in all Millinery will depend entirely on yourself. Practice and more practice is necessary; only then will successful results be assured.

❖   ❖   ❖

(Copyright)

MAKING UP OF STITCHED HATS

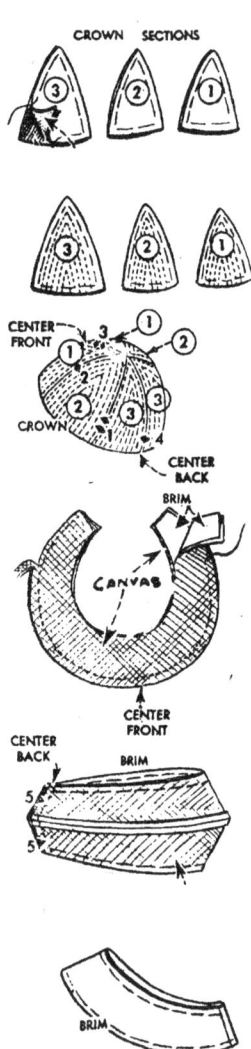

Choose good quality, firm materials. Linens and light weight woollen materials.

Care must be taken when making up to see that the joins in upper material, interlining and under brim do not come one on top of the other. This will cause a lumpy, raised seam and spoil the appearance of the hat.

When cutting under and upper brims, note that they must be right side out; note also that when laying patterns or pattern sections on the material, that the centre front of all parts of the Hat or Bonnet is to the cross of the material.

Cut the crown section singly.

For a pieced crown place the pieces on the cross or bias of the material.

See diagram, clearly illustrating the correct layout on material, showing correct placement of the pattern sections on the bias grain.

When cutting out, allow all seams and turnings. If the material is the type that frays badly, more turnings will have to be allowed.

The Correct Order of Work in Making Up :

When the hat sections are cut out, first mark the centre front and centre back with chalk, thread or pencil. The edge of the paper pattern or the fitting lines need only be marked with pencil or chalk on the canvas or other interlining.

Next join up the seam or seams of all the brim sections. Damp the seams well and press them all open so that they lie flat and frayed or unwanted edges may be trimmed off.

They can be over-sewn if desired, but this is not necessary as they are hidden by the lining.

Give all work that professional finish. It takes a little more time, but is well worth it.

Next baste or tack the upper brim to the canvas.

Next you must place the upper and under-brims right sides facing, with the Canvas or Espartra (whichever you have used) on the top.

The centre front must be exactly matched and basted together firmly. The pieces must be kept flat on the table while working.

Avoid any bulges or bubbles in the material while working, tack neatly, then stitch by machining around the outer edge of the brim as close to the edge as possible. Remove the tacks, then press the turnings open.

Then the interlining must be trimmed away to nothing. Snip off all corners of seam turnings. You must then trim the upper and under brim turnings at the stitched seam to different widths to avoid a hard ridge.

LESSON 129.

MAKING UP OF STITCHED HATS

(Continued)

Next turn the brim right side out with the canvas inside.

Tack very carefully with small stitches around the outer edge of brim.

Roll the seam slightly to the underside of brim as you work for a turned down brim, and for a turned up brim it must be rolled towards the upper side of the brim.

Next it is necessary to tack the under-brim to the interlining at the headline, and it is necessary to work from the centre front in either direction.

Baste the three brims carefully together, seeing the back and fronts are evenly together—markings meeting evenly.

Work from the outer edge of the brims.

Use cotton or silk to match.

Begin to machine on the outer edge; keep the spaces and the stitching even.

Test the head fitting. Correct this if necessary.

Snip turnings ½ in. apart at the inner head line.

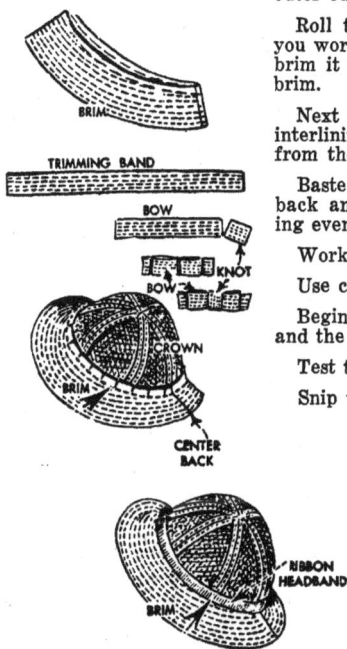

K

LESSON 130.

The Correct Method of Making the Crown

Baste together each section of the interlining if this is being used in the hat.

It is necessary to join the sections together in such a manner that the last seam in the crown runs completely from side to side or front to the back.

NOTE.—It is important to keep exactly to the fitting lines, and take care to see that the head lines and points match perfectly.

Press each seam as you work and then trim away the interlining close to the stitching.

Do not confuse the front of crown with the sides; unless clearly marked to distinguish the front from the sides, the crown will not fit the brim correctly.

Wasted time must be avoided; therefore the time spent to mark each section saves time and worry and confusion when making up the Hat or Bonnet.

Place the crown on the block inside out. Press well with a hot iron.

Next it is necessary to turn up the edges at the headline of the crown. **Tack** securely. Locate the four quarters on both the crown and the brim. Mark same.

Place the crown over the brim, seeing that the quarter marks match on the brim and crown, fitting lines touching.

Tack securely; then try hat on.

To Adjust the Correct Depth of the Crown if necessary.

The crown must be removed from the brim. Mark a new headline and trim away any interlining or turnings.

Next the raw edge of the crown is hemmed to the wrong side of the crown. Then press firmly on a narrow board, or a rolling pin is excellent for this purpose, or a pad made from a blanket.

Tack the crown over the brim turnings, then machine or neatly slipstitch in position.

There is another method of attaching the crown to the brim. This method enables the crown to be joined to brim very neatly.

Cut a bias strip of material to match Hat or Bonnet, the around the head measure, adding 1 in. for turnings.

Join this strip to the inner headline by one edge, and the other edge turned neatly over to edge of brim. This covers the join of crown and brim and is neat.

Be careful in all making to avoid bulky or crooked seams or stitching.

LESSON 131.

The Cutting and Making of Boys or Girl's Sou-Wester Stitched Hat

The head measurement given here is for a 21 ins. head measurement. The hat can be made larger or smaller, as desired.

The quantity of material required: ⅓ yard of 36 ins. to 40 ins.; ¾ yard of 28 ins. to 30 ins.

The pattern consists of four pieces:

(1) The Front Section of Crown.

(2) The Side Section of Crown.

(3) The Back Section of Crown. (All are clearly illustrated in Diagram 1.)

(4) The Half of Brim Pattern clearly illustrated in Diagram 2.

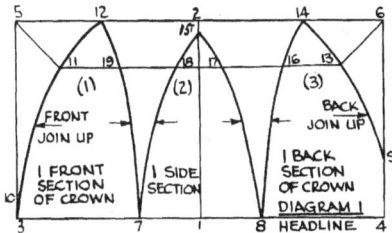

The Band is cut the length of around head measurement, adding ¾ in. for turning. Cut the Band 1 in. in width; allow turnings each side.

Diagram 1.—To Cut the three Crown Sections.

Rule an oblong on paper 11 ins. by 5½ ins.

Rule a line as from 1 to 2 through the centre of oblong.

NOTE.—1 is located half-way between 3 and 4, and 2 is located half-way between 5 and 6.

Measure from 1 to 7 along line 2 ins.

Measure from 1 to 8 along line 2 ins. Mark with points.

Measure from 4 up to 9 (1¾ ins.).

Measure from 3 up to 10 (¾ ins.).

Measure from 5 to 11 on angle shown (1¾ ins.).

Measure from 5 to 12 along line 2¼ ins.

Measure from 6 to 13 on angle shown 1¾ ins.

Measure from 6 to 14 along line 2¼ ins.

Measure from 2 down to 15 (¼ in.).

Rule a line across from 11 to 13.

Measure from 13 to 16 across 1¾ ins.

Measure from 16 to 17 across 1¾ ins.

Measure from 17 to 18 across 1½ ins.

Measure from 11 to 19 across 1¾ ins.

Shape from 3 to 10, from 10 to 11 to 12, through 19 to 7.

From 7 through 18 to 15.

From 15 through 17 to 8.

From 8 through 16 to 14.

From 14 through 13 through 9 to 4.

This completes the three sections of the crown—that is, **One Front Section, One Side Section, One Back Section.** Cut out into three separate pieces, marking each piece Front Side and Back.

LESSON 132.

The Cutting of Half the Brim Pattern

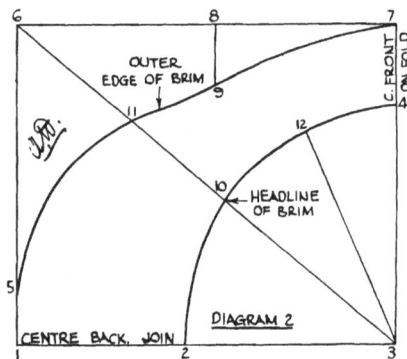

(Diagram 2)

Rule an oblong on brown paper 11¼ ins. by 9¼ ins.

Measure from 1 to 2 along 5¼ ins.

Measure from 3 to 4 up 6¾ ins. Mark with points.

Measure from 1 to 5 up 2 ins.

Measure from 7 to 8 along 5¼ ins.

Measure from 8 to 9 down 1¾ ins.

Rule line from 3 to 6 as shown.

Measure from 3 to 10 on angle line 6¾ ins.

Measure from 6 to 11 down on angle line 4¼ ins.

Measure from 3 to 12 on angle 6¾ ins.

Curve from 4 through 12 and 10 to 2.

The half inner headline of the brim pattern.

Curve from 1 along line to 5 to 11 through 9 to 7, forming half the outer edge line of brim pattern.

NOTE: The line 7 to 4 is the centre front and must have no join.

The line 1 to 2 is the centre back and is joined.

Cut pattern out, marking front and back on the pattern.

The widest part of the brim is placed at the back; the narrow part at the front.

◆   ◆   ◆

LESSON 133.

THE MAKING UP OF THE HAT

**This Hat is suitable for both Girls and Boys up to the age of 7 years.
It may be made up in a variety of materials: Cotton, Gabardine, Holland, Linen, Cesarine, Cretonne, Indian Head, Drill, etc.**

All pieces must be cut double.

The band is cut in single material and the edges turned in and pressed.

All seams must be allowed when cutting out on the material.

The under brim is cut by the pattern.

The headlining is also cut by the 3-crown sections of pattern.

Allow the lining pieces 1 in. longer to turn in at headline of crown.

Stitch the front and side gore of crown together, then the back and side pieces together. (There are six pieces in the crown.)

Then stitch the other three gores together in the same way.

Then stitch together from back to front.

Press well each section as making is proceeded with.

Next stitch the seam at the back of upper and under brim. Press seams well.

Next place the upper and under brims right sides together, centre front and back evenly together.

Machine around the edge about $\frac{1}{8}$ in. from edge of brim.

Turn brim out. Tack around edges. Press well.

Do not stretch outer edge of brim.

Machine stitch around the edge of brim, close to the edge, then add several more rows of machine stitching, following the headline of brim about $\frac{3}{4}$ in. back from the headline, as crown has to be joined on and the stitching will come up close to the headband.

Six to ten rows of stitching will be required, the rows being about $\frac{1}{4}$ in. apart.

Prepare the headband and join.

Tack one side of band to the inner headline edge of brim, placing the lower edge of band over the brim edge about $\frac{1}{4}$ in.

Pin first and then baste securely. Then machine close to the edge of band.

NOTE.—The join of band can have a pointed end for a boy, and a flat bow for a girl.

Place the join at left side of hat. Next pin the top edge of band over the headline edge of the crown.

NOTE.—The centre front of crown must be placed exactly to the centre front of brim.

The centre back of crown must be placed exactly to the centre back of brim.

The crown can be eased in slightly if necessary.

Stitch the band close to the upper edge.

Test the fitting of the hat as the making is proceeded with. This is important and avoids unnecessary work.

LESSON 134.

THE LINING OF HAT

Stitch the Crown pieces together. Press well.

Place lining in hat with raw edges to seams of lining to raw edges of seams in hat.

The seams must be exactly opposite each other.

Pin, then baste lining down seam joins to hold firmly in position.

Turn edge at headline in and baste.

Try hat on again to test head fitting.

Then slip the lining neatly around at the bottom of band, completely covering all joins in the crown.

This hat can be made without an interlining as this style of hat is usually starched and interlining is not necessary.

NOTE: The hat can be made in various colours and two toned effects.

A Blue Hat underlined with brim of White; A Brown Hat with the brim underlined Green; a Navy Hat underlined White or Grey, or all self colours, whichever is preferred.

A contrasting lining can be used to save buying material. This will probably be found among spare pieces.

⬧ ⬧ ⬧

LESSON 135.

DAINTY LACE BONNETS

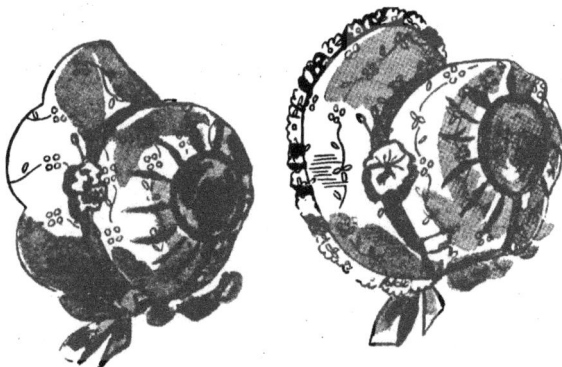

The two little Bonnets illustrated are shown with a scalloped and plain lace trimmed brim.

Using the brim patterns and the crown patterns given in the other lessons, you can cut these Bonnets.

The circular tip is cut out by the edge of a cup placed on brown paper.

The side band of crown is 8 ins. in width and the measurement around head required.

The ends are sloped at back.

Cut this pattern on paper.

This is an excellent test lesson.

Cutting the crown and tip pattern, the top or side band of crown section is gathered or pleated in to the small circular tip.

The back edges faced, or bound, as illustrated.

Pin these Bonnets together on paper first.

Try on and see the effects. Any necessary adjustments can then be made before cutting out on the material.

The trimmings can also be varied; small hand-made flowers are attractive to trim these little Bonnets.

NOTE.—The crowns can also be made without the tip. Try several of these styles. The results will be worth the time spent in making them.

They are also excellent for Sun Bonnets. The brims can be made larger if desired. A large variety of materials can be used.

LESSON 136.

Smart Models for the Teenager

This Easy-to-make Model is attractive and something new.

The old School Hat can be cleaned and re-modelled to look like this.

A bright Velvet Ribbon (or two-toned effect) threaded through the turned back brim and a new style is yours.

A Hood can be purchased for a few shillings and blocked on a dome hat block, the brim turned back and ribbon laced through it.

The result is an inexpensive yet attractive model hat.

Straw can also be trimmed in this way, and even turned up at the side or across the back. Ribbon and flowers may be used as a trimming.

The edges of brim can be bound to add colour to a plain hat.

The hat you are tired of can be made into a new and better model—a different hat with a new look for just the cost of new trimming!

The Small Felt Hat and Little Cap illustrated are easy to make.

Last season's Felt Hat can be re-modelled like new. The brim is cut narrower in front and back, and bound with matching Petersham Ribbon.

The trimming also matches, and is finished with a nice flat bow and ends.

A Sailor Crown block or substitute can be used; the crown is dented in as shown and a new model is created.

The Little Cap can be made from the crown of last season's hat, blocked on a high dome block and folded deep in the centre, finished at side with a pleated ribbon trimming or a smart ornament.

The edges of crown at headline are bound with ribbon to match the trimmings.

Straw hats can also be used, cleaned and remodelled into smart little styles, or an entirely new Hat and Cap can be made.

This Section deals with the Making, Blocking, Trimming, and Re-modelling, and Cleaning of a Variety of Felt Hats

LESSON 137.

There is an endless variety of Colours and Quality of Felt Hoods or Capelines.

When purchasing Felt Hoods there is no need to select them by any head measurement as they are blocked to the size required; only the quality of the Hood and colour is considered.

It is more satisfactory to make the style of hat you desire than to purchase a ready-made one that is one of a style of hundreds made to the same design or style.

Select a simple style for sports and everyday wear and for afternoon wear, or for special occasions a more stylish type or style.

Felt Hats may be made all in one piece—that is, the brim in one piece attached to the crown without a join, or made separate with the crown and brim joined.

In these clearly illustrated lessons I have dealt with both methods of making Felt Hats, and as the Fashions change so rapidly only the plainer types are dealt with here.

You can soon learn to copy more stylish hats, also design your own. By taking notice of models displayed, you can soon create something smart and different.

The cheaper Hoods or Capelines are smaller than the higher priced ones, therefore the smaller ones can be used only for the plainer types.

⋄ ⋄ ⋄

LESSON 138.

The Correct Treatment of Varieties of Felts.

Many of the other types of Felts require different treatment. Test the Felt by cutting a small piece from edge of brim. Notice carefully how it responds to the treatment of heat and water.

Angora Felts are very frail when wet. They require very careful handling. It is necessary when working on these Hoods to work with the palms of your hands. It is quite easy to poke your fingers through them, and if pulled too hard they will easily tear.

After blocking these Hoods it is necessary to brush them with not too stiff a brush, and brush with the pile of the Felt, not against it.

Angora Felts are expensive compared to the other varieties, but are very light and smart.

LESSON 139.

THE GLOSSY FINISHED FELTS

The gloss on these Felts is obtained in the process of making of the Hoods. This gloss is lost as soon as the Hood is steamed.

After blocking the Hood, iron the Hood all over evenly, working with the pile, not against it. Hold a piece of thin lawn or muslin between the Felt and the iron. The iron must not touch the Felt.

Rub methylated spirits or clear glycerine gently into the Felt, working, of course, with the pile. Only a very small quantity of glycerine or methylated spirits must be used at a time.

Brush with the pile, using a soft brush to polish the Felt.

> **NOTE.—Wool Felts are the cheaper variety of Felts and are hard wearing.**

They are excellent for beginners to work on. The better quality Fur Felts wear the best. The cheaper quality marks easily with rain. The Hoods or Capelines are obtainable in a large variety of colours, including white.

LESSON 140.

The Correct Method of Blocking a Felt Hood

(Referred to as a Capeline.)

First it is necessary to steam the crown of the Capeline; a boiling kettle is required, so that there will be plenty of steam.

Hold the rim of the Capeline in the right hand, gradually steaming the crown tip. Keep moving the hood backwards and forwards over the steam to obtain an even dampness.

While the top of the crown is still damp, pull it carefully on to your hat block. It must be carefully eased down with the fingers to fit the top of the block.

Next tie it with a piece of string on the block around the side of the crown, 2 ins. above the headline. The string tied around the crown must be of even depth from headline (all the way around the crown). See the illustration clearly showing this important subject.

Take care not to tear the Felt while working it on to the block. Pin the Felt at the string line with a row of drawing pins. Place a damp clean cloth over the crown section and press well till the crown fits the shape of the block well. Avoid over-pressing as it is easy to mark the felt with the iron, but it is an easy matter to steam and brush the iron marks out.

The crown must be left to dry on the blocks. Then remove the string and then the Hood from the block, and cut around crown at the string line.

You now have the crown separate from the brim. Diagram clearly illustrates the string around crown of hat.

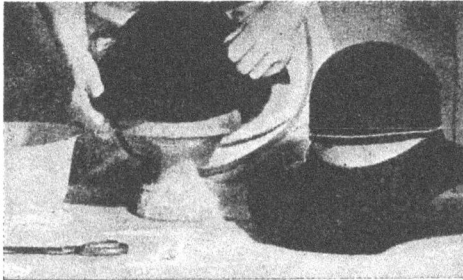

The Correct Method of Placing Felt Hood on Block and the String around Crown.

LESSON 141.

TO BLOCK THE BRIM OF HAT

A Brim Block of suitable shape and size must be used, or a Substitute for a small brim block. A breadboard may be used, or even the flat table.

Place the head block back into the brim and working flat on the table fix the crown at base of block with drawing pins. Press the brim with iron, using damp cloth, until brim is perfectly straight. Press well around the brim close to the headline.

Steam around the opening of brim at base of crown and press a strip ¾ in. wide till it lies close to the crown block. This strip fits inside the crown and the crown is joined to it.

Measure from the crown edge outwards for width of brim required, and chalk mark. Measure evenly all the way around the brim.

A 3 in. (or wider as desired) brim can be marked, and using a razor or razor blade, cut cleanly around the chalk line.

It is better to cut all Felts or Furs with a razor blade, not the scissors. Test a scrap of Felt with both the scissors and the razor blade. See the smooth even cut that is obtained with the razor blade and an uneven cut with the scissors.

After cutting the brim, press again and brush all over the hat with Felt Size. Leave till thoroughly dry.

◆   ◆   ◆

LESSON 142.

The Correct Method of Joining the Brim to the Crown

Pin the crown to the brim before sewing, and try the hat on. If the crown is a little too deep more can be cut off; if you desire it slanted or one-sided, cut more off the opposite side to the slant.

Pin and try on again; then, when right, it can be sewn, and it must be sewn securely, making sure the correct stitches are used.

You can then trim it with either Ribbon, Feathers or Flowers to suit.

The Wiring of the Brim of Hat has been dealt with in another lesson, and fully explained.

LESSON 143.

VELOUR HOODS

These are blocked exactly in the same way as Fur or Wool Felt Hoods, but after blocking it is necessary to brush them hard with a fine wire brush such as used for suede shoes. This will immediately restore the fluffy finish of the Hood.

Before commencing to make up any hat, it is necessary to have the size and shape of block ready to work on. If you have no block, use a substitute as explained in the beginning of the course. Also, it is necessary to have drawing pins, steel pins, chalk, strong cotton, or button-hole twist, same shade as Hood, millinery needles (size 5), Petersham ribbon ¼ in. wide for strengthening the headline, a razor blade, scissors, a clean cloth for pressing, and the illustration of the hat you wish to copy and the measurements that you will be using.

You will require the width of the brim at the front, the sides, and the back of brim and a basin of hot water.

If you think, after testing a small piece of Felt, that the colour is going to run in the Hood (dyes are not the best these days), it will be best to dissolve one tablespoonful of table salt in the hot water for light coloured Felt Hoods, and for dark coloured Hoods place one tablespoon of vinegar in the hot water.

You will also require an old ironing blanket, as the dye will probably mark it, also an iron; a brim board, or a substitute such as a bread board or a large saucepan lid with the breadboard or brim board. Drawing pins are used to hold Felt in place. There is nothing to pin Felt to if a saucepan lid is used.

It is necessary to work fairly quickly, therefore everything must be ready before commencing the making.

Note that while the Felt Hood is wet and hot after pressing, it is easier to work and block into shape. The Felt hardens when it is cold, therefore it is impossible to work or shape the Hood.

⋄   ⋄   ⋄

LESSON 144.

The Correct Method of Making the Crown

Place the Hood into the basin of hot water; remove the Hood from the water. Do not lift the Hood out of the water with the water in the crown of Hood. This will stretch the crown and it will be difficult to block.

Place the Hood on the block, working the crown down on the block, using the palms of both hands. Do not use the fingers as the Felt is very easily torn when wet, as it is then more delicate to handle. (See illustration.)

Tie a piece of string firmly around the headline.

Any surplus fullness can easily be shrunk away with a damp cloth and the iron.

Remember, do not place the iron on the Felt.

The iron will mark the Felt. Use the broad part of the iron in preference to the point.

Next cut the brim off just below the string, using an old razor or a razor blade or a sharp knife. Do not cut with the scissors as it will stretch the brim if you use scissors.

.   Mark the centre front of crown, also the centre back of crown, with chalk or thread. Place the block aside with the crown left on it to dry thoroughly.

LESSON 145.

The Correct Method of Making the Brim

The shape of the brim you desire to make must be considered. Do you wish to make a Straight Brim, a Drooped Brim, a One-sided Turned-up Brim, a Halo Effect, a Roll Brim, or a Turned Up all the Way Around Brim ?

There are many varieties and styles of brims, and as you progress with these thoroughly detailed lessons you will be able to make various shapes on firm brown paper for practice.

Do not attempt to make them in Felt at first as the Felt Hood costs money and if spoilt has to be re-done into a style that suits what is left of the Hood and not the wearer. So be sure that you have made the shape you desire on paper first, then you can with every confidence turn the model out to the style you desire.

Felt, as we know, can be shaped with the means of pressing and pulling into shape, and is easier and quicker to make up than Straw Hats or covered Hats.

When commencing to make the brim, select the best part of the Felt brim for the front of the brim and mark with chalk.

If you are making a style of hat with a brim other than a perfectly flat brim it is necessary to cut through the centre back of the brim and allow it to lie perfectly flat on the table; then arrange the brim pattern you have prepared either from your own design or a pattern cut from the directions given in the Pattern Cutting Section of the course.

You may have an old hat in a design that appeals to you; it is an easy matter to copy it. Unpick the trimming and separate the crown from the brim. You can cut a pattern of the brim on brown paper and re-model the old hat while you have it apart.

After you have arranged the pattern with drawing pins holding it down firmly on the Felt, chalk mark around the outline of the pattern, leaving ¾ in. turning at the headline only.

If the head size is not quite right, it must be re-damped in hot water. You will then find it quite easy to shape it to the size required.

A collar or the end of the block can be used to press it around on, or, as a substitute, an upturned saucepan. You must work fairly quickly; as the Felt dries it will harden. This must be avoided.

If too large, extra fullness can be shrunk away with the hot iron and damp cloth or place the brim on the ironing blanket. The wrong side of the brim must be facing upwards, the right side of brim facing the ironing blanket.

Cover the brim with a piece of dry flannel or thin blanket, using the iron fairly hot. Press in a circular movement.

Try the brim at intervals to avoid shrinking it too much. When you have obtained the right size for the brim and it is perfectly dry, next pin your pattern in position.

NOTE.—When more experience is gained you will be able to cut a variety of styles of brims without any patterns by using your tape measure and measuring the width from headline to edge of brim required and marking with chalk, but there are many types of brims that you first must have a pattern for.

When the right size of brim is marked out, next tack around the headline. Tack also or chalk mark the outer edge of the back join on the felt. Remove the pattern and test the headline fitting. This must be exactly right.

Cut off any extra material at the outer edges and back. No turnings are necessary and none are allowed on the brim edges or back join.

As you will note in joining Felts, the edges are brought together, never overlapped.

The Correct Method of Joining Back of Felt Brim

See Diagram 1, which clearly illustrates the correct method of joining the back of Felt Brim.

The stitch used to join the brim is the "stab stitch." Commence by tying a knot in the thread and stab the needle into the Felt from the wrong side of Felt.

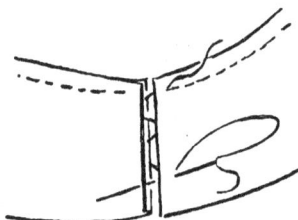

Re-insert the needle in the same hole, but sloping from right to left.

The stitches are made ½ in. apart.

The stitches must be drawn up, pulling the two edges of the felt together. The two edges must meet closely.

I would like you to keep all scraps of Felt in a special box or bag, and select two pieces with a nice even, straight edge and practice this stitch and learn the correct method of joining the Felt edges neatly before you commence joining the brim of your hat.

Diagram 1

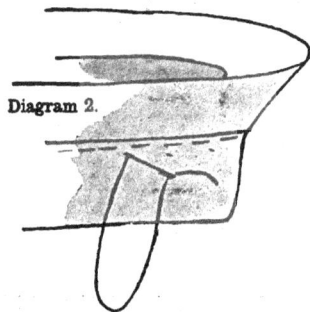

Diagram 2.

You will accomplish much if you learn to join the edges neatly and evenly. This is very important for successful results in making Felt Hats. You will find it easy to straighten the edges of the Felt by using a ruler and a razor blade on a spare piece of board that is kept handy for this purpose.

This will save the table.

Leave ¾ in. turnings at the headline to join the crown to the brim.

Another method of joining the centre back of the brim is to over-sew the two edges together on wrong side of brim, leaving the stitches loose enough to allow the two edges to fall together when the brim at join is pressed flat.

This method may serve in cheap ready-made hats, but for model work no method can equal the first one I have detailed and illustrated in Diagram 1.

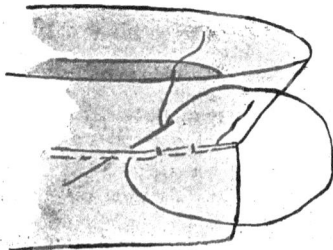

Diagram 3.

There are various other ways of sewing a join in Felt, but I do not recommend any other method than that given here, as I want students to learn and carry out the correct methods and make a success of this undertaking, and throughout this course and all other courses of instruction offered by "MODERN DESIGNERS ACADEMY."

Only thorough Advanced Trade Methods are taught.

LESSON 146.

The Correct Method of Joining the Felt Brim and Crown

First it is necessary for you to snip the headline of the brim at intervals of ¾ in. apart, as clearly illustrated in the lessons, "Shape Making." The snips require to be about ½ in. in depth. Use scissors here, not a razor blade.

When the crown is perfectly dry, remove it from the block. If you remove the crown from the block before it is dry, even slightly damp, it will stretch at the headline, and this must be avoided.

Make up a piece of Petersham ribbon for the head band to fit the head exactly. Mark the centre front and centre back.

Pin the brim of the hat to this band with the snipped turnings on the outside. See that the centre front and centre back of brim is placed at the centre front and back of the Petersham ribbon.

Tack firmly, and try on. If right, stitch the brim to the Petersham, catching in the points as shown in a previous lesson.

◆ ◆ ◆

LESSON 147.

Diagram 2 clearly illustrates the stab stitch, showing the correct position of the needle on the outside of the crown and the correct method of joining brim to crown.

Next place the crown of hat over the Petersham band on the headline of the brim. See that centre fronts and centre backs are in correct position.

Pin first by stabbing the pins into the Felt, then tack firmly and try on.

See if the depth of the crown is correct, as it is easier to alter it at this stage. Check if head fitting is correct with the crown attached; if not, the headline must be stretched.

When sewing the crown to the brim, use the "stab stitch."

◆ ◆ ◆

LESSON 148.

Hemming the Crown to the Brim
(Diagram 3.)

This is another method of sewing the crown to the brim.

Work the stitches in at the brim and out at the crown. Hold the hat towards you while working, and the crown and the brim must be upwards. The stitches must be ⅛ in. in depth and ¼ in. apart.

After the hemming is completed, place the hat on the bock and cover with a piece of flannel or clean cloth, and press around the headline of the hat. The bottom end of iron (not point) must be kept parallel with the brim.

The brim can be pressed if it is necessary. Brim boards are used for pressing the brims, or even the table. The hat should be removed from the block and supported by hand, holding the crown with one hand while pressing the brim with the other.

If the Felt has been marked with the iron, the mark can be removed by steaming and brushing. When steaming, do not forget that the steam is directed to the wrong side of the hat; it will penetrate through to the right side.

When brushing with a stiff brush for ordinary Felts and a wire brush for Velours, brush with the pile of the Felt.

The hat can now be stiffened. First on the inside of the crown and then the underside of the brim, and when dry the hat is ready for trimming and the insertion of a headlining if desired.

(Copyright)

LESSON 149.

The Insertion of Pieces into a Brim or Crown

TWO-TONED EFFECTS USED ALSO AS TRIMMINGS.

These pieces may be inserted into the crown or brim in different shapes—V Pieces, Spot Effects, or attached to the crown or brim by solution. They may be the same Felt as the hat or another piece of Felt. This is where the scrap bag will be found useful.

You can picture a Black Felt Hat with V pieces of Felt (white), or any shade desired, inserted into the crown, or small oval pieces around the headline, or leaves cut out of a contrasting Felt and the veins on leaves stitched on with silver or gold thread or coloured wools.

A Model Hat trimmed in this manner is very expensive to buy ready-made, yet it can be created for practically nothing.

To insert V shaped pieces into the crown or brim, cut the shape on brown paper.

Place it against the crown of hat on the block.

If right size you desire, attach it over Felt with drawing pins. Then chalk mark around it on the crown.

Remove the pattern and cut out around chalk line with a razor blade.

The piece that is cut out is used for the pattern on the contrasting Felt you desire to insert into the crown, and it must be exactly the size and the shape as the piece you cut out.

The stitch to secure it together and the manner of sewing it in place is the same as used in doing the Felt as illustrated in Diagram 1.

This must be very neat; when the stitching is finished the join is pressed.

If more than one piece is inserted, each is inserted in the same manner, then pressed.

You may have a very good Felt hat with a small brim and you may desire a wide brim. This is an easy matter when you know how.

Place the hat on a sheet of brown paper; secure with drawing pins.

Pencil around the outer edge of brim, then measure from this line around in a circle the added width you desire on the brim—2 ins., 3 ins., or whatever width you desire.

Chalk or pencil mark the width all around the circle.

Remove the hat from the paper. Cut out the circle.

You have a piece you cut from a brim previously; if so, this can be used.

If not, you must secure a large size Capeline Felt or Hood, as it is referred to, and cut your extra width of band of Felt from the outer edge of brim of this Felt.

The remainder of brim and crown will make another small hat.

Many various trimmings, bows, etc., can be made from every scrap of Felt.

These bows can be trimmed in various ways.

Suggestions are given in the Trimming Section of the Course.

LESSON 150.

The Correct Method of Fixing the Inserted Pieces in Position

The corners must first of all be tie tacked. You know the stitch you must use for this.

Tucks on a Brim for Trimming.

These tucks show more on the wrong side.

It is necessary to pull the stitching very tight or the thread will show on the wrong side of the hat.

(For the crown this would not matter, but on a brim they must not show.)

PLEATS OR FOLDS IN THE CROWN.

These can be arranged on the Felt crown while the Felt is wet. First tack them into position, then sew them with silk thread; it will mark less than others. When pressing tucks or folds, iron them very lightly under a damp cloth.

• • •

LESSON 151.

The Making of a Folded Felt Hat With Crown and Brim in One Piece

Select a soft Felt Hood or Capeline, as it is easier to work than a hard Felt.

Place the hood in the hot water as previously detailed.

Remove from water.

Place the hood on the block and tie a piece of string or fix with drawing pins around the headline.

Check up the front to back and side to side measure and adjust the string accordingly to measurement required.

Work quickly while hood is damp.

This hat can be made with a brim folded close to the headline of the crown at one part.

It can be turned up in front, at one side or at the back of brim.

Close up to the crown of hat and pressed with a damp cloth.

You will notice that the remaining part of the brim may be still too full; therefore it is necessary to cut this part of the brim away from the crown.

The brim must only be cut just below the string or row of drawing pins and across the width of the brim in one piece.

The position of the cut across the brim will depend upon the style being made. It also depends upon whether the ends of the Felt are to be used as a trimming and finished in a knot or to cross over as ends or form a bow effect or whether a portion must be cut off and an ordinary brim join made.

This join has been explained and illustrated in a previous lesson.

L

LESSON 152.

The Making of a Folded Felt Hat

Note.—If the hat is to have a seam in the brim, then it is necessary to gently stretch the part of the brim that was touching the crown until it becomes less circular.

It is necessary to do this while the Felt is still damp.

The surplus amount must then be cut off, placing the join at the least noticeable place.

Perhaps you can place trimming over the join. The end of a piece of ribbon, a row of small ribbon bows or a feather. But do try to conceal it if possible.

When the brim is joined, press it.

The detached part of the brim can be lapped under the crown for ½ in.; it can be run off to nothing where it joins the crown of hat.

Rejoin the crown to the brim by means of upright hemming.

This stitch is clearly illustrated in a previous lesson.

Another method with the ends of the brim in the form of a tie or bow, the cut can be slanted through the ends of a brim as for ribbon ends. (They are usually sloped not cut straight.)

The cut ends can be stretched instead of leaving them slightly circular.

The detached part can be lapped over the crown and hemmed to the crown.

Next arrange the ends in a number of ways till you approve of one of them.

The ends can be trimmed with rows of narrow braid, stitching, or beads as a decoration, or left plain, and a smart pin or ornament may be inserted in the centre of the cross-over piece as a smart finish.

Work quickly and lightly while Felt is still damp.

When finished and dry, the hat must be strengthened at the headline.

See full details in lessons dealing with this important subject.

A headlining may be inserted if desired. It certainly saves the hat, and it will wear much longer.

Remember to brush the hat well so as the pile runs in one direction.

Look it carefully over; can you see any faults? If so, rectify them immediately.

THE CORRECT METHOD OF CUTTING HAT WIRE.
Avoid twisting the wire. Hold it firmly. Cut it with pliers, not with your scissors. Place the wire between the pliers; grasp them firmly and the wire will cut even.

LESSON 153.

RIGHT.—"MERLE," a lovely model Black Felt, featuring a rolled brim and feather trimmings.

★

BELOW.—"ELITE," an outstanding Model Hat in Navy and White Grosgrain, feather trimmed.

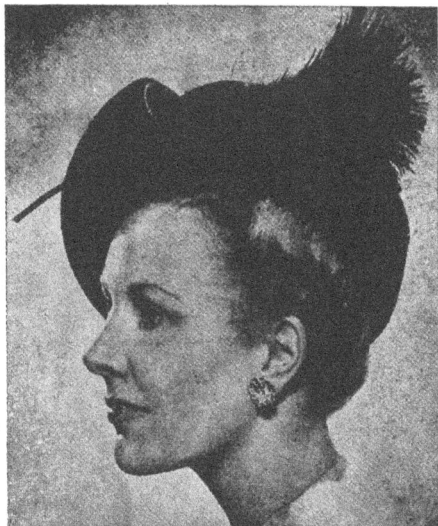

LESSON 154.

THE IMPORTANCE OF TRUE EVEN OUTLINES.

A true-edge outline is important—it is not mere matter of chance.

It must be just right.

The outline of a hat brim must be absolutely true in curve or angle.

Remember to always trim an edge carefully before wiring it.

Try to train the eye to see curves in absolutely correct perspective.

Your success will depend on having "line" just right.

(Copyright)

LESSON 155.

These Exclusive Model Hats are Featuring Various Styles and Trimmings

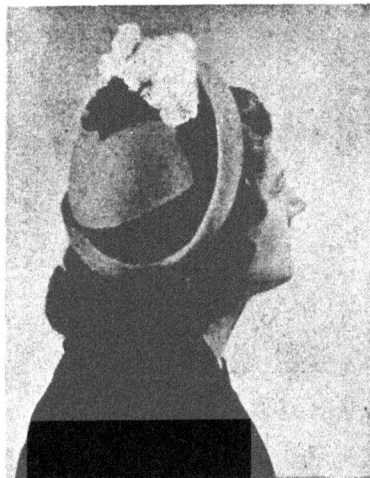

The cost of each is detailed, enabling you to see just how much hats will cost when you make them yourself.

"ESTELL," a smart roll brim model in grey Felt. Trimmed black Velvet ribbon and flowers.

The Cost of Materials:

The Felt Hood costs	7/11
Leno Strip costs	3d
1½ yards Velvet Ribbon	4/4½
Flowers	4/3
Total	16/9½

Materials supplied by courtesy of

ROCKMANS PTY. LTD.

Brisbane   and   Melbourne

• • •

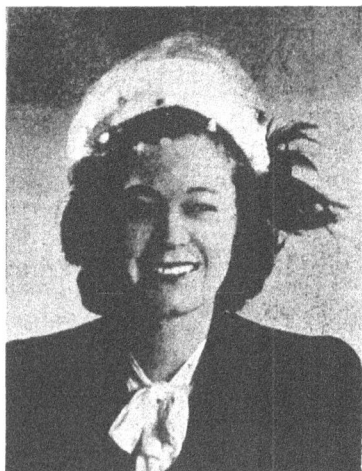

"GLAMOUR," a delightful model white Felt Hat featuring white and black feather trimmings and veiling.

The Materials cost:

The Felt Hood	7/11
10 Hackle Feathers	19/2
½ yard Veiling	1/11½
Head Band and Elastic	10½d
Total	29/11

Materials supplied by courtesy of

ROCKMANS PTY. LTD.

Brisbane   and   Melbourne

LESSON 156.

LITTLE HATS ARE SMART

**FEATHERS, FLOWERS OR RIBBON TRIMMED. VEILING, TOO, ADDS
DISTINCTION TO THE SMALL HAT.
MAKE IT IN VELVET, STRAW, FELT OR GROSGRAIN.**

To Wear for All Occasions.

Metal studs in nickel and gold make smart trimmings for Felt hats.

A self bow of Felt, studded with silver or gold.

Navy Felt with gold is smart.

Grey Felt, silver trimmed, is ideal for the matron.

The brims of last season's hats can be widened by cutting off 2 ins. from the brim and inserting a band of velvet.

This would require wiring to hold brim firmly in position.

Small hats are ideal for winter wear.

Felt, with added Grosgrain bows and a little veiling make entirely new models.

Feathers are always smart and can be changed with the season.

◆ ◆ ◆

LL

(Copyright)

"IRENE"
A lovely English Black Felt Model,
White Ostrich Plume trimmed.

LESSON 157.

Leading Designers Forecast the Fashion Trends for Millinery

For this and the coming season, Bold Hats, Flower Decked Bonnets, broad, soft brims. These are particularly suited to the new hemline and lowered waists, and the fuller skirts.

Short figures need not be afraid to wear big hats, so long as they carry themselves well and keep the hat in scale with the rest of the wardrobe. It will then look new and just right.

Hats to be smart must be simple. The art is in the making and selecting of the correct materials.

A lot of trimming too often indicates a covering for bad line. Hats must have character and form. Felt and Velour, ever classic, stands at the head of the list, especially rich Fur Felt.

Along with bold line, bold colours to lift the colour of smart women's clothes.

Before a hat is selected for anyone, this question must be asked: For what particular costume or frock does the wearer want it?

It is best to get a full detailed description, next to study the figure of the wearer; with hats it is line, next the shape of the head and facial structure.

All this is important, and must be understood before attempting to design hats. **Remember! the right type of hat for the right person. The rest is easy.**

LESSON 158.

These Two Smart Off the Face Halos

Off-the-Face Halos!

RIBBON AND VEILING TRIMMED

Can be Made in Velvet, Grosgrain, Felt, Straw, etc.

Shapes can be obtained in black and white Buckram, ready to cover with Velvet or Grosgrain.

A variety of materials and trimmings may be used instead of above mentioned and ribbon trimmings.

Feathers or flowers can be used on these smart hats.

The shapes are inexpensive and easy to cover.

Follow directions given for making Fabric Hats.

If making these styles in Straw, the crown and brim would be blocked and shaped; also in Felt, the hat would be blocked and shaped.

These styles are smart to wear with Tailored Clothes.

LESSON 159.

Trim in Velvet — Make in Velvet

These are the Hats that will set off the Trim-line Fashion, plain or stitched Velvet or Velvet trimmed.

Velvet has always been fashion's favourite, and no matter how the fashions change you will find Velvet always in demand for small hats and bonnets, for both adults and children's wear.

Designers who concentrate on bonnet styles do so with the sure knowledge that this style will appeal to younger women and girls.

The Empire type of Bonnet is soft, having a draped effect, whereas the early Victorian type of Bonnet is made in Velvet mounted over Espartra and ostrich plume trimmed.

These are very expensive to buy, but can be made much cheaper.

Every type cannot wear the Bonnet.

New suit fashions mean new hat fashions, and these must be right.

For any new fashion obtain catalogues from all leading stores.

See the many styles of hats and how they change, if only a little each season, but they do change. That is the reason why so many milliners have set up in business remodelling hats.

There is big money to be made if you can transform last year's model into an entirely new model this year and next. An old Felt hat can be remodelled like new, and with trimmings of Grosgrain or Feathers is the season's latest.

Even a change of trimming on an old hat gives it that new look.

Cheap Felts are sometimes not worth cleaning as a new hood can be purchased for a few shillings, but a Velour or Fur Felt will be equal to new when cleaned and re-blocked and trimmed with velvet.

LESSON 160.

Design and Make Model Hats to Suit Your Own Individual Personality

It is not only interesting but easy to provide yourself with all the smart hats you require. A hat to match each suit, or frock, for just the cost of the materials.

The Directions for Cutting the Patterns are simple to follow, and clearly illustrated diagrams make the instructions given in the easy lessons so easy to understand that even if you have never made a hat before you can, with the help of this thorough Course of Instruction in "MODERN MILLINERY MADE EASY," make a large variety of different types and styles of smart hats for both adults and children.

Once you thoroughly master these instructions you will find it so easy to make all types of smart hats that really suit the individual personality of the wearer—the type of hats you will be proud to wear.

◆ ◆ ◆

LESSON 161.

THESE TWO MODELS ARE MADE IN FELT, TRIMMED WITH SELF LEAVES AND METAL STUDDING.

The top model is excellent made in Grey Felt and trimmed with navy Grosgrain. The self flowers are studded with silver.

The other model, in beige Felt trimmed with brown Grosgrain and Gilt Studs, is smart for all occasions.

The veiling adds distinction to both models.

These small smart shapes are excellent to wear with tailored suits, etc. A variety of colours and trimmings can be used. Also these models are suitable for re-modelling.

Last season's hats can be remodelled in smart styles. The crowns can be blocked and the brims can be made on any of the patterns given in the Pattern Cutting Section.

The edges of the brims, after being wired, can be curved to the shape desired.

Various types of trimmings—Feathers, Ribbons, Flowers, etc.—can be used.

These models can be made in Grosgrain, Straw, or Fabric. They are easy to copy and will test your ability to copy models.

LESSON 162.

PREVIEW OF AUTUMN

Winter Millinery Fashions show a definite leaning towards soft flattering Pastel Shades, also Fur and Wool Felts in lovely Blues, with special accent on the popular Aqua, Royal, Olive Green, Navy, Browns, Gold and Black are popular shades.

In the ranges of browns the lovely beige, coco, caramel and darker shades of brown. Grey, too, is popular; also wine, mulberry, violet, prune and cherry.

While brims frame the face in a flattering manner, trimmings are placed at varying angles. Violets, roses and velvet ribbon combined are all attractive.

Many models feature trimmings of velvet, or Grosgrain ribbon under the brim. Many under brims are flower trimmed, too.

White ribbon is attractive on black Felt. Coloured veiling is extensively used to brighten a dark Felt.

Black hats trimmed with all black and accessories black and white and navy and white are smart.

Black and green in tonings of moss green with these colours, brown and black, present an established and dignified background.

Remember always that hats are important.

They express each personality more than anythnig else.

The two-toned coloured Felts and Grosgrain Hats are definitely smart for Autumn and Winter wear.

♦ ♦ ♦

LESSON 163.

DO YOU KNOW THE ANSWERS TO THESE 10 QUESTIONS?

(1) How can Hat Brim Shapes be cut without patterns?

(2) What is a substitute for a Hat Block?

(3) What is the best way to obtain experience in the making of all Millinery?

(4) Why must the Inner Headline of Shapes be snipped?

(5) Where are the joins of Crowns and Brims placed?

(6) Why must joins be placed in certain positions?

(7) Why must Canvas Interlinings be trimmed away at turnings?

(8) Why must all work be first Pinned, then Basted?

(9) What type of Straw is Chip Straw and what type of Hats is it most suited for?

(10) What type of Straw is Pedal Straw, and how is it sold?

(Copyright)

LESSON 164.

THE CONVERTIBLE HAT

The convertible hat is the useful type of hat; one that can be changed in a few minutes. It can be transformed for any or all occasions.

The basic Business Hat can be all things to the business girl or woman, provided the hat is the small type.

A plain Tailored Style of Felt or Straw can be changed quickly into a different hat by just adding a large Taffeta or Velvet bow which, when tied around the crown of the hat, completely covers the plain narrow band of ribbon.

Perhaps the brim is a small droop type; turned up at one side with an ornament it becomes a different style. Turn it up in front and add a new feather, and it is another new style. A different style for every day and evening can be yours.

For evening wear a large bow caught with a jewelled clip or ornament all add distinction to the very plainest hat.

◆ ◇ ◆

"Excel" Milliners' Hat Blocks

FIRST CLASS QUALITY.   GUARANTEED AT THE LOWEST PRICES IN AUSTRALIA.

PRICE LIST (including Sales Tax)

No. 1.—Coolie Brim, 14 inch £1 12 6	No. 11.—Fancy Sports Dome £1 5 6
No. 2.—Skull Dome (all sizes) £1 5 6	No. 12.—Plain Domes £1 5 6
No. 3.—Sailor (all sizes) 13 6	No. 13.—Topper Dome £1 5 6
No. 4.—Medium Coolie, 11 to 12 inch ... £1 12 6	No. 14.—Toque Tam £1 5 6
No. 5.—Small Coolie, 9 to 10 inch ... £1 5 0	No. 15.—Sports Dome £1 5 6
No. 6.—Split Tam Beret £1 5 6	No. 16.—Low Tip 12 6
No. 7.—Sloped Sailor 13 6	No. 17.—High Tip 12 6
No. 8.—Bowler Dome 19 6	No. 18.—Sailor Brim £1 3 6
No. 9.—Guttered Crown £1 3 6	No. 19.—Large Brims £1 12 6
No. 10.—Collars 1 6	No. 20.—Fancy Brims, 9 to 10 inch ... £1 5 0

(No. 18, No. 19 and No. 20 Blocks not illustrated.)

The above Prices are Lower than Warehouse Prices and do Not include any Freight.

PLEASE NOTE.—When ordering Blocks, add 6d. extra for cartage to rail. All Blocks are sent with Freight on Rail to be paid by Purchaser. All Orders are Cash with Order, as the above Listed Prices are at Direct Prices. No C.O.D. Prices. Please forward Cheque, Money Order, Bank Draft or Postal Notes in payment for your order to :—

"MODERN DESIGNERS"

(Established 15 Years)

77 QUEEN STREET   —   BRISBANE, Q'LAND

NOTE.—Delivery within three weeks as all Blocks are made to measure and design and are First Quality Seasoned Timbers. Guaranteed not to Split.

LESSON 165.

This Section Deals Thoroughly With Remodelling, Cleaning and Dyeing of Felts and Straws

THE CLEANING AND RE-MODELLING OF HATS

Cleaning Leghorns, Straws: (1) The Bread Process; (2) Soap and Water Process.

Flowers: (1) Cleaning Fluid; (2) Dyeing; (3) Steaming and Pressing.

Milan Straws: (1) Dyed Milan; (2) Natural Milan.

Feathers: (1) Ostrich; (2) Ordinary.

Panamas: (1) Wall Paper Cleaning Process; (2) Bread Process.

Lace: (1) Washing; (2) Tinting.

Straw Braids: (1) Wall Paper Cleaning Process; (2) Cleaning Fluids; (3) Soap and Water Process; (4) Pressing Braid.

Felt Hats: (1) Cleaning Fluids; (2) Art Gum; (3) Fullers Earth.

Velvets: (1) Cleaning Fluids; (2) Steaming and Re-finishing.

Remodelling Pressed Hats: (1) Cutting; (2) Edge Finishes.

Cleaning Leghorn Straws.

Brim Extensions.

We all know that the better quality materials will stand re-modelling several times, whereas the cheaper quality will not. A good quality Leghorn Straw hat may be remodelled, blocked, cleaned and trimmed many times. Do not allow Leghorn Straws to become very soiled. It is advisable to clean them frequently.

NOTE.—The cleaning processes 1 and 2 may successfully be used without taking off the trimming of the hat.

❖ ❖ ❖

LESSON 166.

(1) THE BREAD PROCESS OF CLEANING LEGHORNS.

To keep a fine quality Leghorn Hat in first class condition it is necessary to clean it each dozen times it is worn.

The method of cleaning with bread:

Cut off a thick slice of stale bread. Holding the bread in the right hand, scrub the hat with it. (Do not wet the bread.) The bread will remove any dust or dirt from the straw. Then brush the hat with a good stiff straw brush. If not cleaned thoroughly, repeat the process.

LESSON 167.

(2) THE WALL PAPER CLEANING PROCESS.

When a Straw Hat is very soiled, purchase any good Wallpaper Cleaner or use Talcum Powder and Methylated Spirits mixed into a paste. Scrub the hat with this. Leave to dry and brush well.

(3) THE SOAP AND WATER PROCESS.

When a Leghorn Hat is very soiled and you are going to remodel it, first take off all the trimmings and facings, etc. Brush it well with a stiff brush.

Next stretch the crown over a wooden block (the shape of block and size required) also a stiff Buckram shape may be used.

Next fasten the brim down to the table with drawing pins, placing them about 2 ins. apart around the edge of brim. Place also several drawing pins through the brim to hold it firmly.

Mix up some washing powder or soap flakes into hot water; use warm; apply with a stiff nailbrush and scrub well.

Rinse with clean water and brush. Then wipe dry with a clean towel, absorbing as much of the moisture as possible. Allow the hat to dry thoroughly. Remove the drawing pins from the brim, then press crown and brim well before removing from the block. Use thin muslin over the straw, avoid scorching it with the iron.

◆ ◆ ◆

LESSON 168.

MILANS

(1) **Dyed Milans:** A dyed Milan Straw may be cleaned by dipping a clean cloth first in hot water and then into Ammonia Solution, and scrubbing the straw well with a cloth. Repeat till thoroughly clean.

(2) **Natural Milans:** To clean a natural Milan Straw, place a teaspoonful of Sulphur in a saucer or plate. Cut a lemon in half. Dip the lemon in powdered sulphur, press the lemon down until a fair amount of the sulphur is absorbed in the cut half of lemon.

Now rub the Milan well with the lemon you have dipped in the sulphur. When the sulphur is rubbed off into the straw, dip the lemon into the sulphur again and repeat till you have rubbed the whole hat over and under the brim.

When the whole hat is covered with the lemon and sulphur, allow it to stand for an hour. Then the hat must be brushed all over with a stiff brush.

Oxalide Acid as a Cleaning Process for Straw Hats: The acid must be diluted with water, equal quantities of acid and water mixed. Scrub the hat with the solution of acid and water, then wipe off the acid with a soft cloth, first with weak ammonia.

LESSON 169.

PANAMAS (Straws)

STRAW BRAIDS

(1) **Wall Paper Cleaner process or Talcum Powder mixed with Methylated Spirits.** Straw Hats may be cleaned as a whole or the braid ripped apart and cleaned. This is a lengthy procedure. Mix the Wall Paper Cleaner or Talcum Powder into a paste and scrub the hat. Allow to dry, then brush off with a stiff brush.

(2) **Cleaning Fluid.** Petrol or Petrol and Eucalyptus mixed, White Spirits or any reliable cleaning fluid. Place hat on block, dip a clean cloth into the cleaning fluid, and scrub the straw. Wipe the braid well with it. Leave in the air to dry out.

(3) **The Soap and Water Process of Cleaning Straws.** A good quality straw braid may be scrubbed with a brush dipped in the Soap Flake Solution, add a few drops of Cloudy Ammonia. This will remove any loose dirt from the straw.

Rinse the straw in clean cold water, shake well, wrap in blotting paper, newspaper or old towel. Leave for an hour. Then press. The straw will be equal to new.

Pressing Straw Braids. It is important to always press the Straw Braids on the wrong side of the braid with a medium hot iron. If the iron is too hot it will stick to the straw and spoil it.

◆ ◆ ◆

Handy Hints

Pressed Hats or Blocked Hoods and Capelines. When working, keep all the spare pieces. They will be useful when re-modelling old hats.

Cutting both Straw and Felt Hats. These may be re-cut and re-shaped to look like new. If the shape requires to be changed at the headline the crown must be cut from the brim of the hat.

LESSON 170.

CLEANING FELT HATS

Light shades of Felt Hats can be kept in excellent condition only if they are taken care of and cleaned frequently. They should not be allowed to get very soiled. A good brushing each time they are worn, then dip the brush in methylated spirits and brush again, and when dry brush again with a dry brush. This will keep them like new.

(1) **Cleaning Fluids.** There are numerous cleaning fluids you can use, but you will find the Methylated Spirits excellent. When cleaning the Felt hat, dip a soft cloth in the cleaning fluid and rub it over the Felt with the nap of the Felt, not against the nap. (Rub your hand over a Felt hat; it feels rough one way and smooth another way.) When hat has been well rubbed over, brush the Felt dry with a soft clean brush.

(2) **Art Gum.** This can be purchased at any stationers, and is in the form of a rubber. Art Gum will remove streaks and spots from Felt provided they have not been made by liquid. Rub the Art Gum over the soiled spot. When marks are removed, brush with a stiff brush.

(3) **Powdered Magnesia** as a cleaner. Obtainable in small boxes from any chemist. First brush the hat well and remove any dust. Working on a clean cloth, rub the powdered magnesia well into the Felt. (This is an excellent cleaner for White Felts.) Wrap the Felt hat up in a cloth, leaving the powdered magnesia on it. Leave for a day or more, then brush well with a stiff brush. The Felt will be equal to new.

(4) **Fullers Earth as a Cleaner.** Rub dry Fullers Earth over the hat after first brushing all dust out of the hat. Wrap in a cloth and leave as long as possible—a day or two is advisable—then brush well and remove the Fullers Earth. Block in the usual manner and re-trim.

Note.—For Felt Hats that are slightly greasy at the inner headline, inner ribbon must be removed, the headline cleaned with ammonia or cleaning fluid and a new ribbon replacing the old.

✦ ✦ ✦

LESSON 171.

TO RAISE OLD CROWNS

(1) Set in a Band of Buckram. (2) Set in a Band of Contrasting Felt for Felt Hat, Straw Braid for Straw Hat.

TO WIDEN BRIMS FOR STRAW HATS.

Your old hat can have a New Look with an added band or two of Crinoline Straw on the outer edge. There is plain and fancy Crinoline in a variety of colours and patterns.

Notice carefully that there is a draw thread on the inner edge of the Crinoline, enabling it to be drawn up into a circle and made to fit the edge of the Straw brim.

When beginning to re-model the hat, first brush the straw well, and, if necessary, clean it, using one of the methods already described. The trimmings must also be removed and replaced with new, up-to-date trimmings.

If the hat is worth remodelling, it is worth doing well.

Press well with a damp cloth as previous directions given in another lesson. Brush the hat over with stiffening, as this will give the old straw a fresh new appearance, also reviving its colour.

If you require an added amount on the brim of about $2\frac{1}{4}$ ins. to $2\frac{3}{4}$ ins., purchase Crinoline $1\frac{1}{4}$ ins. wide. When these two rows of Crinoline are added on to the previous brim, after allowing for the $\frac{1}{4}$ in. overlap, the extension on brim will be $2\frac{1}{4}$ ins. finished. If less is required, add only 1 in. of Crinoline.

The Crinoline can easily be removed next season if the styles are worn smaller.

A medium size Sailor Hat shape can be used and with the added width on brim will be the latest model. About three yards of Crinoline should be sufficient.

An excellent idea is to measure around the brim first, allowing 2 ins. for turnings. Hat wire and narrow velvet ribbon to match hat or contrasting colour to trim the hat. A spray of flowers added, and an entirely new model is created!

You will probably find many hats well worth remodelling and you will be pleased with the finished model.

Do not forget all joins at the centre back. Also, if you are adding two rows of Crinoline to the edge of a hat, to add the first row ease the Crinoline up by pulling gently on the draw thread on the inner edge of Crinoline. Ease it up till it fits nicely around outer edge of the hat brim, shaping to fit the edge of brim. Sew the first row on to the binding around edge of hat.

Note.—If this old binding is shabby, replace it with a Velvet one, to match your Velvet trimming.

Join first row neatly at back, then for the second row draw up as first row, pinning it around edge of the last row. Ease up only slightly as you work. Then, when second row is completed, join the centre back of this evenly with the first join. Press well, then measure the amount of wire you will require to fit around brim at the join of the second row of Crinoline.

Widening Brims for Straw Hats

(Continued.)

Make the wire into a circle to fit around brim (as previously described). The wire is then covered with the folded over narrow Velvet ribbon. (Full details covering wire has been previously dealt with in another section).

When wire is covered, pin it around the brim at the join of the last row of Crinoline and sew. **Do you know the correct stitch to use? These have all been explained in previous lessons. It is important to always use the correct stitches.**

Other Straws that look attractive trimmed with Crinoline edges are Knotty Sizal Straw. (This can be bought in hoods and blocked to any shape and size.)

Rapal Straw, with a nice scalloped edge, is excellent also for extensions on straw brims.

A Baku Straw also can be made smart with Crinoline edge and bows of Velvet ribbon.

Sisal Straw also is suited for an extended brim of Crinoline.

Try one old hat with a Crinoline extended edge to see the result.

◆ ◆ ◆

Renovating Flowers

Often Flowers are crushed and perhaps dusty. They are easily cleaned and can be made to look like new.

If the flower is crumpled looking, hold it in front of the steam of a kettle. Leave it to dry. Dust all dirt from flowers with a stiff brush before steaming.

Faded flowers can be dyed. For soiled flowers they can be washed in a cleaning fluid, then steamed. They will look new again.

If you have already learnt the Art of Making Beautiful French Flowers you will be able to make beautiful Orchids, Wax and Paper Flowers for little cost. You can make all the flowers you require, as ready-made flowers are expensive to buy.

This thorough Course of French Flower Making is offered to all who desire to learn the art. All varieties of flowers are taught. Pansies, Roses, Carnations, Sweet Peas, Orchids, Orange Blossoms, Chrysanthemums, Daisies, Daffodils, Frangipani, also Felt-work Cherries, Holly, etc., etc.

The Complete Postal Course is £3/3/-. Write to the Secretary for full particulars.

LESSON 172.

CLEANING LACE

All types of Lace can be cleaned or washed. Any Linen, Cotton or Silk Laces are best washed. Metal Laces are best cleaned.

When washing Laces, wash with Sunlight soap. Rinse well, wrap in a towel till almost dry. Press well.

Cleaning Lace: Any good Cleaning Fluid can be used. Dip the lace up and down in the fluid. Do not wring. Hang over paper to dry.

Coloured Laces may be washed or cleaned. Shake almost dry. Press on wrong side with a warm iron. Black, navy, and dark laces, these often only require a good shaking and brushing and pressing.

Tinting Laces: Cheap laces can be improved by tinting them. Use cold water dye. Wash and rinse in the dye. Press on wrong side. Val. Lace, All-over Laces, Ruffles, etc., all can be dyed to match the hat. Often coloured laces can be bought in the colours required.

◆ ◆ ◆

FEATHERS

Always a popular trimming for Millinery, good quality feathers may be cleaned many times. Pasted together Feathers may be protected when they are placed on a hat for trimming. These are not satisfactorily cleaned and remodelled.

Ostrich Feathers: To clean, shake the feathers free of all dust. Make a mixture of soap flakes and petrol or white spirits. Dip the feathers in and out several times, then dip into a clean bowl of cleaning fluid. Shake and leave to dry.

The tips of feathers may be curled by heating the end of a large nail or knitting needle and winding the ends of feathers around the heated nail (not too hot). Steam will also curl the ends of the feathers, or heat from a flame. Do not hold too close to flame. Take care, as they are very delicate feathers.

Ordinary Feathers: To clean ordinary feathers make a bowl of warm water and soap flakes. Dip feathers in and out till clean. Rinse in luke warm water. Dry, and then brush them till they loosen out natural looking.

LESSON 173.

RENOVATING VELVET

To Renovate Velvet.

First brush well and shake to remove any dust. Next hold the wrong side of the velvet to the steam from a kettle—this will raise the pile of the velvet. Do not press with an iron. Hang up with pins till dry. Brush well with soft brush.

To Renovate Velvet Ribbons.

Clean by sponging the back of ribbon with warm water and ammonia. While damp run the ribbon backwards and forwards over a hot iron, the wrong side facing the iron. This will remove all creases and give the ribbon a new fresh appearance.

To Renovate Silk or Silk Petersham Ribbons.

Wash in lukewarm water and soap flakes. Rinse well; when nearly dry, iron on wrong side of ribbon.

To Renovate Ninon or Chiffon.

Remove dust by shaking well. Wash in warm water, adding borax. Rinse well. Roll on clean cloth and press while slightly damp.

To Clean Light Fawn Felt Hats.

Rub well all over with hot fine oatmeal or Fullers Earth (dry). Brush well.

To Clean Grey Felt Hats.

Rub well with dry, hot bran.

To Raise the Pile in Felt Hats.

Press well with damp cloth and hot iron till dry, then pull the cloth off. This will raise the pile of the Felt.

LESSON 174.

To Prepare the Hat for Re-modelling

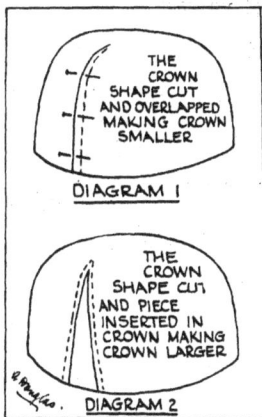

DIAGRAM 1

THE CROWN SHAPE CUT AND OVERLAPPED MAKING CROWN SMALLER

DIAGRAM 2

THE CROWN SHAPE CUT AND PIECE INSERTED IN CROWN MAKING CROWN LARGER

FELT HATS.

First remove the inner head band or lining, and all trimmings, from the hat.

If the Felt has a greasy appearance, brush first with a dry brush to remove all dust.

The Felt can be cleaned with a cleaning fluid, petrol or a mixture of petrol and eucalyptus, or cloudy ammonia added to warm water.

Dip brush in the cleaning fluid and brush well all over till clean. Leave till dry. Brush again with a clean brush, then hold Felt over steam from a kettle and steam it well.

If a Velour Felt, sometimes a good brushing with a fine wire brush will make the Velour like new.

♦ ♦.♦

To Re-model an old Felt Hat

TO LOWER CROWN THE CROWN IS CUT OFF HERE

DIAG. 1

DIAG. 2

FOR HIGHER CROWN INSET PIECE IN THE CROWN

DIAG. 3

CUT AND LACE UP

TO HEIGHTEN THE CROWN.

Cut off the crown about 1 in. above the brim of hat, then stitch on to the crown a band of material or Buckram of the same circumference as the old crown and depth of extra height required.

If a sloping higher crown is required this can easily be obtained by making the inserted band wider on the opposite side to where the slope is required.

Sew the inserted band to the inside of the brim with firm invisible stitches.

The join can be covered with ribbon, feathers or flowers.

Line the join between the crown and the brim on the inside with narrow Petersham ribbon to fit the head of the wearer.

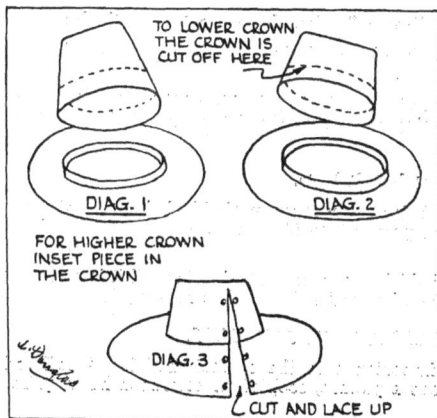

LESSON 175.

To Lower a High Crown

(See Diagram on previous page.)

Remove the crown from the brim of the hat, or, if it has not been previously cut separately, cut off the crown 1 in. or as needed, from the bottom of the crown. If a rounded crown and the style chosen is sloped, cut a little more away on the side of the slope. Sew the crown to the brim and finish off the same as previous directions.

Another method of lowering the crown without removing it is to stitch a wide tuck or several small tucks in it. This makes a smart trimming and can be used only on one side or around the crown; also crown can be made lower by cutting piece out of top. The diagrams clearly illustrate the various methods detailed here.

♦   ♦   ♦

LESSON 176.

To Reduce the Crown Section

(See Diagram on previous page.)

To Make a Hat Smaller in the Crown Section there are two methods:

(1) Shrinking it on a smaller block with a cloth. (2) Cut a V-shaped piece running off to nothing at top of the crown.

With a small leather punch, holes can be punched each side of the cut and narrow ribbon or cord can be used as a trimming to lace up the cut, either at side, back or front of hat.

To Stretch Felt Hats.

If a Felt hat has become too tight for the wearer, probably being wet at some time or other, or the hair style will not permit it to fit as well, wet it and leave it on the hat block till it is dry.

Remove trimming and lining, and hold it over steam of a kettle until it is perfectly stretched to be comfortable again. Re-trim, and it is equal to new again.

SMART RIBBON TRIMMINGS FOR HATS.

The correct trimming is of vital importance to the correct model. A tailored model requires plain trimming, whereas a picture, cocktail or afternoon hat requires flowers and gay ribbon trimmings.

Conclusion

No one, no matter how talented, need expect to make finished and truly professional-looking hats without a great deal of practice. Not everyone can succeed in being a trimmer or a designer, but anyone who is willing to work faithfully and to practice long enough can acquire deftness and skill that will enable her to copy various designs, to do exquisite making, to block and trim in a faultless manner.

In other words, anyone who has the average intelligence and who wills it may train her eyes and hands to do what the mind directs.

Colour, line, neatness, all are essential in millinery.

The author will be pleased to hear from those wishing to have private lessons on any subject. These can be arranged at any time, and include the free use of all millinery hat blocks and brim boards.

There is so much more to be learnt from the actual personal lessons than from this course, which will no doubt form a good groundwork for women and girls who are unable to attend the Academy for private lessons.

I trust that this book will be worthy of recommendation to your friends.

There are numerous other Private or Postal Courses available in "DRESSMAKING, FITTING AND ITS PROBLEMS," "LADIES TAILORING," or "DRESSCUTTING, FITTING AND MAKING BY TAPE MEASURE," or "SHIRT AND PYJAMA CUTTING" (BOYS, YOUTHS AND MEN'S), "CUTTING TO MEASURE AND STOCK CUTTING," or "FRENCH FLOWER MAKING" or "EXCLUSIVE LINGERIE," including Tailored Shorts, Slacks (all types), Bias Cut Garments, Trousseau Sets, Sports Wear, etc., Cutting and Making of Infants, Children's and Teen-age Wear. Cutting to measure and making and smocking, etc., all types of garments including Infants' Smocks, Round Neck Smocked Frocks and Blouses, Boys' Shirts and Trousers, Shorts, etc.

Cutting and making all are included in the Complete Children's Wear Course.

All Books and Fashion Books are included in all Courses. Other Advanced Courses also available.

Write for full particulars to :—

THE SECRETARY,
" M O D E R N   D E S I G N E R S   A C A D E M Y "
77 Queen Street, Brisbane, Q'land.

Many trimmings need deftness of touch; all work must be neat, without stitches showing anywhere. For the beginner, it is advisable to pin trimmings in position, then view them from several angles in your mirror. They can then be re-arranged to suit and then fixed in position.

Do all work well and neatly, and the best results are then assured.

When you have carefully studied and completed the thoroughly illustrated lessons, as fully detailed throughout this advanced Modern Course of Millinery, and have faithfully rendered the problems which have been dealt with, you will become conscious of the fact that there is no better, more thorough, complete course of millinery available than this Course of "MODERN MILLINERY MADE EASY."

There is only one right way of maintaining perfect results; all workmanship is governed by one rule—"THE RULE OF ACCURACY"—and on that alone your success depends. Careless mistakes will only make more work and wasted time.

The procedure of Cutting Patterns and the completion of the work and artistic principles taught throughout this work have all been tried and tested. Beauty can only be achieved through perfect work.

All the secrets of thorough trade methods have been revealed, leaving nothing to guess work. Only first class knowledge is contained throughout this work—

" MODERN   MILLINERY   MADE   EASY."

Other Volumes to Follow

● **Volume 2.**

ADVANCED MODERN CUTTING TO MEASURE, by "Tape Measure" (no tedious drafting, charts, or complicated methods). Covering all Infants, Toddlers and Boys' Wear. Teen-age models. All Outer and Under Garments. Cutting to Measure and Designing as a Profession or for Home Use.

Beautifully illustrated. Contains over 2000 subjects. An Encyclopedia of all Children's Wear, and Exclusive Model Fashions of Infants and Children's Wear.

● **Volume 3.**

ADVANCED MODERN CUTTING TO MEASURE, by "Tape Measure" (Part I). The modern perfect method of DRESSCUTTING TO MEASURE of Adults' Frocks, Suits, Skirts, Collars, Sleeves, Blouses, Bodices, etc., etc. Designing, fitting and its problems thoroughly dealt with. Each subject fully detailed and beautifully illustrated.

A Thorough Trade Training.

● **Volume 4.**

ADVANCED DRESSCUTTING TO MEASURE, by "Tape Measure" (Part 2). Advanced Dresscutting, Ladies' Tailoring (Man tailored Costume and Coat and Skirt Cutting to Measure), Draping, Bias-cutting, Modelling, Fitting, Advanced Styling, Raglans, Dolmans. Fancy Sleeves, Fancy Bodices, etc., etc., Capes, Frills, etc., etc.

A thorough Professional Trade Course of Instruction. Fully detailed and beautifully illustrated.

● **Volume 5.**

EXCLUSIVE LINGERIE. The cutting to measure of all types of Model Lingerie, Tailored Shorts, Slacks, Overalls, Shorts, Dresses, etc., etc., Model Hostess Gowns, Pyjamas, Bias-cut Garments, Exclusive Trousseau Wear, etc. Model Styles of all Lingerie.

A complete thorough Professional Trade Course of Training. Fully detailed and beautifully illustrated.

● **Volume 6.**

EXCLUSIVE FRENCH FLOWERS MADE EASY. The making of beautiful Artificial Fabric, Paper, Wax, Felt, Flowers, Orchids, Violets, Daisies, Orange Blossom, Frangipani, Pansies, Daffodils, Poppies, Roses, etc., etc. All popular varieties. Felt Work, Cushions, etc. Novelties for Home Decorations.

Fully Detailed and Illustrated.

● **Volume 7.**

ADVANCED DRESSMAKING (Part I). Covering all Making, Finishing, Fitting of Garments, Cutting to Measure of Skirts without Patterns, Bias Cutting, all Tucking, Shirring, Braiding, Belt Making, Flower and Bag Making, Rouleau Trimmings, Model Blouse Fashions, Setting and Fitting Sleeves, making Shoulder Pads, Darts, Drawn Thread Trimmings, Quilting and Needlework, etc., etc.

Fully Illustrated.

● **Volume 8.**

ADVANCED DRESSMAKING (Part 2). Children's Dressmaking, Boys and Girls' Coat Making, Boys' Shirt and Trouser Making, Frock, Pyjama Making, etc., etc.

All Children's Sewing fully detailed and illustrated.

● **Volume 9.**

THE MODERN DRESSMAKER. The Principles of Fitting, etc. All Needle Work, Trimmings and Finishings, etc., Smocking, Bound Button Holes, all types of Pockets, Placquets, Sleeves and the Correct Methods of Setting and Fitting and Finishing, etc.

Fully Detailed and Illustrated. Everything You Should Know About Dressmaking.

● **Volume 10.**

DRESS FITTING AND ITS PROBLEMS (Part 1). The Correct Balance. All Fitting Faults and Their Remedy. Fitting Disproportionate and Abnormal Figures. Long and Short Back and Front Balance. Fitting High and Low Bust Figure types. Excessive Bust Development. Fitting Sloping Shoulders. High Square Shoulders. Disguising Disproportion. Successful Fitting of All Garments, etc., etc. The Cause and the Remedy.

All Fully Detailed and Illustrated. An Encyclopedia of all Fitting for the Trade.

● **Volume 11.**

ADVANCED DRESSMAKING (Part 4). Covering Up-to-date Methods of all Secrets of Successful Dressmaking, Padded Work, Loops, Flare and Frill Cutting, etc.

All Essential Details of the Correct Finishings. All Important Subjects in Dressmaking.

● **Volume 12.**

YOUTH AND MEN'S SHIRT AND PYJAMA CUTTING. A Thorough Large Trade Training. Stock and Order Cutting. Cutting for all Figure Types.

For Further Particulars and Prices, write to—

THE NEW ART PUBLISHERS

77 QUEEN STREET - BRISBANE - QUEENSLAND

Lightning Source UK Ltd.
Milton Keynes UK
UKHW042149111218
333852UK00001B/45/P

9 781446 501221